WRITERS IN A LANDSCAPE

WRITERS IN A LANDSCAPE

Jeremy Hooker

Cardiff
University of Wales Press
1996

British Library Cataloguing in Publication Data.

A catalogue record for this book is available from the British Library.

ISBN
0-7083-1362-0 (hardback)
0-7083-1391-4 (paperback)

Typeset by Action Typesetting Ltd, Gloucester
Printed in Wales by Dinefwr Press, Llandybïe

Contents

Acknowledgements

'From graven image to speech: Edward Thomas's prose' is a revised and expanded version of a chapter which I contributed to *The Art of Edward Thomas*, ed. Jonathan Barker (Bridgend: Poetry Wales Press, 1987). A shorter version of 'Thomas Hardy, John Cowper Powys and Wessex' was published in *The Powys Review* Nos. 27 and 28, ed. Belinda Humfrey. Some of the ideas developed in the book began life in talks which I have given at Powys Society annual conferences, to the Edward Thomas Fellowship, and to the Richard Jefferies Society, and in the course, 'Writing and Place', which I have taught to undergraduates. I am grateful to all those who have encouraged me in these ventures, and collaborated with me in discussing the ideas.

Preface

My main focus in this book is upon the work of four writers –
Thomas Hardy, Richard Jefferies, John Cowper Powys and
Edward Thomas – and their interpretations and imaginative
'shaping' of places and landscapes in the south and south-west
of England. The historical period with which I am concerned is
the modern, from the 1870s to the 1930s, with extensions, in my
considerations of William Golding's *The Spire* and V. S. Naipaul's
The Enigma of Arrival, to more recent times.

The vital interests of the book are diverse, complex and far-
reaching. Since place is a ground of personal and historical experience, there is a sense in which the literary concern with place
comprehends *everything*. In the modern period, this experience
includes agricultural depression and the disintegration of rural
society, urbanization and increasing secularization, Empire, the
First World War and its aftermath. My concern with history in
this book, however, is not only with social events and movements. I am concerned also with questions of identity, national,
personal, and sexual, which arise in response to the crisis of
modernism. My explorations involve myth and a sense of the
sacred, and the binding relationships that constitute religious
experience. I seek to understand ways of imagining aimed at
transcending the limitations of the historical situation and
achieving spiritual enlargement, in the double sense of freedom
and expansion of being. It is above all in the context of the writers' *arts of seeing*, especially as applied to places and landscapes,
that I explore these concerns.

Having described what the book is about in broad terms, I
want in the rest of this Preface to outline the personal relationship with my subjects that has helped to shape my approach to
them. I was brought up in the south of England during and after
the Second World War, and I know the actual, changing places

and landscapes that the writers whose work I study in this book recreated imaginatively, and which their readers have described as 'Hardy's Wessex' or 'Jefferies Land' or 'Edward Thomas Country'. My father was a landscape painter whose paintings, often of movements of light and shadow on southern rivers or seashore, were part of my home from the beginning. He had a great love of Constable, so that while still a boy, before I had looked closely at any Constable painting and long before I had read C. R. Leslie's *Memoirs of Constable*, I had imbibed his ideas about seeing and feeling and painting his own places, and about finding his art 'under every hedge and in every lane'.[1] During the same period – I am talking about the time when I was eleven or twelve years of age – my perception of nature was strongly influenced by reading Richard Jefferies' essays. What I remember from before reading Jefferies are pleasures of a boy's active life in the countryside – playing, bird-nesting, fishing; what I recall from the first reading of essays in *Jefferies' England* is an intense, delighted, but also somewhat melancholy perception of the natural world.

When I re-read a Jefferies essay such as 'Haunts of the Lapwing' today, I can still feel the original excitement that it engendered in me. Now, however, I can analyse its causes, whereas at the time I would probably have said I liked the 'atmosphere' Jefferies evokes.

> Coming like a white wall the rain reaches me, and in an instant everything is gone from sight that is more than ten yards distant. The narrow upland road is beaten to a darker hue, and two runnels of water rush along at the sides, where, when the chalk-laden streamlets dry, blue splinters of flint will be exposed in the channels.[2]

So the essay begins, at once conveying a sense of the force of nature and exemplifying Jefferies' art of seeing, here confined to a narrow space but revealing the wonder of things through his vivid images. Jefferies goes on to describe the lapwings he sees as 'the only things of life that save the earth from utter loneliness'. The 'Winter' part of the essay concludes: 'From their hereditary home the lapwings cannot be entirely driven away. Out of the mist comes their plaintive cry; they are hidden, and their exact locality is not to be discovered. Where winter rules most ruthlessly, where darkness is deepest in daylight, there the slender plovers stay undaunted.'[3]

The seeing carries considerable feeling – it is, I would say now, a lyrical vision – and reveals the sensibility of the seer: a man who is lonely, tender, stoically enduring, attached to an earth that he knows to be a precarious 'home'. But while Jefferies is present in his words, he is also open to nature, which he sees with something of the feeling for the 'wholly other' that Rudolf Otto defines as the sacred.[4] Jefferies had no time for organized religion – he even described churches in the landscape as 'repellent structures'[5] – but his writing manifests that 'translation from the sacred to the secular' which Robert Rosenblum perceives in Northern Romantic art, a translation in which 'we feel that the powers of the deity have somehow left the flesh-and-blood dramas of Christian art and have penetrated, instead, the domain of landscape'.[6] Constable had 'felt that the *supernatural* need not be the *unnatural*'.[7] Walking in the fields with a humble mind, he had seen Nature as 'God's own works'. The Nature Jefferies worshipped, like many of his fellow Victorians, was godless and without design.

It is characteristic of Jefferies, however, that in responding to Nature as force he also sees the significant detail and the uniqueness of each thing. It might almost have been he rather than Constable who wrote: 'The world is wide; no two days are alike, nor even two hours; neither were there ever two leaves of a tree alike since the creation of the world; and the genuine productions of art, like those of nature, are all distinct from each other.'[8] Thomas Hardy has a similar vision of uniqueness and distinction, especially in respect of intense moments shared by lovers, which he or they often see retrospectively, and in the context of a Nature that has no regard for the individual. I first read some of Hardy's novels at about the same time as I read Jefferies, and it was their 'atmosphere' I liked, which meant their treatment of Nature. This I would now describe as their simultaneous expression of impassioned subjectivity, manifested in imagery of particular places and things, and depiction of the littleness of human beings against landscapes and in face of natural forces.

The reading was an element within my discovery of my own places, which were in certain respects recognizably the same as those Hardy and Jefferies had written about, and in other

respects quite different. The historical changes were plain to see
in the material structures and alterations and inventions of the
twentieth century. But there was also a changed life-experience –
one which, I later realized, Hardy and Jefferies had partially
anticipated, and Hardy had called 'the ache of modernism'.[9] Not
that any concept is adequate to the life-experience of a given
period, or adequate for any individual in a cosmos that, as John
Cowper Powys says, 'runs to personality'.[10] This is one reason
why writers write, of course, in order to express what is
uniquely different about their feeling and seeing. Before I
thought much about these things, however, at about the age of
seventeen, I encountered Edward Thomas's poems and
responded to them rather as I had to Jefferies' essays. At that
time, it was poems such as 'Thaw' and 'Tall Nettles'[11] that moved
me most. Rather than being poems of Edward Thomas's extreme
self-consciousness, these seem to be about Nature rather than
about him, and have a clarity in their detailed perception of hidden or unregarded, 'common' things. I liked Edward Thomas for
liking 'this corner of the farmyard ... most', and for liking 'the
dust on the nettles'. I too was awed by 'the land freckled with
snow half-thawed' and by creatures that saw 'what we below
could not see'. Again, as in Jefferies, it was the sense of the non-
human, a wholly other Nature, to which I responded. Those
things that were meanest to conventional vision really mattered
for simply being, and we lived in a world full of energies and
inexhaustible mysteries, which precise images could point to but
not capture.

After visiting the Lake District in 1855, Nathaniel Hawthorne
wrote: 'On the rudest surface of English earth, there is seen the
effect of centuries of civilization, so that you do not quite get at
naked Nature anywhere. And then every point of beauty is so
well known, and has been described so much, that one must
needs look through other people's eyes, and feel as if he were
seeing a picture rather than a reality.'[12] What I have been saying
about my own experience may seem to bear this out. But
Hawthorne was writing as an American, who saw England in
contrast to American landscapes. One of the truths we realize in
reading Jefferies and Hardy and Thomas, however, is that in
English landscapes and places, the minute particular – lapwings
in a winter field, rooks returning to their nests – can convey a

sense of a non-human and undomesticated Nature. It is also true that Thomas and Hardy, especially, prefer, like Constable, to depict landscapes with human associations, but this does not mean that they do not sometimes reveal 'naked Nature', as a powerful force that animates even the smallest thing. At the back of this tradition of English writings about Nature as a power – a tradition which begins with Wordsworth, but also diverges from his optimistic perception of the fit between Nature and the human mind – is the EXISTENCE Coleridge felt as 'the presence of a mystery, which must have fixed thy spirit in awe and wonder'.[13] I do not claim that it is the *same* presence in each case, however. Hardy, for example, was moved by a Bonington landscape to 'feel that Nature is played out as a Beauty, but not as a Mystery'. He wanted 'to see the deeper reality underlying the scenic, the expression of what are sometimes called abstract imaginings'. In his later novels he sought to create equivalents to the 'late-Turner rendering' with a way of seeing that is awakened 'to the tragical mysteries of life'.[14]

The art of seeing as exercised variously by the writers with whom I am concerned in this book is an art that subverts conventional vision and goes behind the 'scenes' to disclose realities that they hide. In each instance, it arises from a 'distance' – from a form of displacement with complex socio-historical and personal causes, that refines and sensitizes the writers' 'sense of place'. During the period from the late sixties when I was beginning to write seriously as a poet and critic, my thinking about this subject was quickened by the experience of seeing my original home country from the distance of another culture – the Welsh – which was in crucial ways radically different from that of the south of England. At the same time, I became increasingly critical in my questioning of pictorial conventions.

I will not say much here about complications of seeing since I treat the subject extensively in the following pages. I must, however, refer briefly to its importance for my own writing about place, since it has a bearing on my treatment of the writers discussed in this book. I was brought up and went to school near Boldre in the New Forest, where William Gilpin, the father of the picturesque, had held the living in the later eighteenth century. Looking closely at place in poems which I wrote in Wales in the seventies, I developed a historical sense that made me sharply critical of the picturesque as a way of seeing. I saw how much it excluded of the life of the people who were the makers of the landscape, as well as of the life of nature. In 'Prospect of Boldre Church', for example, I brought nature and history – specifically the sinking of HMS *Hood* and the subsequent loss of life (the lost sailors are commemorated in the church) – to bear on the picturesque scene:

> the sea
>
> Outside the frame: colder
> For fires quenched in a flash,
> For steel made a harrow
> Useless on the ocean bed;
>
> Even here, enclosed
> Above oaks above
> A full river, the sea
> Open, spirited shipless.[15]

My aim in the poem was to break an image or picture of place by opening it to the historical and natural forces that it belied, the forces that actually shape place.

In writing the poems in *Solent Shore* I was, among other things, resisting my own tendency to nostalgia. This is an element in most English 'poetry of place'. In an essay in an earlier book[16] of that title I discuss the 'context of loss' which, in my view, strongly affects the character of English poets of place after Wordsworth, and attaches them to past poets whom they identify with particular places. The connection between an enhanced 'sense of place' and the experience of displacement is one that I explore further in the present book. All the writers I discuss here were, in one way or another, unsettled, and came to see their original or ideal country in the light of their separation from it. Nostalgia was a temptation to them, but a temptation which, to varying degrees, they usually resisted, with arts of seeing that counter false vision, including ideas of an England that never existed, and picturesque renderings of landscape and place. But it is not my intention to draw a simple opposition between 'reality' and 'myth'. As my discussion of Edward Thomas reveals, his poetry is energized by a struggle to break out of picturesque and nostalgic formulations, and it is partly religious feeling, projected on to Nature, that opens him to a larger sense of identity as a human being.

As Yi-Fu Tuan has said: 'Oppressive society and a rich beauti-ful countryside are fully compatible. The countryside can always look innocent, for the instruments of rural exploitation exist most conspicuously as law courts and money markets which are all in the city.' Tuan proceeds to praise Raymond Williams for having 'shown ... that if we look closely and with imagination, the Eng-lish landscape will reveal a darker meaning'.[17] I acknowledge an intellectual debt to Raymond Williams and the school of criti-cism which, operating in and across a number of disciplines, examines literary texts in the context of the 'real' history, inter-prets landscapes as ideological constructs, and lays bare the power relations concealed in ideas and images of countryside and nation. Williams and the writers who follow him have done a great deal over the past twenty-five years to make us aware of 'a darker meaning' in English and other landscapes.

I too am involved, in this book, with the relation of seeing and vision to shaping historical, social and political influences upon writers and their work; but I am also concerned with a sense of the sacred and experiences of mystery, which I consider in their own terms, as well as in relation to the crisis of religious belief and its symbolic language which is a defining feature of the Vic-torian and modern periods.

When I first read *The Country and the City*, at the time of its original publication in 1973, I recognized it as a necessary book that would influence all subsequent thinking on its subject, mine as much as anyone's. At the same time, I was disturbed by Williams's tendency to subsume the particular in the gen-eral, as witnessed by the kind of judgement that lumped J. C. Powys together with a number of other writers and dismissed his 'country-based fantasy'. Thus, the whole Powysian world vanishes without a trace in a paragraph in which Williams talks about the falsification of 'the real land and its peoples', and says 'a traditional and surviving rural England was scribbled over and almost hidden from sight by what is really a suburban and half-educated scrawl'.[18] There is truth in Williams's criticism, if one reads the Powys novel by the light of the values of social realism (but not much truth, if one is prepared to admit the real strangeness of actual human experience). It is a criticism, how-ever, that has nothing to say about an essentially religious spirit, a sense of the sacred, which is present in Constable in an orthodox form, but manifests itself very differently in Powys's work.

I first started to read the writings of John Cowper Powys in the early seventies, and I found them profoundly liberating from narrow and rigid concepts of personal and human identity. Powys's writings are about freedom; they are liberating through what they show and what they teach – for he was also a teacher – about the exercise of 'the power within us to create and to destroy',[19] the power of the human soul. Powys is a Romantic libertarian in the tradition of William Blake, and he both renews an idea of the power of the imagination that is accessible to all, and anticipates the new ecological awareness that condemns our species chauvinism and listens with respect to all the non-human voices of the planet. It is above all in his treatment of the human imagination as a *natural* power that Powys affirms and enables freedom.

In *A Glastonbury Romance*, for example, as Sam and Mat Dekker look at the ruin of a medieval church, carvings 'telling the story of the Nativity and of the Massacre of the Innocents' – a religious story about birth and death – disclose 'in that rich confusion of organic shapes a general impression of earth-life', revealing 'what far-removed opposites in Nature the mind of man can reduce to an imaginative unity'.[20] In fact the drive of Powys's developing fiction was to show the multiverse underlying the universe, and the reality of individual creative consciousness – by no means an exclusively human phenomenon – which can survive the dissolution of ideas of order and unity and be at home in a world that is partly of its own making. One may not go all the way with Powys in his thinking, and there are other ways of depicting the sacred 'spirit of life'. But Powys's titanic imaginative world, in which the primary element is water, the medium of absolute potentiality, is a great affirmation of the inexhaustible possibilities of freedom. His achievement was to renew the idea and power of the imagination in the service of 'the *magical* view of life',[21] at a time when scientific and socio-historical determinism dominated the intellectual field.

I have written above of 'the forces that actually shape place'. By this I mean all the powers of nature, and historical and cultural forces, which include the power of the individual mind. It is a primary conviction animating my thinking in this book that the 'shaping spirit of Imagination' is not the least of the forces that make the identity of place. Wallace Stegner, the American writer, has even gone as far as to say 'no place is a place until it has a poet'.[22] I agree with Stegner in spirit but I would not couch my sense of the relation between writer and place in these words. The terms I prefer denote rather a reciprocal action of shaping, an action expressed most succinctly by David Jones in the Preface to *The Anathemata*, when he says 'one is trying to make a shape out of the very things of which one is oneself made'.[23] He is referring to the motifs that are his material, religious and cultural and historical 'things', things that made him before he shaped them in the form of a work of art. The material is personal too, of course: it is one's experience of childhood, of family and ancestry, of friendship, of love gained or lost. It is from the totality of human needs and influences and aspirations, from all that has made him or her a particular human being, unconscious as well as conscious, blind as well as seeing, that the writer shapes an imaginative world. And that world affects other people's sense of the actual places on which it is based, and may even become part of it, as in Hardy's Wessex. Yet the places continue to exist outside the writer's vision; they live on, and change, and are experienced and seen and interpreted differently by other people, constituting a human reality that reveals the limits of any one vision, at the same time as it is known partly through images, through what writer and painter have shown. My subject in this book is a complex reciprocal relationship. If 'no place is a place until it has a poet', no poet is a poet without the implaced motifs and material of which he or she is made.

All the writers considered in this book are men. Is that because David Sopher was right to suggest that attachment to home is 'perhaps always to some degree a male myth'?[24] In my view, no. A comparison of the culturally conditioned and possibly gender-influenced differences between the male and female 'sense of place' would make a fascinating subject. The geographical bounds of my field of study would have permitted such a comparison, if I had extended its temporal framework to include the time of Jane Austen, or if I had introduced such strikingly contrasting modern writers as Mary Butts and Sylvia Townsend Warner. It seems to me only right that I should acknowledge the existence of these choices, especially in the Preface to a book that includes discussions of *male* ideas of gender differences. It should be clear from this Preface, however, that I concentrate mainly on Hardy and Jefferies, Thomas and Powys in this book because they are the principal writers who helped me to see landscape and place. I learned to look partly with their eyes, and I learned to question both what I saw and their ways of seeing.

1
Landscape of childhood

There are two images that will help initially to illuminate the ground that I shall explore in this book. I take the first from Helen Thomas, who in her memoirs recalls visiting Ivor Gurney in Dartford Asylum in 1932. She took with her maps of Gloucestershire where her husband, Edward Thomas, had often walked.

> Ivor Gurney at once spread them out on his bed and he and I spent the whole time I was there tracing with our fingers the lanes and byways and villages of which Ivor Gurney knew every step and over which Edward had also walked. He spent that hour in revisiting his home, in spotting a village or a track, a hill or a wood and seeing it all in his mind's eye, with flowers and trees, stiles and hedges, a mental vision sharper and more actual for his heightened intensity. He trod, in a way we who were sane could not emulate, the lanes and fields he knew and loved so well, his guide being his finger tracing the way on the map.[1]

It had been evident to Helen Thomas on an earlier visit that Ivor Gurney 'identified Edward with the English countryside, especially that of Gloucestershire'. Now, tracing the places with his finger, Ivor Gurney 'had Edward as companion in this strange perambulation and he was utterly happy, without being overexcited'. Helen Thomas does not speak about lines or marks or names on the maps, but of 'lanes and byways and villages'. She knows that for Ivor Gurney the maps *are* the places.

Most readers will find this a deeply moving image, as did Helen Thomas. It also has a significance which extends beyond its revelation of the intense love of his native places that inspired Ivor Gurney as a poet and a musician. Gurney was strongly attached to Gloucestershire from childhood, but first the war and then his incarceration in the asylum sharpened his vision, as this image shows. His poems depict a land strongly marked by evidence of historical continuity, from the Roman period until the twentieth century, and the continuity is associated with an idea of community, which is a compound of the poet's youthful friendships and strongly idealized images of popular and literary and musical good fellowship, drawn from the Elizabethan age in particular. It is not my present purpose to analyse the effect of the war on Ivor Gurney's sense of England, his identification of England with Gloucestershire, or his obsession with his country's post-war betrayal of the 'honour' due to him as a soldier, a poet and a musician.[2] I want instead to dwell on the image of Ivor Gurney absorbed in the maps, or rather the places, which he revisits with the dead poet, Edward Thomas, as his companion.

The image, I suggest, is an extreme instance of a not uncommon experience among poets following Wordsworth, who have identified themselves with places with an intensity born of loss. They have seen places in terms of an idealized community, but their identification with place has been an expression of their isolation, and has been with fellow poets, seen as 'poets of place', rather than with a 'people'. It is an experience that may be traced through the nineteenth century and into the modern period, in Matthew Arnold's elegy for Wordsworth as 'a sacred poet', for example, and in Lionel Johnson's elegy for Arnold.[3] While Ivor Gurney identified Edward Thomas with England, he sometimes perceived himself as the voice of his country. In 'Larches', for example:

> I must play tunes like Burns, or sing like David,
> A saying-out of what the hill leaves unexprest,
> The tale or song that lives in it ...[4]

What Gurney actually voices in his songs, however, is not the spirit of a land imbued with the expression of a people, but real isolation occasionally softened by imaginary companionship.

Ivor Gurney's predicament was all the more tragic in that he was also, in the tradition of *Lyrical Ballads*, a seer of the common life. 'The Escape', for example, is comparable to Coleridge's statement in *Biographia Literaria* of Wordsworth's object, in his poems in *Lyrical Ballads*, to awaken 'the mind's attention to the lethargy of custom', and make people *see* the world before them. Gurney's poem is at once his credo and a wonderfully compact reaffirmation of the Romantic doctrine:

> I believe in the increasing of life: whatever
> Leads to the seeing of small trifles,
> Real, beautiful, is good; and an act never
> Is worthier than in freeing spirit that stifles
> Under ingratitude's weight, nor is anything done
> Wiselier than the moving or breaking to sight
> Of a thing hidden under by custom – revealed,
> Fulfilled, used (sound-fashioned) any way out to delight:
> Trefoil – hedge sparrow – the stars on the edge at night.[5]

In a movement characteristic of a number of Gurney's poems, a 'small trifle' – 'Trefoil' – is connected in a single vision to the cosmos – 'the stars on the edge at night' – which is simultaneously centred in place, since, here, 'the edge' is Cotswold Edge. Tragically, the crucial term missing from Ivor Gurney's vision connecting microcosm and macrocosm was a shared human world.

Edward Thomas was able at times in his poems to express something approaching a sense of community, or communion of spirits, in the English countryside. One of the finest examples of this is 'As the Team's Head-Brass'. The poem is especially poignant for the sense it conveys of the war encroaching on the land, not only in such significant details as 'the fallen elm', the talk about the war, and the death of the ploughman's mate in France, but also in the feeling that the action – the ploughing, the lovers entering and leaving the wood, the conversation between ploughman and poet – occupies the last moment of an epoch, before death descends upon them all and the world they share falls to pieces. What is significant within this context of suspense, however, is that ploughman and poet communicate easily and at a deep level, because they speak a common language. It is not only that they speak the same language, without any awkwardness of class difference, but that they share their feelings and thoughts, directly and intuitively. In this sense, it is almost as if they are one, and even for a reader who knows the poem well, a moment's inattention can result in the confusion of speakers. Communication between people at this level is extremely rare in Edward Thomas's poems, and his experience of its difficulty, as a fact of the society in which he lived, had a shaping effect upon him as man and writer.

Ivor Gurney was removed, literally, from the world he had once shared with his friends, and idealized as the ground of

community and historical continuity. It is against the achievement of 'As the Team's Head-Brass' that the extent of his loss can
be best measured. 'The Mangel-Bury', a poem Gurney wrote in
the asylum, begins:

> It was after war; Edward Thomas had fallen at Arras –
> I was walking by Gloucester musing on such things
> As fill his verse with goodness ...

He then describes, in images that recall the war and suggest his
neurasthenic condition, coming upon a mangel-bury, and helping a farmer load the vegetables onto a cart. But he has no contact with the man, except in his mind:

> We threw them with our bodies swinging, blood in my ears
>   singing;
> His was the thick-set sort of farmer, but well-built –
> Perhaps, long before, his blood's name ruled all,
> Watched all things for his own. If my luck had so willed
> Many questions of lordship I had heard him tell – old
> Names, rumours. But my pain to more moving called
> And him to some barn business far in the fifteen acre field.[6]

Unlike the world of 'As the Team's Head-Brass', the world of
'The Mangel-Bury' affords no relationship between the poet and
the farmer, and the one exists for the other only as a fantasy
of racial continuity and possession – in effect, an exaggerated
image of the kind of belonging he has lost. What actually impels
the poet, as an isolated and nerve-torn man, is pain. The image,
however, has an obverse: Ivor Gurney absorbed in the maps, that
are his places in ways that the actual country could never be. But
it is not only a tragic individual case we encounter in the double
image; it is also the end in English poetry of a line of relationships, which, in Wordsworth, connects not only the poet and the
solitary figure in the landscape, but relates them both to an idea
of humanity founded upon participation in a divinized natural
world.

The other image to which I referred at the beginning of this
chapter is from V. S. Naipaul's *The Enigma of Arrival*. In this
novel, a writer resembling Naipaul himself describes the journey
by aeroplane from Trindad to England that 'had given me my
first revelation: the landscape of my childhood seen from the
air'.[7] Seen from above, that which on the ground was 'so poor to

me, so messy', was 'a landscape of logic and larger pattern'. In effect, he has seen where he comes from for the first time: at 'the moment of departure, the landscape of my childhood was like something which I had missed, something I had never seen'.

Naipaul is highly conscious of the ironies of what he is showing: the external vision that reveals what was not seen among the 'mess' of living, 'a landscape of clear pattern and contours'; indeed the home ground seen 'like a landscape in a book, like the landscape of a real country'. I consider Naipaul's treatment of the complexities of seeing, in the context of post-colonial migration of peoples, later. Here, I want to use his image to illuminate the ground of my explorations in this book.

Places may exist in landscapes, and may be seen as landscapes, but they are not landscapes. Places are where people live, where they are enwombed, embedded in the communal and the familiar. The experience of place may be positive or negative, according to circumstances and individual outlook: a slave is tied to place against his or her will, and the outsider's idea of belonging may not correspond to what the native feels. It is quite possible not to *see* place, because it is too close, too well known. Landscapes, by contrast, are primarily visual phenomena. They are conventional ways of seeing that have been developed in Europe since the seventeenth century; literary landscapes are products of painted *landskips*, landscape gardens, books, and they are aesthetic and social constructs.

Landscapes have a history, which is strongly marked by the manipulations of the powerful – enclosers, improvers, masters of landed estates, arbiters of taste – and the dispossession of the powerless. Broadly speaking, literature of place in the Romantic and modern periods, from John Clare to Thomas Hardy, is the art of the displaced: those who, for a variety of reasons, which do not necessarily include their physical eviction from home ground, are either sufficiently 'removed' to see place as a landscape, or who exist in the uneasy but creative state of tension between a sense of communal belonging, and separation from the place and the people, which may include their own families. Removal may be physical, and enforced by politics or economics, as it was by enclosures and by the agricultural depresson beginning in the 1870s, which drove many labourers from the land; or it may be more subtle, and essentially a form of self-division, as it was in the case of Thomas Hardy. Removal, in this sense, enables the writer to see the ground he stands on with peculiar intensity, even his family and their values, but at a psychological and sometimes a social distance, because he is no longer part of it. The emphasis upon seeing is significant. Place is that which we perceive with all our senses; in psychological terms it is associated with the mother, with a condition of original oneness. This is one of the reasons why childhood is so important in literature of place, because it is associated with the primary state of belonging, which is at once secure and a condition of absolute potential. And it is why childhood was associated with revolutionary energy in the Romantic period, first in hope of the creative new beginning, and later as a form of turning inwards and looking towards the past, as desire for renewal was frustrated in the realm of social and political action.

If landscape is that which we see, place, when we learn to see it, may become landscape. And when the landscape is the writer's original place, it may move him to his depths. In this case, though, the landscape will probably be associated with an obscure sadness, a yearning, and an elegiac mood, for it is then the original country that can never be re-entered, a condition of complete being, Eden, or the Golden Age. As the religious feeling becomes identified with Nature, and therefore associated with landscape and place, the latter, too, is a locus of the sacred, a 'centre' where wholeness of being may be sought. It was largely through the influence of Wordsworth that landscape during the nineteenth century came to take the place of a much older form of worship: the Psalmist's Book of Nature, in which 'The heavens declare the glory of God; and the firmament sheweth his handiwork.'

George Eliot wrote with peculiar emotional force about the connection between childhood and place, in *The Mill on the Floss* (1860):

> We could never have loved the earth so well if we had had no childhood in it ... What novelty is worth that sweet monotony where everything is known, and *loved* because it is known?
> ... These familiar flowers, these well-remembered bird-notes, this sky with its fitful brightness, these furrowed and grassy fields, each with a sort of personality given to it by the capricious hedgerows – such things as these are the mother-tongue of our

imagination, the language that is laden with all the subtle inextricable associations the fleeting hours of our childhood left behind them.[8]

The emotional tone of the passage is reminiscent of Romantic poetry, especially that of John Clare who wrote of his childhood places with 'the mother-tongue' of his imagination. This is not, however, the tongue in which George Eliot writes, for even where she recaptures the emotion born of attachment, as in this passage, she writes, also, as the detached thinker, the intellectual, the woman who had to be separated from her childhood ground before she could write thus about 'our imagination'.

A comparable mixture of emotion and detached generalization characterizes the following passage from Mircea Eliade's *Myths, Dreams and Mysteries*:

> Even among Europeans of today there lingers an obscure feeling of mystical unity with the native Earth; and this is not just a secular sentiment of love for one's country or province, nor admiration for the familiar landscape or veneration for the ancestors buried for generations around the village churches. There is also something quite different; the mystical experience of autochthony, the profound feeling of having come from the soil, of having been born of Earth in the same way that the Earth, with her inexhaustible fecundity, gives birth to the rocks, rivers, trees and flowers. It is in this sense that autochthony should be understood: men feel that they are *people of the place*, and this is a feeling of cosmic relatedness deeper than that of familial and ancestral solidarity.[9]

Again, as in George Eliot's treatment of the connection between childhood and love of the earth, the words have an emotional resonance which arises not only from what is being affirmed, but from the writer's *historical* consciousness: his detached view of 'Europeans of today' and their feelings, and his knowledge that such awareness is a product not of 'cosmic relatedness', but of history. The intensity of the sense of belonging reveals a self-consciousness about the relationhip, and marks the writer's separation from place.

Yet, if 'the mystical experience of autochthony' belongs rather to the dream-life of modern men and women than to their social reality, it is a potent dream, which reveals deep human needs. Eliade's thinking offers a challenge to cultural materialism, which may be summed up by his observation that 'The more a consciousness is awakened, the more it transcends its own historicity'.[10] What is ultimately at issue is not only the conviction that men and women have integral spiritual and material needs, but an enlarged idea of human potential.

John Clare wrote that 'there is nothing but poetry about the existence of childhood', and 'there is nothing of poetry about manhood but the reflection and the remembrance of what has been'.[11] His poetry transcends the sentiment, as not all nineteenth- and twentieth-century English pastoral poetry does. In Clare, attachment to place constitutes more than nostalgia for an idea of the past; it is both an emotional commitment and a philosophy of man and nature, involving a quality of care and responsibility in opposition to a political system based on a mean and distorting view of human needs. At best, Romantic thinking about childhood transcends an infantile clinging to the past, and attempts to carry original creative energy from the past into the present, into the adult life, and a world in need of renewal and enlargement. To Coleridge, in *Biographia Literaria*, 'To carry on the feelings of childhood into the powers of manhood; to combine the child's sense of wonder and novelty with the appearances, which every day for perhaps forty years had rendered familiar ... is the character and privilege of genius.' In *Nature* (1836), Emerson described 'the lover of nature' as 'he whose inward and outward senses are still truly adjusted to each other; who has retained the spirit of infancy even into the era of manhood'.

From the beginning, in his Wordsworthian 'Domicilium',[12] Thomas Hardy's perception of his home area had an elegiac quality, and was marked by his awareness of the past, and his recognition of change. The landscapes of southern England bear the signs of a long and continuous human occupation: wooden and stone henges, tumuli, prehistoric and medieval field patterns underlying modern fields, and so on. The identity of the area is due in part to this, but owes more to its recreation as a literary landscape, in the writings of William Cobbett and Jane Austen, for example, and above all in the novels and poetry of Thomas Hardy. Jane Austen and William Cobbett were both very much concerned with their times. So was Hardy, of course. In his writings, however, the historical sense, which discloses the past in the present, Roman skeletons in Casterbridge gardens, or signs of evolutionary or prehistoric beginnings in cliff face or heath, is revealed as a response to modernity, which disrupted traditional patterns of life. In Hardy, therefore, what may appear to be a sense of continuity is rather an awareness of historicity and epochal differences. There is a tendency in his work to naturalize the human, and to explain character in terms of environment, but there is also a counter-emphasis, on the distinction between the human and the natural, and the uniqueness of the individual soul. His landscapes live because they are, in more than one sense, arenas of conflict, and because each is, as he said of Turner's water-colours, 'a landscape *plus* a man's soul'.

Hardy's sense of what might be called place-time, and his view of the human situation as a theatre in which domesticity and wildness interact, or conflict, is evident as early as 'Domicilium'. Hardy begins the poem by orientating his home and proceeds to set it in its natural context between woodland and heath. He establishes an intimacy between the inhabitants and their natural surroundings as much by his use of local names ('honeysucks', 'heathcroppers') as by their proximity to one another, but he is careful to separate human projections from the reality of non-human Nature: 'Wild honeysucks/Climb on the walls, and seem to sprout a wish/(If we may fancy wish of trees and plants)/To overtop the apple-trees hard by.' The movement of the poem is at first outward, in space, from the house among its trees and flowers to 'The distant hills and sky'. Hardy then introduces time into the scene, through an oak, 'springing from a seed/Dropped by some bird a hundred years ago', and 'days bygone –/Long gone', when his grandmother would walk with him and answer his question about the look of the place 'when first she settled here'. Her answer identifies time with change – 'Fifty years/Have passed since then, my child, and change has marked/The face of all things' – and emphasizes how wild the place formerly was:

> 'Our house stood quite alone, and those tall firs
> And beeches were not planted. Snakes and efts
> Swarmed in the summer days, and nightly bats
> Would fly about our bedrooms. Heathcroppers
> Lived on the hills, and were our only friends;
> So wild it was when first we settled here.'

Technically and in emotional maturity, there is of course an enormous difference between this early poem and the great sequence of poems which Hardy wrote more than fifty years later after the death of his wife. The sense of place-time in 'Poems of 1912–13', however, is recognizably the same as that of the young poet. The sequence begins with 'The Going', an event that left Hardy 'here', where he 'Saw morning harden upon the wall', an image that unites time and place at their most desolate and unyielding, as a kind of domestic solitary confinement for the lonely and grieving poet. 'Your great going', he says, 'Had place that moment, and altered all.' Not 'took place', which would have been the expected construction, but 'had place', an expression in which Emma's death takes possession of the house, wedding Hardy to loss.

The movement of the sequence as a whole is from 'here' to 'there': from death to life, the present to the past, Dorset to Cornwall. Already in 'The Going', it seems that it is the living poet who is dead, and his dead wife who is alive. From 'the yawning blankness/Of the perspective', Hardy turns to the past, and life in all its danger and exciting vitality:

> You were she who abode
> By those red-veined rocks far West,
> You were the swan-necked one who rode
> Along the beetling Beeny Crest,
> And, reining nigh me,
> Would muse and eye me,
> While Life unrolled us its very best.

Initially Hardy identifies himself as 'a dead man held on end/To sink down soon', but the *abiding* image of Emma, which he establishes in 'The Going', and which dominates the sequence, derives from his treatment of where she 'abode': the high and dangerous Cornish cliffs, where she was fearless and free.

'Poems of 1912–13' are, in more than one sense, an act of restoration. It is an act by which Hardy returns the woman who was his 'long housemate' to the liberty of her 'olden haunts'. In several of the greatest poems, 'After a Journey', 'Beeny Cliff', 'At Castle Boterel', he is able, as it were, to rejoin her temporarily, in memory, and what he then recaptures is the younger woman, the figure of romance, in the place that for him was 'pre-eminently ... the region of dream and mystery'.[13] Indeed, the Emma of the poems is seldom his wife, the woman who had lived with him

for nearly forty years and who had recently died. She is rather
the young woman, and the woman before she met him. In several poems Emma is the child. Thus, in 'Rain on a Grave', Hardy
says she will form 'the sweet heart' of the daisies, the flowers she
'Loved beyond measure/With a child's pleasure/All her life's
round'; in 'Lament', he associates her with snowdrops, which
'she would have sought/With a child's eager glance'; and in 'I
Found Her Out There' he imagines her shade returning underground to the west, until she joys in the throbs of the sea 'with
the heart of a child'. Hardy identifies Emma with wild flowers,
birds, the sea, horses, and her childhood; she is 'a ghost-girl-
rider', 'the woman riding high above with bright hair flapping
free'; she is more a spirit of place than she is a ghost.

In view of this, and armed with what we think we know about
the failure of Hardy's marriage, it would be easy enough to
argue that his concern in the poems is not Emma, but his
romance of the young woman. But in my view it would be truer
to see the sequence as an act of restoration. Donald Davie, in his
fine essay, 'Hardy's Virgilian Purples', says: 'The status of
Emma's *being*, now that she is dead – more than ever this metaphysical question seems to be the question that the poems ask,
and ask about.'[14] One way of understanding this would be to say
that in 'Poems of 1912–13' Hardy is in pursuit of Emma's inner-
most identity, her soul, not to possess it, but to restore it to its
original freedom. He links her with things that first engaged his
deepest feelings, first expressed in 'Domicilium' – Nature, and
the place that exists in Nature, between the domestic life and the
wild. He associates her with living things, but he does not identify the human with the non-human. As the young man did *not*
'fancy wish of trees and plants', so the old poet distinguishes
absolutely between love, 'a time of such quality', and 'primaeval
rocks', that 'record', beyond all 'transitory' manifestations of
geological time, 'that we two passed'. What exactly Hardy
means by this may be disputed. It seems indisputable to me,
however, that Hardy associates Emma's spirit with the Cornish
rocks and sea – which is his image of that which endures.

If the predominant impression of 'Poems of 1912–13' is the
transcendence of time, that is a mark of their difference from
most of Hardy's other work, for he was not only time-conscious,
but a writer who persistently thought and felt and saw in terms

of place-time. Hardy was, as it were, born into a world far older than that of his predecessors, since the vistas of geological time had been opened up in the decades immediately before his birth. His sense of the age of the earth and of the evolutionary process is a shaping influence upon his 'Wessex'. If the physical sciences helped to undermine Hardy's religious faith, they also provided him with the image of 'a cleft landscape', in which the beginnings of life were revealed, and to which he responded with imaginative awe.

A remarkable expression of this is the scene in Chapter XXII of *A Pair of Blue Eyes*, in which Henry Knight, clinging to the Cliff without a Name, and in imminent danger of falling to his death, comes face to face with the fossil trilobite. 'It was a creature with eyes. The eyes, dead and turned to stone, were even now regarding him.' What Knight saw was 'himself at one extremity of the years, face to face with the beginning and all the intermediate centuries simultaneously'. With evident imaginative relish, Hardy provides his character with a vision of 'time closed up like a fan', which displayed evolution in reverse, from 'fierce men, clothed in the hides of beasts', back to 'elephantine forms', 'huge-billed birds', 'crocodilian outlines', 'dragon forms and clouds of flying reptiles', 'fishy beings of lower development', and so to 'the lifetime scenes of the fossil confronting him'. It takes 'less than half a minute' for Knight to see the images with his inner eye.

The emphasis is upon seeing: the dead eyes of the fossil trilobite, which nevertheless 'were even now regarding' Knight, and the man's intelligence, with which he is capable of both seeing his place in Nature, as one of 'the strugglers for life', and realizing 'the dignity of man'. Hardy observes, of 'the varied scenes' Knight saw, 'There is no place like a cleft landscape for bringing home such imaginings as these.' And, he might have added, no time like the age of Lyell and Darwin. Armed with their discoveries and theories, it is of course Hardy who 'cleaves' the landscape, and sees in a moment the epochs of evolutionary time. The moment that discloses time in depth, and places which provide such moments, are characteristic of Hardy's way of seeing and feeling, and they have helped to produce a symbolic language of time and place and landscape. In opening place to a vista of 'the beginning', Hardy made a vast temporal space available to the writers who followed him, and who have, for the most part, interpreted it differently.

T. F. Powys is in many respects a writer quite unlike Hardy: an allegorist preoccupied with theodicy, an equivocal mystic, and a whimsical and ironic comic writer, who humbles the human intelligence in face of the absolutes of Love and Death. Yet, like his brothers, Llewelyn and John Cowper Powys, T. F. Powys was influenced by Hardy, especially in his rendering of landscape. In his novel *Mockery Gap*, for example, he describes night falling on 'the blind-cow rock',[15] 'giving the true bass note to the colours of the evening, the blackness of despair':

> Clouds that earlier in the day had been but shining vapour, now became real and yet more real and grew sensibly darker. The cliff, the fields below, the church that waited for the night, even the tiny shining of the little water-brooks, were beginning to express the supreme loneliness of lonely silence – of the beauty that dies.
>
> Shadows, born of the shadow of the blind cow, began to creep here and there like monstrous toads and thick vipers. The shadows became more and more monstrous as the sun dropped, while some amongst them now showed a likeness to him that is called Man, a dweller upon the earth.[16]

The influence of Hardy on this, and especially of the opening chapter of *The Return of the Native*, is unmistakable. Both passages are portentous, and strain for effect, yet are impressive, too, and succeed in sounding the 'bass note'. Both use landscape to present an image of man: in Hardy, 'slighted and enduring', in Powys, 'a dweller upon the earth'. Powys, however, is concerned with the 'monstrous', with evil, with death and beauty, and with 'eternal truth', and translates his landscape (or seascape) into metaphysical terms. He is preoccupied with seeing, like Hardy in the scene at the Cliff without a Name; with 'the true look of the land ... to be seen by those who have eyes to see'. But who does see, when the ultimate reality is hidden, and may be known, perhaps, only by those blinded by death?

Llewelyn Powys's treatment of the same natural phenomenon, in his essay, 'The Blind Cow',[17] is much more straightforward. To him, it symbolizes 'the obdurate reality of matter'. Yet he has the 'fancy' that out of nature 'there does rise a certain whisper of hope challenging to the sottish absolute domination of the Blind Cow'. He describes a heightened moment walking along the shingle, when he 'might have been walking upon a shoal of infinity, upon a sea-bank of eternity, actual but at the same time transcendental'. In this mood he comes upon a guillemot fouled with oil. 'Down to my very marrow-bones I knew for certain that the Blind Cow rules all.' He is confirmed in his conviction that 'All life destroys other life to live'.

> In death alone is the hope of the unhappy, in that utter annihilation that brings a fortunate peace to restless life. Make no doubt, there never has been a particle of truth in those simple and beautiful words of Jesus. They represent the passionate wish of a deluded poet, and that is all. 'Are not five sparrows sold for two farthings and not one of them is forgotten before God?'

In both brothers' writing (and at times in that of John Cowper Powys, too) one can hear the prophetic note, the note, perhaps, of their father's sermons, but, instead of his evangelical Christianity, Llewelyn Powys is the atheist preacher, and T. F. Powys the 'dark' mystic. For both the Blind Cow is associated with death, but for Llewelyn Powys it symbolizes 'determined unimplicated matter, against which the sensitive spray of life throughout the millenniums has dashed itself in vain', while for T. F. Powys the waves that struck the rock in its 'dead state' 'became intense and living'. He invokes 'the Name, and the terror and love of it that hides so silent behind the tomb'. The Name 'must for ever hide, too, the ultimate truth. God, for ever and everlasting, life without end – God'.[18] Would it be too simple to say categorically that the rock symbolizes death, and the sea eternity? Probably. In his funny and disturbing stories T. F. Powys stretches language and human understanding to their limits, and shows that what we do not see, and do not know, may be the divine reality.

There is a mystical element in other writers whose work I consider in the following chapters. In Richard Jefferies, not only in *The Story of My Heart* and essays such as 'The Dawn' and 'Nature and Eternity', but in *Bevis* and in his more pedestrian work, where, entering a wood, he finds himself at 'the gates of another world'.[19] In Edward Thomas's discovery in south country landscapes of 'a region out of space and out of time',[20] and in John Cowper Powys's 'marginal' intuitions. All the writers are modern in the sense that they live in the culture of a dying religion, and with a language permeated by that condition. But their responses to the common situation are different. What this means in effect is that 'mystical' and 'religious' are words whose meaning cannot be taken for granted, and then imposed on the writers, but only revealed through explorations of the individual vision. John Cowper Powys, writing in the early years of the Second World War, summed up 'what has happened in our time'. 'Individual men and women', he claimed, 'in great numbers all over Europe have ceased to believe in the soul.'[21] What he means by the soul is 'that great magician', which he understands, in Blakean terms, as creator and destroyer of the whole universe of metaphysics and philosophy, and capable of transforming the individual through his or her imaginative capacity. Richard Jefferies said of himself: 'Never was such a worshipper of earth. The commonest pebble, dusty and marked with the stain of the ground, seems to me so wonderful; my mind works round it till it becomes the sun and centre of a system of thought and feeling.'[22] He uses the same word as Powys, but his emphasis is different: 'The chief use of matter is to demonstrate to us the existence of the soul.' The common ground between John Cowper Powys and Richard Jefferies is not that they assign the same meaning to the word 'soul', but that each has a sense of human potential, a capacity for the individual to change his or her life, and for human beings to create a new world. My concern in this book is accordingly not only with the history to which the writings about landscape and place respond, but also with the desire for enlargement of being, and for glimpses of the infinite and the eternal, expressed in mysticism and the use of myth, and by which the writer seeks to transcend historicity. I am concerned with complications of the art of seeing, in response to political and religious issues. However complicated vision becomes, it should be remembered nevertheless that it arises, in each instance, from places known and loved in childhood, and seen with the growing mind, and that the original sense of wonder remains part of the later experience, even when it is an experience of separation and isolation. Gratitude, also, is part of my subject, in the sense that the writers considered in this book would have understood what the painter Stanley Spencer felt about his birthplace and the chestnut trees he loved for 'just being'.[23]

2

Richard Jefferies: The art of seeing

Vincent Van Gogh wrote to his brother Theo at the end of September 1888:

> If we study Japanese art we see a man who is undoubtedly wise, philosophical and intelligent, who spends his time how? In studying the distance between the earth and the moon? No. In studying the policy of Bismarck? No. He studies a single blade of grass.
>
> But this blade of grass leads him to draw every plant and then the seasons, the wide aspects of the countryside, then animals, then the human figure. So he passes his life, and life is too short to do the whole.[1]

This serves well as a general description of the art of the writer Richard Jefferies, a contemporary of Van Gogh, and whose vision, as I shall later show, had affinities with that of the Dutch painter. In his writings on Nature and rural English society Jefferies frequently starts with the particular, with something seen at a certain time in a specific place. He then moves from close observation of the plant, animal or natural feature to cover a widening expanse, and thus reveals the life of a locality in depth, including people and their social organization. This is one of several respects in which he differs crucially from Gilbert White, whose 'artist's eye for landscape'[2] Jefferies compared to Turner's. But White, 'the great observer', described animals and birds, not people. Even in *Hodge and his Masters* (1880), one of his journalistic and apparently less artistic works, Jefferies usually begins his sketches by picturing a small detail, action or incident, and proceeds to introduce the human character into the context of place. He then draws out the social significance of what he shows, so that he depicts the individual within both his natural and social world.

Jefferies describes movements in space that are often movements in time, too: across the seasons, but also between present and past, and present and future. The farthest physical reach of his characteristic movement is from blade of grass or particle of dust to sun and stars. In his later writings, the movement is from the seen to the unseen, from the known to the unknown, and from the world of traditional and customary ideas to a larger idea, an idea that has yet to be thought. Jefferies' writings about nature are alive to hearing, taste, smell, and especially touch, and his frequent combination of the senses reveals the life beyond appearances and produces sensuous delight. It is from the seen, however, that he often starts. His seeing is aesthetic – he is consciously a painter of word-pictures which disclose the inadequacy of nineteenth-century vision and of the landscape-painting that he described in Amaryllis at the Fair (1887) as 'nature in a dress-coat' – but it is not only aesthetic. What gives Jefferies' art of seeing extension and depth is his ability to see nature in several capacities simultaneously: as an observer; as a naturalist; as a hunter; as an explorer; and as a farmer's son, who understands the significance of what he sees to the farmer, the labourer and the poacher. Moreover, his position is, in several respects, that of a mediator, including a mediator between the country life of which he writes, and the townspeople who, in the main, formed his readership. As his writing moves from the particular, so it usually moves through, or combines, observation, information, imagination and speculation.

Jefferies' description of 'the common rushes' in 'The Pageant of Summer' is a classic instance of his capacity to both ennoble and defamiliarize the lowly object, and also, with near vision, to enlarge the world. It was a capacity which he shared with other Victorians, poets and naturalists, such as Tennyson and Philip Henry Gosse, who were very different from him in temperament and belief. The 'myth' of Jefferies overemphasizes his intellectual isolation, whereas in fact there were important points of contact between his mode of perception and that of other Victorians. What most distinguishes Jefferies from his contemporaries are a quality of personal expression, and the lengths to which he took his art of seeing, which resulted in extreme intellectual iconoclasm.

One reason why critics have found Jefferies hard to classify is ᵗ he was a writer of extremes. In terms of gender stereotypes, ᵇʰ are, as I shall later show, important when discussing ᵉˢ, he was preoccupied with male ideas of power and mas-

tery. But he had, too, a tender and spiritual perception of nature
– indeed, a quality of love – which he identified with the heroines of his fiction. In the following passage, for example, we see
with Amaryllis's eyes:

> They were the white wild violets, the sweetest of all, gathered
> while the nightingale was singing his morning song in the April
> sunshine – a song the world never listens to, more delicious than
> his evening notes, for the sunlight helps him, and the blue of the
> heavens, the green leaf, and the soft wind – all the soul of spring.
>
> White wild violets, a dewdrop as it were of flower, tender and
> delicate, growing under the great hawthorn hedge, by the mosses
> and among the dry, brown leaves of last year, easily overlooked
> unless you know exactly where to go for them.[3]

These, we know, are Jefferies' feelings, but it is easier for him to
identify them with Amaryllis than to present them directly as his
own. Indeed, where Jefferies expresses his spirituality most
directly, in *The Story of My Heart* (1883), it seems to me that he
communicates less effectively than he does when he dramatizes
and embodies his feelings in his mature fiction, or in the semi-
narrative form of his later essays. In this passage, he writes with
special knowledge, a knowledge born of care for the things other
people disdain ('a song the world never listens to'; the violets are
'easily overlooked'). The nightingale is not a bird only, but utters
'all the soul of spring', and the beauty of the violets is their
purity ('a dewdrop as it were of flower'), as well as their sweetness, tenderness and delicacy. If the song and the violets are
neglected by the world, so are the feelings they provoke in Jefferies, feelings which the increasingly mechanical and imperialis-
tic society in which he lived marginalized by ascribing them
exclusively to women.

A late essay, 'Meadow Thoughts' (1884), begins, as much of
Jefferies' writing does, with his original home, the small farm at
Coate near Swindon:

> The old house stood by the silent country road, secluded by many
> a long, long mile, and yet again secluded within the great walls of
> the garden. Often and often I rambled up to the milestone which
> stood under an oak, to look at the chipped inscription low down –
> 'To London, 79 miles'. So far away, you see, that the very inscrip-
> tion was cut at the foot of the stone, since no one would be likely to
> want that information. It was half hidden by docks and nettle

despised and unnoticed. A broad land this seventy-nine miles – how many meadows and corn-fields, hedges and woods, in that distance? – wide enough to seclude any house, to hide it, like an acorn in the grass. Those who have lived all their lives in remote places do not feel the remoteness. No one else seemed to be conscious of the breadth that separated the place from the great centre, but it was, perhaps, that consciousness which deepened the solitude to me.[4]

Again, as he did with the common rushes and the wild white violets, Jefferies magnifies the part and enlarges our sense of the whole. Here, he restores depth, breadth and remoteness to part of Wiltshire, to the 'secluded' house, hidden 'like an acorn in the grass', and thus expands the constricted world of mid-Victorian England. 'An hour or two only by rail' again becomes the seventy-nine miles felt by the observer rooted in one place, and the distance shrunk by the railway is restored to 'a great, broad province of green furrow and ploughed furrow between the old house and the city of the world'. So far, it would appear to be an essay about belonging, which bears out what Jefferies says about the country: 'It is necessary to stay in it like the oaks to know it.' That is how Gilbert White knew Selborne, of course. But it is not exactly how Jefferies knew the country round Coate, which his admirers would call 'Jefferies' Land'. Even as the opening paragraph of 'Meadow Thoughts' unfolds, the feeling of shared seclusion becomes a sense of personal solitude, and also of separation from nature, as Jefferies notes: 'everything is so utterly oblivious of man's thought and man's heart'.

In order to gain a fuller view of 'Jefferies' Land', it is first necessary to ask a basic but difficult question: who was Richard Jefferies? In a letter[5] written towards the end of his life, Jefferies wrote: 'I am only too proud to say I am a son of the soil and to add that my family have been farmers and landowners for nearly 300 years, a pedigree as good I think as many titled names can claim.' In a memorable sentence, Edward Thomas described Jefferies in relation to his native land as 'the genius, the human expression, of this country, emerging from it, not to be detached from it any more than the curves of some statues from their maternal stone'.[6] He called Jefferies an 'earth-spirit', and in words that implicity acknowledge the feminine side of Jefferies, he described him as 'a rib' taken from the side of the land, the 'immense Maternal Downs'.[7] There is nothing in the plain facts of Jefferies' life to account for this myth-making. His own father said of his writings after his death: 'How he could think of describing Coate as such a pleasant place and deceive so I could not imagine, in fact nothing scarcely he mentions is in Coate proper only the proper one was not a pleasant one.'[8] The father could not understand his son's need to idealize. And perhaps that need would have been less great if the reality had been more ideal. Most of the time between the ages of four and nine, Richard lived away from Coate, with his aunt in Sydenham. From 1866 to 1873 he worked irregularly as a reporter on local newspapers in North Wiltshire and South Gloucestershire. A fragment of early writing, 'Hyperion',[9] which seems to be autobiographical, describes 'a youth in an obscure country village, quite lost in the rudest and most illiterate county of the West, who passed a great part of his time reading books, dreaming, so much so that he was useless on the farm'. For all its idealizing of Jefferies' original home, *Amaryllis at the Fair* describes extreme family tensions and is a novel full of violent feeling, while in his last essay, 'My Old Village', Jefferies speaks of the unfriendliness of the villagers towards him and of their mutual 'incompatibility'. It would seem, therefore, that his life at Coate was, at least, not idyllic. From 1877 to 1882 he lived in Surbiton, and during the same period, in 1878, his father sold up at Coate and moved to Bath where he worked as an odd-jobbing gardener. Jefferies lived in West Brighton from 1882 to 1884, in Eltham from 1884 to 1885, and in Goring from 1886 until his death in the following year. It is evident from this skeletal account that the writings for which he is best known, whose setting is Coate and the surrounding area, were written retrospectively and at a geographical distance. They were written, moreover, after the beginning of the great agricultural depression which profoundly affected life in the English countryside, and against a background of urban growth, that transformed not only London, which, as a writer and journalist, he knew well, but also the Swindon of his boyhood and young manhood. Jefferies' writings as a whole are true to the complexity of his life and circumstances; it is only parts of his work that help to sustain the myth.

It is Raymond Williams who, in *The Country and the City*, notes 'a myth of Jefferies' and sets out to correct it by describing the 'reality';

The suburban writer and journalist, recreating the country of his adolescence on the struggling smallholding; the sick man, perhaps the most brilliant imaginative observer of trees and animals and flowers and weather in his century, going on looking and writing until he said at the end: 'nothing for man in nature ... unless he has the Beyond'...; the ambitious, hardworking young man, writing in the interest of landed proprietors and employers ...[10]

This is indeed a useful corrective, but it can be taken too far. Thus, an anthology of Jefferies' prose such as that edited by Richard Mabey for the Penguin English Library, *Landscape with Figures* (1983), virtually effects what might be called a spiritual emasculation of the author. Mabey rightly draws attention to an important aspect of Jefferies' work, but one could hardly gather from reading his anthology why Q. D. Leavis should have described Jefferies as 'a many-sided and comprehensive genius'.[11] The problem for the critic or anthologist of Jefferies is, of course, that the journalist who contributed articles to journals such as *The Live Stock Journal and Fancier's Gazette* is the same man whose writing is often discussed and anthologized in books about mysticism.[12] In his balanced study, *Richard Jefferies*, W. J. Keith justly says of the 'apparent dichotomy between the reporter and the mystic' in Jefferies that 'the two must be appreciated together and not in isolation'.[13] It is, I believe, in looking at Jefferies' art of seeing that we can perceive the one man whose diverse writings only appear to fragment.

In going over home ground 'Meadow Thoughts' returns us to writings of Jefferies' early maturity, notably *Wild Life in a Southern County*, *Round About a Great Estate*, and *The Amateur Poacher*. There is, however, a great difference. These books were published in 1879 and 1880, before the breakdown of Jefferies' health in 1881, after which his seeing, subtilized by pain and disappointment, became sharper and more philosophical. It also became at once harder in its realism and more idealistic. Jefferies had an acute sense of the eternal 'Now', and of the presence of the past in the countryside, but his way of seeing was modern, as Turner and Van Gogh were modern painters. One of the key passages for understanding this is in 'Walks in the Wheat-Fields' (1887), where he praises Turner's *Rain, Steam, and Speed* as 'a most wonderful picture'. 'Turner painted the railway train and made it at once ideal, poetical, and classical.' Jefferies then shows

the relation between the real and the ideal in his art of seeing.
'He who has got the sense of beauty in his eye can find it in
things as they really are, and needs no stagey time of artificial
pastorals to furnish him with a sham nature. Idealise to the full,
but idealise the real, else the picture is a sham.'[14]

As Jefferies shows in his portrait of Felise in *The Dewy Morn*
(1884), having the sense of beauty in the eye depends upon love.
'Her love made earth divine.' In Edward Thomas's words, the
'clear concentrated sight and patient mind' which distinguish
Jefferies' imagination are born of love. To this it should be added
that Jefferies, as I think Alain A. Delattre[15] was the first to
demonstrate, had an eidetic memory. Professor Delattre quotes
'A Roman Brook' (1883):

> The brook has forgotten me, but I have not forgotten the brook ... I
> wonder if any one else can see it in a picture before the eyes as I
> can, bright, and vivid as trees suddenly shown at night by a great
> flash of lightning. All the leaves and branches and the birds at
> roost are visible during the flash. It is barely a second; it seems
> much longer. Memory, like the lightning, reveals the pictures in the
> mind. Every curve, and shore, and shallow is as familiar now as
> when I followed the winding stream so often.[16]

It is evident from this passage that there is no contradiction
between recalling 'things as they really are', and idealizing them
in the light of a strong emotion such as love or nostalgia.

The enlargement effected by Jefferies in 'Meadow Thoughts' –
a geographical and imaginative enlargement, which restores
depth and living detail to the drastically foreshortened view –
recalls the *pedestrian* style which, although Jefferies never aban-
doned it, characterizes the nature books of his early maturity. In
these, he is an explorer, who opens up the farm and fields, and
the hills and villages near Coate, as contemporary pioneers were
at work in North America, and Livingstone and Stanley opened
up East Africa to the white man in the 1870s. From an early age,
Jefferies had identified himself with the archetypal adventurer:
'Ulysses was ever my pattern and model: that man of infinite
patience and resource.'[17] His father as a young man had worked
as an itinerant labourer in America and Canada, and Richard
had been excited by his stories. The boys in *Bevis* remake their
small corner of Wiltshire in images of the globe, and Jefferies as a
young naturalist fancied 'that this country is an epitome of the

natural world', and saw in Coate Water an illustration of 'the great ocean which encircles the world'.[18] In his sense of living connection to the cosmos, Jefferies is the English writer who most resembles D. H. Lawrence. Rather than dwell on this at present, however, I wish to examine the pedestrian style of Jefferies as he explores English places, taking us on foot over the ground, moving slowly, or standing or sitting still, practising his art of seeing, as Constable did, under every hedge.

The title of *Round About a Great Estate* suggests a pattern in which the artistry is implicit in the way of seeing: going round and about over the ground, observing things, seeing their connections, so that a detailed, living world gradually enlarges before us. In his Preface to *Wild Life in a Southern County*, Jefferies writes:

> There is a frontier line to civilization in this country yet, and not far outside its great centres we come quickly even now on the borderland of nature.[19]

But, he continues, the difficulty confronting the explorer of nature and humanity in 'the veritable backwoods of primitive England' is that one thing cannot be separated from another; the subjects are 'closely connected'. He therefore arranges his chapters 'to correspond in some degree with the contour of the country', beginning high on the Downs, and following a stream down to the village and the hamlet; the stream becomes a brook, which he follows to 'a solitary farmhouse'; he then explores the fields, hedges and copse around the farm, and finishes in the Vale. The movement between Hills and Vale, or from the Vale to the Hills, with Coate as the centre, occurs often in Jefferies' writings; only in the later writings, in *The Story of My Heart* (1883), for instance, the movement on foot changes from an exploration to map the terrain into a spiritual ascent from the known to the unknown.

A passage characteristic of Jefferies in exploratory mode in *Wild Life in a Southern County* shows us the progress of an ant through grass on the Downs. The ant has 'no path through the jungle':

> Coming to a broader leaf, which promises an open space, it is found to be hairy, and therefore impassable except with infinite trouble; so the wayfarer endeavours to pass underneath, but has in the end to work round it. Then a breadth of moss intervenes, which

is worse than the vast prickly hedges with which savage kings fence their cities to the explorer, who can get no certain footing on it, but falls through and climbs up again twenty times, and burrows a way somehow in the shady depths below.

Next, a bunch of thyme crosses the path: and here for a lengthened period the ant goes utterly out of sight, lost in the interior, slowly groping round about within, and finally emerging in a glade where your walking-stick, carelessly thrown on the ground, bends back the grass and so throws open a lane to the traveller. In a straight line the distance thus painfully traversed may be ten or twelve inches ... [20]

Jefferies goes on to say that from this daylong process 'some faint idea may be obtained of the journeys thus performed, against difficulties and obstacles before which the task of crossing Africa from sea to sea is a trifle'. Jefferies is quite conscious of what he is doing, as the references to African exploration show. 'Unexplored England' was the title of a book he had in mind to write in 1878, at the same time as he was thinking about the book that became *Wild Life in a Southern County*, in which his explorations of Wiltshire clearly owe a good deal to his reading of contemporary accounts of African exploration. The ant as he describes it is itself an explorer, and by its means Jefferies opens up the interior, and pushes back the frontier of the unseen and the unknown. The process he discovers among the grass enlarges the world, making ten or twelve inches the space of the ant's laborious struggle, as in 'Meadow Thoughts' he recovers the breadth and depth of the land from the train journey of 'an hour or two only'.

In 1886, in *The Mayor of Casterbridge*, Thomas Hardy wrote about the England of country people in the 1830s: 'To the liege subjects of Labour, the England of those days was a continent, and a mile a geographical degree.' In 1826, William Cobbett spoke to a woman aged about thirty who had never been more than two and a half miles from her Wiltshire village. Jefferies lived at a time when the rural England which Hardy described and Cobbett had experienced was more a memory than a reality. In fact, the whole world was being expanded and contracted simultaneously: expanded by the opening up of continents, and contracted by the development of means of communication and locomotion that spanned them. Britain was at the centre of this process, and at home the movement of people to towns and the growth of the railways and of new means of communication, which contributed to the centring of consciousness upon London and the manufacturing districts, tended to shrink the country, marginalize 'wild England', and diminish the sense of the sacred in nature which for many Victorians was their religion. It was to this process that Jefferies' enlargement of vision was a response. His art of seeing was a way of restoring the mind to a 'natural' scale, insect or human, and thus awakening a sense of wonder at what the attentive and receptive eye can actually see. But the physical vision had metaphysical implications.

John Pearson, in a talk about *The Rise of Maximin*,[21] Jefferies' adventure novel serialized in the *New Monthly Magazine* in 1876–7 but not rediscovered until 1975, has said that Jefferies was alarmed as well as fascinated by contemporary discoveries in central Africa because they 'were leading to a removal of that sense of mystery which Jefferies found so essential to a full life'. Pearson quotes a passage from Jefferies' early novel *Restless Human Hearts* (1875) in which he says:

> The world has grown so small. Time was ... when there was a Verge, an Edge, beyond which there was an unknown something for man to seek. All the continents are found now, the geographers assure us that no more remains to be discovered. Excepting only a few small spots, and these, too, narrowing daily, the whole surface of the earth has been surveyed and mapped out and reduced to scale.

As Pearson observes, 'this paradox of expansion making smaller is accompanied by a feeling of near-claustrophobia, and a sense that the world is worn-out'. Jefferies' response to his reduced and exhausted world took two main forms: an art of seeing that enlarged and re-enchanted the natural domain, and fictional recreations of an age of adventure, through a return to either an idealized childhood or an imagined past, in *Wood Magic* (1881) and *Bevis* (1882), *The Rise of Maximin* and *After London* (1885). The literary forms are distinct, but a common spirit animates them. The values of the adventure stories infiltrate Jefferies' mysticism, which reflects both the imperial spirit and corresponding Victorian ideas of gender. There are closer connections between Jefferies' prayer for 'power of soul' in *The*

Story of My Heart, his Caesarism, and his idea of mastery in *After London* than has been recognized. I shall return to this theme in my next chapter.

There is no disjunction between the man who sees the ant traversing ten or twelve inches of the Downs and the man who can sometimes remind us of Thomas Traherne:

> If we had never before looked upon the earth, but suddenly came to it man or woman grown, set down in the midst of a summer mead, would it not seem to us a radiant vision? The hues, the shapes, the song and life of birds, above all the sunlight, the breath of heaven, resting on it; the mind would be filled with its glory, unable to grasp it, hardly believing that such things could be mere matter and no more. Like a dream of some spirit-land it would appear, scarce fit to be touched lest it should fall to pieces, too beautiful to be long watched lest it should fade away. So it seemed to me as a boy, sweet and new like this each morning; and even now, after the years that have passed, and the lines they have worn in the forehead, the summer mead shines as bright and fresh as when my foot first touched the grass. It has another meaning now; the sunshine and the flowers speak differently, for a heart that has once known sorrow reads behind the page, and sees sadness in joy. But the freshness is still there, the dew washes the colours before dawn. Unconscious happiness in finding wild flowers – unconscious and unquestioning, and therefore unbounded.[22]

Earth fills the mind with 'glory'. In 'Footpaths' (1880) Jefferies wrote: 'For such is the beauty of the sunlight that it can impart a glory even to dust.'[23] It is his eye, observing a sunlit particle of dust as closely as he watched the ant, that sees the glory. It is not the glory of God Jefferies sees, as it was for Traherne, nor does he see a world in a grain of sand. But the intensity with which he sees 'mere matter', whether it is a flower or the dust, leads him towards a sense of its complete otherness, its existence beyond all perceptions, images, concepts. The seeing is visionary, with the dawn freshness of his boyhood, but it is realistic too, with a political dimension. In my view, it makes as much sense to abstract either the 'political' or the 'mystical' Jefferies as it does to talk about two Van Goghs: the painter of 'dark' studies of labourers, and the painter of landscapes filled with the sun. Jefferies was impressed by *Leaves of Grass*; he too knew, like Whitman, that 'nothing is consistent that is human'.[24] His unity comprehends divisions and contradictions, and his early work contains possibilities which his later writings develop.

Jefferies is so well able to create an illusion of immediacy that it is initially a shock to realize that his finest descriptions of Coate farm and the country of north Wiltshire were written retrospectively and somewhere else. In 'Meadow Thoughts' he wrote: 'It is ten years since I last reclined on that grass plot, and yet I have been writing of it as if it was yesterday, and every blade of grass is as visible and as real to me now as then.'[25] What Jefferies shows in fact is that it is necessary to see a place from, or in awareness of, some distance in order to be intensely conscious of it. His life and work exemplify the pattern of modern writing about place. Distance is an essential ingredient in all seeing, and in writing about place this is usually true not only physically, but in a social sense. We do not normally see what we are part of, so that writing about place is rarely by people who 'stay in it like the oaks'. A John Clare or a Richard Jefferies is made as much by loss as by what he feels he once held. Hence the importance to a sense of place of chosen or enforced mobility, of estrangement, alienation, exile. Although Jefferies moved nearer London partly in order to further his ambitions, he too was affected by the history that obliged men like his father to give up their farms, and many agricultural labourers to leave the land for the cities, or emigrate to the New World or the colonies. Jefferies wrote in 'After the County Franchise' of the difficulty of making a home, a settled place with long associations, in the 1880s. Coombe Oaks was such a place: 'a grown house, if you understand; a house that had grown in the course of many generations, not built to set order; it had grown like a tree that adapts itself to circumstances, and, therefore, like the tree it was beautiful to look at.'[26] Jefferies betrays his anxiety that the reader might not understand, for he is probably a man situated as he is, in a 'modern style' rented villa, which can never be a 'home'. In Jefferies' case, as in that of many others, his sense of his original home was heightened by his later homelessness.

But Jefferies was evidently never really close to the people of his village, or perhaps to his own parents, either. His eye for people was extraordinary, and to begin with, at least, it had an anthropologist's, or even a naturalist's, detachment:

The labourer's muscle is that of a cart horse, his motions lumbering

> and slow. His style of walk is caused by following the plough in early childhood, when the weak limbs find it a hard labour to pull the heavy nailed boot from the thick clay soil. Ever afterwards he walks as if it were an exertion to lift his legs.

So Jefferies wrote in one of the letters[27] to *The Times* with which he first made a name for himself. In *Hodge and his Masters*, in particular, Jefferies wrote as a self-appointed pedagogue and social critic, and his observations of 'young Hodge' or 'country girls' or men at work in country or city have an unpleasant tone. He is a voyeur, and a spy snooping and writing on behalf of authority. He sounds like a prig and a snob, and the seriousness with which he takes himself as a pedagogue can be comic. All of which, I think, reflects the insecurity of his social position: he is, as it were, *between* the labourers and the farmers, and *between* the agricultural world and his urban, middle-class readership – between them, and separated from both. This is a peculiarly English phenomenon, a product of a class society, which calls to mind V. S. Pritchett's description of George Orwell as 'a writer who has "gone native" in his own country'.[28] Jefferies belongs in part with the Victorian and modern writers and artists who have reported the findings of their travels in 'unexplored England' – with W. H. Hudson and the Newlyn Group of painters, for example, but also with Orwell and Evelyn Waugh, in both of whom David Gervais perceives the 'detached stance of the anthropologist and the traveller'.[29]

Social separation is a cause of the scientific detachment manifested in the letter to *The Times*. But how effective Jefferies' observation could be when combined with sympathetic feeling. Fifteen years later, in the last months of his life, Jefferies dictated to his wife 'My Old Village', with its portrait of the labourer John Brown:

> He went to work while he was still a child. At half-past three in the morning he was on his way to the farm stables, there to help feed the cart-horses, which used to be done with great care very early in the morning. The carter's whip used to sting his legs, and sometimes he felt the butt. At fifteen he was no taller than the sons of well-to-do people at eleven; he scarcely seemed to grow at all till he was eighteen or twenty, and even then very slowly, but at last became a tall big man. That slouching walk, with knees always bent, diminished his height to appearance; he really was the full

size, and every inch of his frame had been slowly welded together by this ceaseless work, continual life in the open air, and coarse hard food.[30]

Jefferies may not have changed his political views essentially – first and last his belief rests on 'the good master' – but as his description of John Brown, and his treatment of Roger the Reaper in one of his finest essays, 'One of the New Voters' (1885), show, fellow feeling came with an enlargement of his social and political understanding. Jefferies was not the least of the great Victorians to react to the forces producing change in his age by making ever stronger connections and distinctions; in short, by developing a moral vision. At times he recalls Ruskin, but the fruitful tension between the eye for beauty and the moral sense is all his own.

This may be seen in the following passage from 'One of the New Voters':

Look at the arm of a woman labouring in the harvest-field – thin, muscular, sinewy, black almost, it tells of continual strain. After much of this she becomes pulled out of shape, the neck loses its roundness and shows the sinews, the chest flattens. In time the women find the strain of it tell severely. I am not trying to make out a case of special hardship, being aware that both men, women, and children work as hard and perhaps suffer more in cities; I am simply describing the realities of rural life behind the scenes. The golden harvest is the first scene; the golden wheat, glorious under the summer sun. Bright poppies flower in its depths, and convolvulus climbs the stalks. Butterflies float slowly over the yellow surface as they might over a lake of colour. To linger by it, to visit it day by day, at even to watch the sunset by it, and see it pale under the changing light, is a delight to the thoughtful mind. There is so much in the wheat, there are books of meditation in it, it is dear to the heart. Behind these beautiful aspects comes the reality of human labour – hours upon hours of heat and strain; there comes the reality of a rude life, and in the end little enough of gain. The wheat is beautiful, but human life is labour.[31]

The passage resolves complex tensions, of which that between aestheticism and conscience is only one. It is a forceful demonstration of the memorable, epigrammatic conclusion, and the force results from Jefferies' ability to see both 'the first scene' and 'the realities of rural life behind the scenes'. He thus expresses a great truth, a truth which his urban and leisured readers might otherwise have overlooked. His perception of the human cost of labour balances his passion for the visual, and for female beauty. The picture of the woman labouring in the harvest-field is the obverse of the portrait of Felise in *The Dewy Morn* (1884) and of the *Venus Accroupie* in 'Nature in the Louvre' (1887); the obverse and the complement, as Jefferies' worship of female beauty sharpened and embittered his perception of the physical ravages of field-work. His feeling is the more intense because his love of the female form was closely bound up with both his worship of Nature and with something essentially feminine in himself. He saw in 'the living original' of the *Venus Accroupie*, 'the human impersonation of the secret influence which had beckoned me on in the forest and by the running streams', and the expression of 'the deep aspiring desire of the soul for the perfection of the frame in which it is encased, for the perfection of its own existence'.[32] In his Introduction to an edition[33] of *The Story of My Heart*, Andrew Rossabi writes: 'Significantly in his next book, *The Dewy Morn*, Jefferies' soul becomes what she always was – a woman, the beautiful Felise, perfect child of nature, pure and fresh as the dawn, the embodiment of love.' This is a crucial insight. The identification of something essential in Jefferies himself with the woman helps to explain the passion of his vision. Jefferies' way of seeing the field-woman reflects his position as a mediator between agricultural labourers and his more or less leisured readers, and combines the feelings of a man who has ancestral and familial roots in the working land with the scientific detachment of a naturalist and the aesthetic pleasure of a word painter. It also expresses the emotion of a man who sees the violation of the essence of Nature, and of his soul's 'deep aspiring desire'.

According to Edward Thomas, the elements of Jefferies' imagination are clearness, concentration, patience, love. But Jefferies' art of seeing also involved what in *The Amateur Poacher* he called 'the in-bred sportsman's instinct of perception',[34] and conjoined primitive instinct and animal cunning and sensitivity to human empathy. He could see into deep, dark water, if it were not muddy, and he teaches the art in 'A Brook'. He could adopt the viewpoint of animal or fish, and look out of undergrowth or water at the human intruder. 'Mind under Water' is a remarkable instance of his use of the keenest senses to enter into the world of creatures, and by so doing to reveal man anew. He frequently pictures natural scenes – and blames the painters for being too conventional to see what he calls 'Nature's imagination'. He himself supplies their lack with numerous pictures in words, pictures containing light and shade, stillness and movement, clarity and mist, the old and the new in the landscape, as well as colour, line and depth. His pictorial vision also manifested a brilliant imagism, which forms a stylistic link with Edward Thomas and modern poetry.

But of course, Jefferies' imagining was not a matter of seeing alone. In 'Wild Flowers', he speaks of the 'touch of thought', and says: 'To the heaven thought can reach lifted by the strong arms of the oak, carried up by the ascent of the flame-shaped fir.'[35] To Bevis, the stars 'were real, and the touch of his mind felt to them'.[36] Jefferies speaks of 'feeling to' the sun and the stars, and in *The Story of My Heart* he prays *with* or *through* the elements. 'The Sun and the Brook' (1882) delineates a remarkable reciprocity between Nature and the human senses and mind:

> From tree, and earth, and soft air moving, there comes an invisible touch which arranges the senses to its waves as the ripples of the lake set the sand in parallel lines. The grass sways and fans the reposing mind; the leaves sway and stroke it, till it can feel beyond itself and with them, using each grass blade, each leaf, to abstract life from earth and ether. These then become new organs, fresh nerves and veins running afar out into the field, along the winding brook, up through the leaves, bringing a larger existence. The arms of the mind open wide to the broad sky.[37]

This was essentially the experience of Bevis lying at night on 'the green path by the strawberries' that 'was the centre of the world'. For Bevis, 'The heavens were as much a part of life as the elms, the oak, the house, the garden and orchard, the meadow and the brook. They were no more separated than the furniture of the parlour, than the old oak chair where he sat, and saw the new moon shine over the mulberry tree.' All 'were in the same place with him'.[38] His is a supreme experience of belonging, of a centred existence, connected to all things near and far. For him, 'there was no severance'.

Yet, in *The Story of My Heart* and in his later writings generally, Jefferies often stresses the opposite of this connection: absolute separation between man and nature, and between mind and matter. This is not a mere contradiction, however: in Jefferies' thought, separation and being part of the whole existed in a dialectical relationship, compelling him to express and explore both states in his writings. Both were closely bound up with his interpretation of the nature of Nature.

Jefferies' later conclusion that there is no design in nature was latent in his earlier way of seeing, as this passage from *Round About a Great Estate* shows:

> The very dust of the road had something to show. For under the shadowy elms a little seed or grain had jolted down through the chinks in the bed of a passing waggon, and there the chaffinches and sparrows had congregated. As they moved to and fro they had left the marks of their feet in the thick white dust, so crossed and intertangled in a maze of tracks that no one could have designed so delicate and intricate a pattern.[39]

His perception of the 'maze ... that no one could have designed' leads ultimately to the assertion of *The Story of My Heart*: 'There is no god in nature, nor in any matter anywhere, either in the clods on the earth or in the composition of the stars. For what we understand by the deity is the purest form of Idea, of Mind, and no mind is exhibited in these.'[40] This may be the statement of a disillusioned Platonist – in 'Nature and Books' (1887) Jefferies says that 'it took me a long time to read Plato, and I have had to unlearn much of him'[41] – but in any case it seems to follow from Jefferies' mode of perception. In 'Hours of Spring' (1886) he writes: 'You never know what a day may bring forth – what new thing will come next ... You never know what will come to the net of the eye next ... There is no settled succession, no fixed and formal order – always the unexpected.'[42] This leads him on to say: 'Nature has no arrangement, no plan.' What is evident, certainly, is that nature's profusion and unexpectedness outrun his speed of perception and of notation, and that in responding to nature's *otherness*, he rejects all ideas of its order and correspondence with the mind.

In a late manuscript, edited by Samuel J. Looker and published under the title 'The Old House at Coate', Jefferies writes:

> When at last I had disabused my mind of the enormous imposture of a design, an object, and an end, a purpose or a system, I began to see dimly how much more grandeur, beauty and hope there is in a divine chaos – not chaos in the sense of disorder or confusion but simply the absence of order – than there is in a universe made by

pattern. This draught-board universe my mind had laid out: this machine-made world and piece of mechanism; what a petty, despicable, microcosmus I had submitted for the reality.[43]

Jefferies' mysticism, therefore, was based on the opposite of a natural theology, such as that of the early Ruskin or Philip Henry Gosse; but it was no less optimistic. 'Logically, that which has a design or a purpose has a limit ... I look at the sunshine and feel that there is no contracted order: there is divine chaos, and, in it, limitless hope and possibilities.'

The mysticism born of belief in 'divine chaos' and 'limitless hope and possibilities' had its corollary in Jefferies' absolute scepticism of all 'contracted order'. Thus, in *The Story of My Heart*, he came to see himself standing 'bare-headed before the sun';[44] bare, that is, of all philosophy not his own, and all religion, facing the source of life, and the unknown. Jefferies became the ultimate iconoclast, who cast down all images and all conceptions of the Beyond. He rejected even his own perceptions; as he wrote in his notebook: 'I look out and see – I cannot see.'[45]

In 'Nature and Books' Jefferies runs through the whole world of human knowledge in his attempt to answer the question: 'What is the colour of the dandelion?' He goes to one source of information after another: his own descriptive powers, a book on colour, works on optics, spectrum analysis, the theory of the polarization of light, the colours used in painting, the language of the studio, botany, and so on. But he does not find the answer. 'There is nothing in books that touches my dandelion', he says, with a nice use of the sensuous word 'touches', which means both 'equals' and 'explains'. Jefferies values modern science with its empirical method, and invokes it in support of his iconoclasm:

Our Darwins, our Lyells, Herschels, Faradays – all the immense army of those that go down to nature with considering eye – are steadfastly undermining and obliterating the superstitious past, literally burying it under endless loads of accumulated facts; and the printing-presses, like so many Argos, take these facts on their voyage round the world. Over go temples, and minarets, and churches, or rather there they stay, the hollow shells, like the snail shells which thrushes have picked clean; there they stay like Karnac, where there is no more incense, like the stone circles on our own hills, where there are no more human sacrifices. Thus

men's minds all over the printing-press world are unlearning the
falsehoods that have bound them down so long; they are unlearning, the first step to learn. They are going down to nature and taking up the clods with their own hands, and so coming to have
touch of that which is real.[46]

It is possible to see an irony in the fact that Jefferies has
employed the science or art of observation, fathered by Gilbert
White and dear to many clergymen in the nineteenth century, in
order to affirm the complete emptiness not only of the Church,
but of all religions. Such is the mystical cast of his own thought,
however, that it is not surprising to find modern theologians
such as John Robinson[47] admiring him, or his writing being discussed and anthologized in books on mysticism. From the closing lines of *The Amateur Poacher* which invoke the presence of 'a
something that the ancients called divine' in the open air, to the
mysticism of 'divine chaos', Jefferies has worked for enlargement
of mind and spirit. Looking at the common rushes or the wild
white violets, he expanded the realm of mystery. Contemplating
the indescribable dandelion, he brings down the whole edifice of
traditional thought and worship. To have 'touch of that which is
real', however, he believes that science must work with imagination, or what he calls 'the alchemy of nature'. 'Let us not be too
entirely mechanical, Baconian, and experimental only; let us let
the soul hope and dream and float on these oceans of accumulated facts, and feel still greater aspiration than it has ever
known since first a flint was chipped before the glaciers.'[48] Jefferies' *thinking* can seem vapid: abstract, and closer to a vague
scientific utopianism than to the self-transcendence of true mysticism. It is in his expression of wonder that he is most original:
wonder at the human mind or soul, and wonder of the mind in
face of the commonest natural phenomena.

As Vincent Van Gogh admired and emulated the Japanese
artist who began by studying a single blade of grass, so Richard
Jefferies started by looking closely at particular things, and was
led across a widening field in space and in time towards the
whole. There are other parallels between Jefferies and Van Gogh.
One of these is their sense of the aesthetics of work in the fields –
both how the reality of work may be depicted, and how labour
affects the labourer and his or her way of seeing. Jefferies' classic
statement of this theme is in 'One of the New Voters'. If there is a

visual equivalent to what Jefferies shows in his description of the woman working in the harvest-field, it is not Millet, I think, but Van Gogh in his paintings of the sower and the mower, especially *Mower in the Barley Field at Noon*, in which the bent figure with the curved sickle is at once distinct and part of the forces present in the swirling colours of barley field and sun. Van Gogh paints the dynamic rhythms of passion, both the life-energy and the suffering. His landscapes, like Jefferies' harvest-field, are fields of force, in which the figures are at once channels of life-energy and consumed by the energy they serve.

Another important point of contact between Jefferies and Van Gogh is their displacement of religious feeling onto Nature. Consider Van Gogh's late canvases: sunflowers, sun-wheels, sun-bursts, flame trees, the earth on fire, the human figure consumed in the furnace of the wheat-field, all in whirling, spiralling, dynamic motion, caught up in a fierce wind; the bush burns, a voice speaks from the whirlwind, and we can *see* it speaking. The vision enlarges and terrifies; is at once natural and divine. Then consider Jefferies bare-headed before the sun, and his effort almost to the end of his life to develop the ideas of *The Story of My Heart* under the heading 'Soul Life' or 'Sun Life', and the numerous passages in which he celebrates the sun. In *Bevis*, for example, his ecstasy at sunlight is located where it began, at his boyhood home, 'the centre of the world', where 'round about it by day *and* night the sun circled in a magical golden ring':

All the light of summer fell on the water, from the glowing sky, from the clear air, from the sun. The island floated in light, they stood in light, light was in the shadow of the trees, and under the thick brambles; light was deep down in the water, light surrounded them as a mist might; they could see far up into the illumined sky as down into the water.

The leaves with light under them as well as above became films of transparent green, the delicate branches were delineated with finest camel's-hair point, all the grass blades heaped together were apart, and their edges apparent in the thick confusion; every atom of sand upon the shore was sought out by the beams, and given an individual existence amid the inconceivable multitude which the sibyl alone counted. Nothing was lost, not a grain of sand, not the least needle of fir. The light touched all things, and gave them to be.[49]

No wonder Bevis should exclaim: 'It's magic.' With regard to this, it is interesting to recall Kenneth Clark's observation in *Landscape into Art* that, 'Above all, Van Gogh, like Turner, had the northern sense of light as a source of magic.'[50] Jefferies depicts the sun as a painter, delineating the branches 'with finest camel's-hair point'. But the sun is much more than a painter; it is the great creative force which causes what it paints to be: 'The light touched all things, and gave them to be.' Every thing, 'every atom of sand', is singled out and 'given an individual existence'. Jefferies' sense is pagan, but he ascribes attributes of the Judaeo-Christian God to the sun. Images of Providence haunt the passage: 'Nothing was lost, not a grain of sand, not the least needle of fir.' But the sun is magical, not a providential deity, and Bevis ascribes the magic to Circe. The sun creates and illuminates; it can also consume and destroy.

In September 1888, Van Gogh wrote: 'I want to paint men and women with that something of the eternal which the halo used to symbolize, and which we seek to confer by the actual radiance and vibration of our colouring.'[51] In his *The Sower* painted in the same year, the biblical reference is explicit, and the dark figure is actually haloed by the great sun, and all is radiant and vibrant with colour. It is a painting which cannot be reduced to biblical symbolism, but which embodies strong religious feeling, as conventional religious paintings of the age, such as *The Light of the World*, do not. The traditional religious iconography is absent from Van Gogh's paintings, but instead of the light concentrated upon Christ or the Virgin Mary, a new radiance and vibration animate and irradiate the earth and his human figures. Similarly, D. H. Lawrence's language and symbolism divinize the natural forces which unite men and women with each other and with the cosmos; the sun is a living power in Lawrence's world. In Jefferies' writings the light is more chaste, more classical, and rather an intimation of ideal beauty than of sexual desire. His nature mysticism persistently employs terms and images from neo-Platonism and the tradition of medieval Christian mysticism, with its emphasis on light and vision, on transfiguration, and on unknowing, unseeing, in the approach to God. Although Jefferies frets at having to use words like 'soul' and 'immortality', he uses them, nevertheless, and embodies his vision in traditional imagery. He focuses on blade of grass, common rush, or atom of sand, and reveals it as a thing of wonder. Enlarging his area of attention, he gradually intensifies awareness of the surrounding world. Finally, he relinquishes the visible to 'divine chaos' with its 'limitless hopes and possibilities'. In Jefferies, therefore, the art of seeing reaches the point at which a potent religious imagery, having shed its original meaning, serves a new freedom. The results of this process are creative, but also destructive.

For Jefferies' isolation is, finally, terrible. It is painful to see the logic of his thinking and mode of perception, reinforced by something ingrained in his personality, cutting him off from almost every one and every thing, from human society but ultimately from Nature and the universe as well. As he wrote in his notebook near the end of his life: 'by no course of reasoning however tortuous can I fit my mind to the universe. My mind is separate from this designless thing altogether.'[52] And, a little later: 'I have been through nature, I am weary of nature, nothing there. I have been through books, nothing there ... in long illness, I have let my mind think in on itself. Nothing there. I have been to the edge of the end – no resource – nothing to rest on.'[53] The illness speaks for itself, and the neurasthenia which anticipates Edward Thomas's socially conditioned 'evil', his 'isolated selfconsidering brain'. From such things as the common rush and the dandelion Jefferies has come 'to the edge of the end' – to death, but also to the brink of the unknown. He has exhausted the possibilities of vision: 'We find the same earth everywhere because we look with the same eyes; we want some more eyes, and a different mind.'[54] It is a tragic paradox of a writer such as Jefferies and a painter such as Van Gogh that they are not as spiritually isolated as they feel themselves to be. Their creative response is to what many people feel: the constrictions of a materialistic civilization, the narrowness of the prevailing social mentality, and the perceived emptiness and hypocrisy of established religion. They are among the few capable of fulfilling the widely felt need to see and feel anew, and it is partly that which isolates them. It is another paradox that the very intensity of vision by which Jefferies came to know his blindness, and to see in everything the unknown beyond his reach, should be one of his great gifts to his readers.

3

'Which way is England?':
Richard Jefferies' *After London*

After London, or Wild England (1885) is a novel of complex and
contradictory emotions and impulses, in which we see Richard
Jefferies responding to the crisis of his times. The novel is about
an England in which civilization has relapsed into barbarism,
but the cause of the catastrophe is uncertain. As the chronicler
who relates what is known of the history says:

> All that seems certain is, that when the event took place, the
> immense crowds collected in cities were most affected, and that the
> richer and upper classes made use of their money to escape. Those
> left behind were mainly the lower and most ignorant, so far as the
> arts were concerned; those that dwelt in distant and outlying
> places; and those who lived by agriculture. These last at that date
> had fallen to such distress that they could not hire vessels to trans-
> port themselves. (16)[1]

Here, the fictional history corresponds closely to actual causes
of anxiety in English society in the 1880s: 'the immense crowds'
that had gathered and were continuing to gather in cities; inten-
sifying class divisions and tensions, which mocked the idea of
'one nation' and threatened outright conflict, thus causing trepi-
dation among the propertied classes; agricultural depression,
which for the past decade had been ruining farmers and causing
an exodus of labourers from the land, so that to people brought
up in a period of prosperity the very foundations of rural England seemed rent asunder. In these and in other respects, *After
London* is a critique of Victorian England, and a novel which, for
all its concern with barbarism and wildness, is born of the crisis
of modernity. More curiously, it provides mirror images of the
period in English society. I shall return to these, but I want first
to consider what is at once a broader, and, for Jefferies, a more
personal, impulse behind the novel's creation.

J. R. Seeley's *The Expansion of England* was first published in

1883, two years before *After London*. There is a curious relationship between the history book and the novel, considered as different responses to England in the later years of the nineteenth century. Seeley tells the story of an England that 'is far greater now than it was in the eighteenth century; ... far greater in the eighteenth century than in the seventeenth, far greater in the seventeenth than in the sixteenth'. Now, England's 'prodigious greatness ... makes the question of its future infinitely important and at the same time most anxious'.[2]

True to the contemporary imperial spirit, Seeley is not only vainglorious about English superiority, but concerned with the anxieties of empire, especially the dangers of foreign rivalry that a world-power incurs, and the moral responsibility to subject peoples. If we relate *After London* to the literature of empire, to which, in a sense, it belongs, we can see that the anxieties were not only political or social, or even moral, but also had to do with concepts of manhood (and womanhood). Seeley adduced 'facts ... to show natural aptitude for colonisation and a faculty of leadership in our race', and spoke of 'a good number of Englishmen ... who have exerted an almost magical ascendancy over the minds of the native races of India'.[3] Jefferies, too, was preoccupied with leadership and the 'magic' of superior gifts. In a broader perspective, his concern in the novel is with human power, and with that power as it conflicts or interacts with the power of Nature. It is in the fiction, too, that we can see intimate anxieties concerning questions of manhood, and the corresponding male idealizations of the female.

I will quote or refer to the closing words of *The Amateur Poacher* several times in this book, because they contain a great deal of Jefferies in a small space, and because they are germane to the argument of the book as a whole. I give them here in their larger context:

> Let us be always out of doors among trees and grass, and rain and wind and sun. There the breeze comes and strikes the cheek and sets it aglow: the gale increases and the trees creak and roar, but it is only a ruder music. A calm follows, the sun shines in the sky, and it is the time to sit under an oak, leaning against the bark, while the birds sing and the air is soft and sweet. By night the stars shine, and there is no fathoming the dark spaces between those brilliant points, nor the thoughts that come as it were between the fixed stars and landmarks of the mind.

Or it is the morning on the hills, when hope is as wide as the world; or it is the evening on the shore. A red sun sinks, and the foam-tipped waves are crested with crimson; the booming surge breaks, and the spray flies afar, sprinkling the face watching under the pale cliffs. Let us get out of these indoor narrow modern days, whose twelve hours somehow have become shortened, into the sunlight and the pure wind. A something that the ancients called divine can be found and felt there still.[4]

There is a little word-painting in the second paragraph, but, more importantly, we hear in the passage Jefferies' cadences, and his personal accents: the prophetic note, and the controlled ecstasy, whose obverse in later writings is a barely controlled despair. Here, though, the affective thought is founded on a security that is at once local and cosmic, close to Traherne's and the opposite of Pascal's, 'between the fixed stars and landmarks of the mind'. Jefferies voices his desire for enlargement, and convinces us that he knows it, in both senses: expansion of mind and spirit, and freedom. This is a major concern of much of Jefferies' writing, and it is, I think, central to *After London*. It was a concern affected by social and historical pressures, but it involved Jefferies' mysticism, too.

It will be useful at this point to juxtapose some words of Jefferies with an idea of John Cowper Powys. Writing in *Autobiography* of his childhood in the Derbyshire Peak, Powys recalls 'the dim feeling of immensity' produced by a hill, and comments: 'How magically sagacious is childhood in its power of arriving at boundless effects through insignificant means!' It was not a great hill, he tells us, but to him as a child it was sublime. 'Many aspects of children's days are silly enough', Powys continues, 'but how often the whole course of our subsequent history becomes an attempt to regain this sorcery, this power of finding the infinitely great in the materially small.'[5] Powys calls this power *'the ecstasy of the unbounded'*, and it may be related to Jefferies' words in 'Wild Flowers': 'Unconscious happiness in finding wild flowers – unconscious and unquestioning, and therefore unbounded.'[6] Jefferies, too, is referring to his childhood experience of the world, 'sweet and new like this each morning', but not to a capacity lost with childhood. It is what the man felt in 'the morning on the hills, when hope is as wide as the world'.

For Powys, 'this sorcery, this power of finding the infinitely great in the materially small' is a function of the imagination, a function which the child has but the adult must struggle to regain. Jefferies certainly knew the sorcery of which Powys writes. *Bevis*, for example, is full of 'magic'. Bevis himself, self-forgetful in his play-acting, becomes his heroes, and transforms the world around him, an actual place known in detail, and enlarged by active exploration, into an imaginary world. He and Mark both choose to play-act, and are convinced in the act, passionately changing the real into the ideal. Jefferies, who usually keeps a certain humorous detachment from the boys, also shares both their delight in adventure and the spirit of magic which they find in Nature. Bevis and Mark are at once secure at the centre of a world, and explorers of the terrestrial globe, remaking their surroundings as Central Africa, the Himalayas, the Mississippi, the New Sea, and so on:

> 'What a long way we can see,' said Mark, pointing to where the horizon and the blue wooded plain below, beyond the sea, became hazy together. 'What country is that?'
> 'I do not know; no one has ever been there.'
> 'Which way is England?' asked Mark.
> 'How can I tell when I don't know where we are?'[7]

In the boys' world, there is magic in the fact that all things have 'secrets'; they do not invent the magical quality of Nature, but they have the essential ability – the imagination – to perceive and respond to it, and thus to experience 'the ecstasy of the unbounded'. This, in turn, depends upon their inability to reflect upon experience. As Jefferies says of Bevis's sense of being centred within the sun's 'magical golden ring': 'Bevis, as you know, did not think: we have done the thinking, the analysis for him. He felt and was lost in the larger consciousness of the heavens.'[8] *After London* is, in certain respects, an adult continuation of *Bevis*. But the major difference is that the later novel has to recreate the unexplored England which Bevis and Mark enjoyed by virtue of their very unconsciousness of adult problems and perspectives; and it has to incorporate Jefferies' thinking about England, the country which the boys took so much for granted that they could pretend not to know where it was.

In one of his main roles as a writer – it was how he made a living – Jefferies was an explorer of rural England for the benefit of the urban reader. But, as I have already shown, he was anxious

about the diminution of the unknown, which the expansion of
the known world in his time entailed. While the British Empire
had a number of frontiers, and the English countryside was one
of them, imperial and industrial Britain was at the centre of the
process by which the unknown world was being opened up and
the margin of mystery contracted. And this is the process *After
London* counteracts, imaginatively, by returning civilization to
barbarism, by naturalizing urban and industrial society, and by
re-enchanting a Nature divested of mystery. But if Jefferies
unmakes the Empire, he does so in order to make a 'wild England' in which his imperial spirit can triumph.

In *After London* Jefferies obliterates the shrunken, known
world of late Victorian England and recreates the country partly
in an image of barbarous times, and partly in the image of England as it was known to him as a boy. Then, Coate Water was the
New Sea and there were exciting adventures to be had among
the surrounding swamps and thickets, and exploring the Downs
and Savernake Forest. The writing of *After England* was an act of
imaginative enlargement, which restored the space and mystery
of the wild and afforded freedoms which the reality of England
in the later nineteenth century precluded. But the emotions of
the novel are too complex for it to be described solely as regres-
sive – a nostalgic recreation of the imaginative 'space' of childhood, capable of evoking 'the ecstasy of the unbounded'. The
novel is both deeply personal and addresses vital *modern* issues –
psychological alienation, anxiety at the urban and industrial
growth of England, and at the secular disenchantment of the
world. As a prophecy of ecological disaster, it is even more
timely now than it was in 1885, since we have the powers of
destruction which Jefferies imagined. Even some specific references to Victorian history are not outdated, since Jefferies is evidently anxious about 'internal colonialism', in the form of English treatment of the Irish, Welsh and Scots.

The opening paragraphs of *After London* are especially haunting:

> The old men say their fathers told them that soon after the fields
> were left to themselves a change began to be visible. It became
> green everywhere in the first spring, after London ended, so that
> all the country looked alike.
> The meadows were green, and so was the rising wheat which

had been sown, but which neither had nor would receive any further care. Such arable fields as had not been sown, but where the last stubble had been ploughed up, were overrun with couch-grass, and where the short stubble had not been ploughed, the weeds hid it. So that there was no place which was not more or less green; the footpaths were the greenest of all, for such is the nature of grass where it has once been trodden on, and by-and-by, as the summer came on, the former roads were thinly covered with the grass that had spread out from the margin.   (1)

The eye for natural detail shown here greatly reduces the sense of *human* catastrophe, which might have been seen in unreaped wheat and ruined crops. Nature is the subject, not human kind. And Nature is active, a fruitful invader, 'greening' the country, returning it to what it once naturally was. Nature, marginalized by urban civilization, has recovered the centre, as 'the grass had spread out from the margin', covering the former roads.

After London replaces the centre with the margins in more than one respect. It restores Nature to the place taken by industry and the great cities – which was the crisis of 'modernism' which many people experienced in the 1880s. It also reverses the contemporary political situation by having the Irish and the Welsh oppress the English. As the chronicler says:

No blame can, upon a just consideration, be attributed to either of these nations that endeavour to oppress us. For, as they point out, the ancients from whom we are descended held them in subjection many hundred years, and took from them all their liberties.   (27)

And, centrally, the novel is about a marginalized man who becomes the Leader.

After London is a strange, distorting mirror of England in the early 1880s. In wild England the relation between England and its Celtic conquests is reversed, so that the English heartland is threatened by the Irish and the Welsh. The novel also displaces contemporary class antagonisms onto the barbarous realm, with Bushmen representing the underclass which the Victorian middle class feared. In political terms, the novel reproduces its author's mixed responses to his times: his liberalism with regard to the Celtic 'problems' and, in some respects, to social organization; his individualism; his conservatism in respect of issues of heredity and hierarchy; his imperialism and its corresponding gender stereotypes.

After London has its compensatory elements, too. It is a middle-aged and dying man's imaginative recreation of the world of his boyhood. It is a sick man's version of heroic manhood, and a story of recognition successfully achieved by an obscure genius. Its epigraph might be: 'My strength is not enough to fulfil my desire.'[9]

The psychology of the hero, Felix Aquila, is particularly interesting. It is impossible not to see him as, to some degree, a self-projection of the author. But Jefferies shows insight into what makes Felix difficult and unattractive, and writes about him with detachment as well as fellow feeling. Felix is what we would now call an outsider: an alienated, isolated man who broods within himself. He is initially what Edward Thomas, following Turgenev, would have called a 'superfluous man': a man without social or political power, living on the margins of his society.

Felix becomes a hero through his voyage on the Lake which has drowned the middle part of England, roughly from London to the Bristol Channel. But before his voyage, 'Felix's own position was bitter in the extreme. He felt he had talent. He loved deeply, he knew that he was in turn as deeply beloved; but he was utterly powerless' (75). That is the crux: his lack of power, and his desire for it. It helps to explain what otherwise might seem a contradiction in his motives for undertaking his voyage. In his heart, Felix is unable to condemn Baron Thyma, father of his beloved Aurora, for desiring 'a better alliance' for his daughter than with him. It is to make himself worthy of Aurora that he undertakes his voyage: 'This was the strongest of the motives that had determined him to seek the unknown' (88–9). Felix is an aristocrat, and he shares the social values of the aristocrats. But we are also told of his 'hardness of heart, that unutterable distance, as it were, between him and other men, which lay at the bottom of his proposed expedition' (123). Thus, his sense of distance from his peer group, together with his desire of power, makes him intensely competitive: he needs to prove himself – against them, but in their eyes. He needs, above all, to establish claims to manhood, claims which partly are, and partly are not, those of his aristocratic caste.

That Jefferies was preoccupied by concepts of manhood is evident throughout his writings. It may be seen, for example, in his description of the keeper in *The Gamekeeper at Home* (1878): 'freedom and constant contact with nature had made him every inch

a man; and here in this nineteenth century of civilised effemi-
nacy may be seen some relic of what men were in the old feudal
days when they dwelt practically in the woods';[10] or in Jefferies'
idealized portrait of his father, the Shakespearean Iden (named
after Iden the gardener in the Second Part of *King Henry VI*), in
Amaryllis at the Fair. Iden has all the qualities of the Jefferies hero
except worldly success: he is a man of culture and intellect, an
observer who draws his thoughts from Nature, he has been an
adventurer like Ulysses, and he is a home-maker who cares passionately for his land. The ideal of manhood was bound up with
authority and a capacity for leadership, as may be seen in Jefferies' frequent references to farmers as 'masters' who, in caring
for the land, govern their labourers and direct their toil, in his
praise of Julius Caesar in *The Story of My Heart*, and in the mas-
terful Bevis with his dictatorial treatment of his peers as well as
of labourers and servant girls. Manhood, in *After London* and
elsewhere in Jefferies' writings, is also associated with physical
strength, or with its equivalent in endurance and skill.

The contrasts between Felix and his brother Oliver, and Felix and
Lord Durand, are obvious. Given his physique, Felix clearly cannot
be the conventional knight. Another contrast is that between the
courtier Lord John and Felix's father, Sir Constans Aquila:

> He [Lord John] was a handsome man, with clear-cut features,
> somewhat rakish from late hours and dissipation, but not the less
> interesting on that account. But his natural advantages were so
> over-run with the affectation of the Court that you did not see the
> man at all, being absorbed by the studied gesture to display the
> jewelled ring, and the peculiarly low tone of voice in which it was
> the fashion to speak.
>
> Beside the old warrior he looked a mere stripling. The Baron's
> arm was bare, his sleeve rolled up; and as he pointed to the tree
> above, the muscles, as the limb moved, displayed themselves in
> knots, at which the courtier himself could not refrain from glanc-
> ing. Those mighty arms, had they clasped him about the waist,
> could have crushed his bending ribs. The heaviest blow that he
> could have struck upon that broad chest would have produced no
> more effect than a hollow sound; it would not even have shaken
> that powerful frame.   (79)

The difference is marked between the courtier who displays 'the
jewelled ring' and the noble gardener whose 'muscles ... dis-

played themselves in knots'. One has acquired the trappings of distinction, the other is distinguished by nature. But the contrast has implications which may not bear close analysis. The 'natural advantages' of the courtier 'were so over-run with the affectation of the Court that you did not see the man at all'. Sir Constans, the gardener, is superior to Lord John because he is close to Nature. Yet the superiority is expressed in terms of muscle power and potential for violence. Sir Constans's sons, Felix and Oliver, look on at the scene filled with 'anger and disgust' at 'the spectacle of the Baron in his native might of physique' humbling himself to the courtier.

Now, at the end of the twentieth century, we have good reason to ask whether there are better qualifications for manhood than a capacity to conquer and to kill. Jefferies in *After London* can help us a little in answering the question, but not much.

Compared to Oliver, Felix is a stripling. He is, however, a man of knowledge, and he makes up with his mind for what he lacks in physical might. He is 'independent and determined to the last degree' (48); 'method, organization, and precision, were the characteristics of his mind' (60). His knowledge includes 'an abridged history of Rome'. Indeed, his character accords with Jefferies' Caesarism, as defined in *The Story of My Heart*, and Felix in his England is 'the one man filled with mind', and the man who 'comes nearest to the ideal of a design-power arranging the affairs of the world for good in practical things'.[11]

To the real man corresponds the true woman: Aurora, named after the Roman goddess of the dawn. He is courageous and scientific and a founder of empire. She is pure and faithful and cultured and religious. There is a good deal of boyish fantasy in the exploits stemming from this pairing of ideals. But the ideals also correspond to a dream or fantasy of empire, and account for a good deal that, from a modern point of view, was wrong with the imperial heyday of Victorian society, including gender stereotypes and the misuse of human power. It is all too easy, though, to assume the moral high ground in discussing Victorian sexual attitudes, and it should be added that Jefferies, like other Victorian men (Thomas Hardy and Francis Kilvert come to mind), could value both purity and sensuousness, and write tenderly and reverently about women, as few modern writers can. The question of Jefferies' treatment of sexuality cannot be left here, however, partly because, as I have already indicated, he tended to project his spiritual aspirations into his creation of female characters, and partly because, in his very innocence of our political correctness, he could be extremely revealing in his expression of male attitudes. The following passage from *The Story of My Heart* is almost shockingly naked in this respect:

> To shoot with a gun is nothing; a mere touch discharges it. Give me a bow, that I may enjoy the delight of feeling myself draw the string and the strong wood bending, that I may see the rush of the arrow, and the broad head bury itself deep in shaggy hide. Give me an iron mace that I may crush the savage beast and hammer him down. A spear to thrust through with; so that I may feel the long blade enter and the push of the shaft. The unwearied strength of Ninus to hunt unceasingly in the fierce sun. Still I should desire greater strength and a stouter bow, wild creatures to combat. The intense life of the senses, there is never enough for them. I envy Semiramis; I would have been ten times Semiramis. I envy Nero, because of the great concourse of beauty he saw. I should like to be loved by every beautiful woman on earth, from the swart Nubian to the white and divine Greek.[12]

A pretty bunch of murderers and lechers, male and female, Jefferies envies; yet he seems to be curiously innocent of what he is revealing as the savage and predatory hunting imagery, with its connotations of sexual violence, modulates effortlessly into the euphemistic fantasy of being 'loved by every beautiful woman on earth'. As in his portrayal of Aurora, Jefferies' treatment of women is usually the opposite of this.

Felix's adventures educate him in the ways of men. He learns to overcome 'the ancient prejudice, the ancient exclusiveness of his class' (157), in shaking hands with the servant, or slave, whose hospitality he has accepted. The action corresponds with his theoretical condemnation of servitude. He learns to see society from the point of view of 'common and illiterate men', grooms and retainers, who 'read man, in fact, as an animal' (171). 'They stripped man of his dignity, and nature of her refinement.' He does not share the degradation of these men, however; rather he learns from the existence of the evils they have revealed to him.

The lessons Felix learns are secondary to his great purpose, which is revealed in his reflections on the strait he comes to on his voyage:

Who held this strait would possess the key of the Lake, and would
be master of, or would at least hold the balance between, the kings
and republics dotted along the coasts on either hand. No vessel
could pass without his permission. It was the most patent illustration of the extremely local horizon, the contracted mental view of
the petty kings and their statesmen, who were so concerned about
the frontiers of their provinces, and frequently interfered and
fought for a single palisaded estate or barony, yet were quite oblivious of the opportunity of empire open here to any who could seize
it.   (140)

Manhood is defined by mastery, and mastery is the means to
empire. Unlike 'the petty kings and their statesmen', with their
'contracted mental view', Felix has the largeness of mind to see
'the opportunity of empire'. He puts into practice with his exploration, like Caesar, 'the ideal of design-power arranging the
affairs of the world'. In wild England he is the one man of vision.
As an explorer of the unknown land, and as a strategist, he is
equivalent to the Jefferies who, in *The Story of My Heart*, ventures
to the end of the world of ideas.

Felix eventually becomes leader of the shepherds, who look on
him 'as a being of a different order to themselves', and salute
him 'as one almost divine' (232). Among them he becomes judge,
healer, and ultimately 'the Leader'. Towards the end of the novel
he directs the shepherds to clear 'the land by the river in order
that he might erect a fortified dwelling suitable to his position as
their Leader in war' (240). Earlier he had visited the spot 'accompanied by ten spears. The second visit only increased his admiration of the place and his desire to take possession of it' (237). Taking possession, being regarded as almost divine, leading
supposedly simpler and less technically skilled people: the boyish fantasy merges seamlessly with the ideology of empire.

At this point, Felix 'the Leader' has abolished the 'unutterable
distance' between himself and other men, but he has done so by
removing himself entirely from anyone who might claim to be
his equal. He does not consort with individuals, he leads shepherds, and is accompanied by 'spears'.

Having been conducted by shepherd guides to the sea, Felix
'forgot his anxieties and his hopes, they fell from him together,
leaving the mind alone with itself and love'. The passage continues:

For the memory of Aurora rendered the beauty before him still more beautiful; love, like the sunshine, threw a glamour over the waves. His old and highest thoughts returned to him in all their strength. He must follow them, he could not help himself. Standing where the foam came nearly to his feet, the resolution to pursue his aspirations took possession of him as strong as the sea. When he turned from it, he said to himself, 'This is the first step homewards to her; this is the first step of my renewed labour.' To fulfil his love and his ambition was one and the same thing.   (238)

In fact, Jefferies exaggerates Felix's independence and idealizes his ambition. In reality his ability to follow his 'old and highest thoughts' depends upon the shepherds as a labour force. If 'to fulfil his love and ambition was one and the same thing', his love is bound up with a concept of manhood which is founded on 'taking possession' – of place, of people, and of his beloved Aurora. In this respect, the conclusion of *After London* accords with the romantic resolution of conventional Victorian novels which equate love with property values. Earlier, we learn that treasure-seekers perish on the noxious site of London but Felix escapes with a diamond bracelet which, he later thinks, 'would be a splendid present for Aurora. Never had he seen anything like it in the palaces; he believed it was twice the size of the largest possessed by any king or prince' (212). Apparently without Jefferies noticing, his idealistic hero is really a successful materialist. The novel ends, however, with Felix 'moving rapidly westwards', still pursuing his odyssey. But it is not with Homer that the equation of love and ambition, and the emphasis upon mastery and possessions, belong; this particular mental and emotional pattern of *After London* belongs firmly to the romance of empire.

After London is, among other things, an imaginative response to the disenchantment of Victorian England: to the secularization of society and the loss of mystery, as religion failed and as Nature 'lost its social authority'.[13] Jefferies restores the power of Nature, as he turns the centre of England into the great Lake and surrounds it with the great Forest, which in fact had not been known in these islands since prehistoric times. And he re-enchants nature, with 'superstitions' such as the 'ladies of the fern':

These were creatures, not of flesh and blood, and yet not incorporeal like the demons, nor were they dangerous to the physical man, doing no bodily injury. The harm they did was by fascinating the

> soul, so that it revolted from all religion and all the rites of the
> Church. Once resigned to the caress of the fern-woman, the unfor-
> tunate was lured farther and farther from the haunts of men, until
> at last he wandered into the unknown forest, and was never seen
> again. These creatures were usually found among the brake fern,
> nude, but the lower limbs and body hidden by the green fronds,
> their white arms and shoulders alone visible, and their golden hair
> aglow with the summer sunshine.   (112)

On the face of it, this fear of revolt 'from all religion and all the
rites of the Church' sorts ill with the 'pagan' Jefferies.[14] Even if
we identify the fear with Felix, and relate it to his adoration of
the religious Aurora, this is still true, since Felix shares both his
author's independence of thought and worship of purity.
Indeed, it is hard not to see a fear of female sexuality in the danger to man of the 'ladies of the fern', and in Jefferies' idealization
of the pure woman. He writes in *The Story of My Heart* of his
belief 'in the flesh and the body, which is worthy of worship – to
see a perfect human body unveiled causes a sense of worship'.
But he goes on to say that 'increase of physical beauty is
attended by increase of soul beauty. The soul is the higher even
by gazing on beauty.'[15] A fictional instance of this occurs in *The
Dewy Morn*, when Martial, concealed in the fern, gazes at Felise's
knees:

> This wondrous loveliness purified and freed his soul from the
> grossness of material existence.
>   Such is woman's true place, to excite thus the deepest, the best,
> the most exalted of man's emotions.[16]

Jefferies is very much a Victorian in his idealism; but the problem with his worship of purity is, it seems to me, not the
reverence itself, but its relegation of human desire to a form of
material 'grossness'. Jefferies' female characters – the most con-
vincing by far is Amaryllis – are partly idealizations of the real,
and partly embodiments of the spirit of Nature with which he
identified; they are not lacking in credibility and vitality, but it
has to be said that acquaintance with them helps to show what
Thomas Hardy was up against when he presented Tess Durbeyfield as 'a pure woman'.

Religion in its beneficial form is represented by Aurora who is
'deeply imbued' with the 'moral beauty' of 'the old faith', with

its tenets 'such as the duty of humanity to all, the duty of saving and protecting life, of kindness and gentleness' (121–2). Significantly, the few who adhered to this form of primitive Christianity 'had no power or influence' (122). Aurora's power is over the soul of the essentially pagan Felix who is 'simply untouched' by the faith itself. He has gained from wandering alone in the Forest a deep impression of 'the mystery of existence', but as for religion, 'like the wild creatures of the forest, he had no ears in these matters. He loved Aurora, that was all' (123). In other words, Aurora is his religion, a state of affairs with dangerous implications for the human needs of the woman and the man.

As I have shown, *After London* is a novel imbued with the spirit of imperialism: in its concept of manhood and leadership, in its emphasis upon taking possession of places and of people, in its predominantly male values. And the maleness of the novel is evident, not least, in its heroine who, unlike Amaryllis and Felise, is less a woman than she is a Victorian male ideal.

Purity evoked a strong emotional response in Jefferies: the Lake, like Aurora, is pure. Corruption and rottenness evoked a correspondingly strong negative emotional response. The following passage describes Felix's penetration into 'the deserted and utterly extinct city of London':

> He had penetrated into the midst of that dreadful place, of which he had heard many a tradition: how the earth was poison, the water poison, the air poison, the very light of heaven, falling through such an atmosphere, poison. There were said to be places where the earth was on fire and belched forth sulphurous fumes, supposed to be from the combustion of the enormous stores of strange and unknown chemicals collected by the wonderful people of those times. Upon the surface of the water there was a greenish-yellow oil, to touch which was death to any creature; it was the very essence of corruption.   (206)

'The wonderful people' are those of Jefferies' own time, the people of the century of progress. What they have left 'was the very essence of corruption'. In 'that dreadful place', the very elements in which Jefferies found something divine – earth, water, air, 'the very light of heaven' – were poison. But why should Jefferies want to visit such a fate, albeit a fictional one, upon London? Several reasons, arising from the anxieties of the times, suggest themselves – the growth of urban and industrial England, increasing pollution, the apparent conquest of Nature by the new mechanical powers, metropolitan centralization and the concomitant marginalization of the countryside. To these we may add the fact that, while Jefferies was fascinated by London, and by no means always treated it negatively in his writings, it also meant to him the place where people do not *see*. This may be illustrated by a passage from *Amaryllis at the Fair*:

> I have never walked up Fleet Street and the Strand yet without seeing a starving woman and child. The children are indeed dreadful; they run unguarded and unwatched out of the side courts into the broader and more lively Strand – the ceaseless world pushes past – they play on the pavement unregarded. Hatless, shoeless, bound about with rags, their faces white and scarred with nameless disease, their eyes bleared, their hair dirty; little things, such as in happy homes are sometimes set on the table to see how they look.
>
> How *can* people pass without seeing them?[17]

Jefferies, then, saw in London the centre of the moral failure of his age. It was as he said of Robert Godwin in *The Dewy Morn*, his fellow citizens 'possessed the faculty of not seeing – the faculty of no imagination'.[18]

The moral condemnation is powerful, but does not exhaust what needs to be said about Jefferies' art of seeing in *After London*. In writing about Jefferies' visual imagination, I have emphasised its positive aspects. But Jefferies also experienced what might be called the pain of seeing. In 'Wild Flowers', for example, he reveals both his eidetic memory and its cost to him: 'To-day, and day after day, fresh pictures are coloured instantaneously in the retina as bright and perfect in detail and hue. This very power is often, I think, the cause of pain to me. To see so clearly is to value so highly, and to feel too deeply.' Later in the same paragraph he speaks of Nature's 'new mazes', the 'design without plan' which 'cannot be reduced to set order', with the result that 'The eye is for ever drawn onward and finds no end'. His eye is consequently 'wearied yet insatiate'.[19] The ocularcentric mode can isolate the perceiver as well as exhaust the mind, and its magnifications, and abstractions of the part from the whole, the detail from the design, can produce phantasmagoria, and symptoms of neurosis and even madness. It is evident that in Jefferies' case sight both helped to reveal the wonders of Nature to him, and increasingly separated him from the world he could see. It is fitting, therefore, that Felix's nightmare should manifest itself as the illusion that he can actually see his own eyes, which burn with the fire consuming the corruption of the city: 'His head felt enlarged, and his eyes seemed alight; he could see these two globes of phosphoric light under his brows. They seemed to stand out so that he could see them' (204). This is the logic of ocularcentrism taken to extremes. It is ironic, but also significant, that Felix's eyes, his principal means to vision, should also ultimately show him the opposite of all he holds dear, and share in the combustion of civilization.

After London is a story about male power. Yet this is surely not the abiding impression of the novel, which is rather of the power of Nature. The main reasons for this are the descriptions of Nature, especially in Part 1, where Nature is shown invading the centre of England and pushing the humans who remain into the margins, and Felix's feeling for 'the mystery of existence', which corresponds to Jefferies' own. It seems probable that the intensity with which Jefferies visualized and felt the miasma and the nightmare effects of the London swamps owed something to the illness that was poisoning his being. And health meant the past, and the country of his boyhood and youth. There is, then, a special poignancy about the description of Felix's escape from 'that dreadful place':

> The canoe had left most of the islets and was approaching the open Lake when, as she passed almost the last, the yard caught the over-hanging branch of a willow, the canoe swung round and grounded gently under the shadow of the tree. For some time the little wavelets beat against the side of the boat, gradually they ceased, and the clear and beautiful water became still. Felix slept till nearly noon, when he awoke and sat up. At the sudden movement a pike struck, and two moorhens scuttled out of the water into the grass on the shore. A thrush was singing sweetly, whitethroats were busy in the bushes, and swallows swept by overhead.
>
> Felix drew a long deep breath of intense relief; it was like awaking in Paradise. (210–11)

The Paradise in which Felix awakes might be the shores of Bevis's New Sea; it is the English countryside as Jefferies has often described it: an intensely active natural world, with the man watching and listening, enjoying the beauty. This is the earth described in 'Wild Flowers', of which Jefferies asks, if we

'suddenly came to it man or woman grown, set down in the
midst of a summer mead, would it not seem to us a radiant
vision?' It is with an enforced relaxation of will that Felix, borne
by the canoe, has drifted to this Paradise. For the time being, his
male will in abeyance, he merely watches, touches the grass, listens to the song of the birds. He is like the boy or man 'finding
wild flowers – unconscious and unquestioning, and therefore
unbounded'. Now, Felix simply enjoys 'the mystery of existence'.
'His whole body, his whole being was resigned to rest' (211).
Here, and on the Lake, he experiences 'the ecstasy of the
unbounded'. In the main, that is what Jefferies has recreated
wild England for – the mind's submission to the power of
Nature, and sheer enjoyment at the active and contemplative
experience of Nature. The adult has reconstructed the real but
ideal and imaginary space in which the boy could look around
him and ask, 'Which way is England?'

It would be wrong, though, to use this perception to under-
play the political meaning of the novel. The passage quoted
above may be the still centre of *After London*, but the realistic
political centre of the novel lies elsewhere. Felix recovers his
energy and his will, and voyages on to prove himself as a man –
and to fulfil Jefferies' fantasies – by leading shepherds and slay-
ing gypsies, and becoming a power in the land.

Jefferies' actual situation – the situation of a sick man, and a
man of genius condemned to obscurity – accords much more
closely to Aurora's interpretation of 'the spirit of the ancient
Greeks' than to Felix's virtual deification as the Leader:

> In some indefinable manner the spirit of the ancient Greeks seemed
> to her in accord with the times, for men had or appeared to have so
> little control over their own lives that they might well imagine them-
> selves overruled by destiny. Communication between one place and
> another was difficult, the division of society into castes, and the iron
> tyranny of arms, prevented the individual from making any
> progress in lifting himself out of the groove in which he was born,
> except by the rarest opportunity, unless specially favoured by for-
> tune. As men were born so they lived; they could not advance, and
> when this is the case the idea of Fate is always predominant. The
> workings of destiny, the Irresistible over-powering both the good
> and the evil-disposed, such as were traced in the Greek drama, were
> paralleled in the lives of many a miserable slave at that day. They
> were forced to endure, for there was no possibility of effort.

> Aurora saw this and felt it deeply; ever anxious as she was for the good of all, she saw the sadness that reigned even in the midst of the fresh foliage of spring and among the flowers. It was Fate; it was Sophocles.
>
> (114–15)

Aurora herself takes the part of Antigone, and the ancient drama is performed on the grass 'in the sunlight', to the song of birds. The play is about a political situation, but it is here linked closely with Nature. In his male will, Felix is a man of Roman virtue, a would-be Caesar. He is thus a man of his time, a man of J. R. Seeley's expanding England, who found in the classics models of imperial manhood. But he is also a man 'forced to endure', and his acknowledgement of Fate takes the form of his submission to the power of Nature. In this, he looks beyond his time, both to an older world which worshipped 'something that the ancients called divine' in the open air, and to a new world which will recover the sense of the sacred in Nature. The underlying drama of *After London* is the conflict between Roman will and Greek submission to Fate, or between a male idea of human power and the power of Nature, which for Jefferies was intimately involved with both his spiritual aspirations and his idealization of woman.

4

From graven image to speech: Edward Thomas's prose

Before the revival of critical interest in Edward Thomas in the late sixties and seventies, it was quite common for critics to dismiss his prose as a whole indiscriminately as hack work. Now, though, we are more in danger of overestimating the continuity of his development, and the consistency of his prose with his poetry. Edward Thomas certainly emerges as an impressive writer from Edna Longley's selection of his prose, *A Language Not To Be Betrayed* (1981). It is, however, an anthology which represents Thomas mainly as a literary critic, and he was the outstanding English critic of his generation. Moreover, he established in his criticism, at least as early as *Richard Jefferies* (1909), and with increasing confidence in his books on Maurice Maeterlinck and Walter Pater, published in 1911 and 1913 respectively, the principles of the poetry that he had still to write. Indeed, he did more than establish the principles; he wrote of language and style with the poet's authority. Yet he continued to write prose that was partially vitiated by the weaknesses characteristic of his earlier work.

In a relatively short writing life, Edward Thomas wrote more than thirty books, edited over a dozen more, and produced a vast number of book reviews. He wrote in a variety of forms - description, diary, itinerary, biography, criticism, fiction, autobiography, prose poetry – and frequently mixed them. His books about nature and the country, in particular, mix description and observation with reverie, imaginative recreation, and lightly disguised spiritual autobiography. The loosely defined 'country' book, aimed at a largely urban middle-class readership nostalgic for a pastoral England, was a permissive form; but it is still remarkable how liberally Edward Thomas interpreted his commissions, especially in putting so much of himself into the landscapes. The permissiveness was, at best, a mixed blessing; at worst, it exacerbated the morbid self-consciousness which Thomas himself diagnosed as his greatest ill. The restless, unsatisfactory nature of much of the prose manifests acute formal problems, which Thomas finally overcame only in his poetry. They were not only formal problems, however, but related intimately to problems with the self. Thomas's prose is in part the record of his struggle to achieve an adequate means of self-expression, a struggle which required him to resolve the problem of knowing and believing in the self he desired to express. This in turn meant, in terms that he used in *The Country* (1913), finding something larger than the self 'to rest upon'. In this sense, Edward Thomas's quest, like that of many Romantic and modern writers who have sought to lose and find themselves in Nature, was essentially religious.

Edward Thomas's first book, *The Woodland Life* (1897), consists of articles and a nature diary which he wrote while still in his teens. As he noted in his maturity, the young writer had 'a grandiloquent turn'. He had a gift of observation as well, and a microscopic eye, and the ability to arrange his observations. Thus, he perceives a dead leaf:

> On the green mound lies a dead oak-leaf, sober brown and nothing more to the first glance. Through the winter it has lain there, while some of its fellows yet cling wizened and wan about the saplings. Its scalloped edge has kept intact in spite of wind and rain and frost. With the process of the months it has darkened and curled, till now it is a semi-cylinder of the hue of old leather; but underneath the plain brown surface shows a beautiful variety of shades – amber streaks, strange mottlings of chestnut, red and tawny, and, breaking through all, a bloom of faint gold. Each different tinge glows richly as the sunbeams light up the glossy curving surface. It is a last remnant of winter and of the bygone year, pillowed among the tender growths of early spring – sere brown set in the midst of youthful verdure.[1]

In the progressive revelation of what 'the first glance' misses, this resembles the descriptive writing of Richard Jefferies, whose great influence on his life and work Edward Thomas acknowledged. Jefferies frequently begins with a small, easily overlooked detail of animate or inanimate nature, and magnifies it until its character, function, and place in the environment are revealed. In 'The Pageant of Summer', for example, he begins with rushes:

Green rushes, long and thick, standing up above the edge of the ditch, told the hour of the year as distinctly as the shadow on the dial the hour of the day. Green and thick and sappy to the touch, they felt like summer, soft and elastic, as if full of life, mere rushes though they were. On the fingers they left a green scent; rushes have a separate scent of green, so, too, have ferns, very different from that of grass or leaves. Rising from brown sheaths, the tall stems enlarged a little in the middle, like classical columns, and heavy with their sap and freshness, leaned against the hawthorn sprays. From the earth they had drawn its moisture, and made the ditch dry; some of the sweetness of the air had entered into their fibres, and the rushes – the common rushes – were full of beautiful summer.[2]

The juxtaposition of the two passages indicates Thomas's debt to Jefferies, but is more revealing of differences. Jefferies is one of the great natural observers of the Victorian age, a period rich in the arts of seeing, in which natural history combined with poetry and painting to produce, in Ruskin and Tennyson and Hardy and Gerard Manley Hopkins, for example, not only minutely detailed perception, but an ocularcentric mode that was both physical and metaphysical. Even among these writers, Jefferies had no equals when it came to natural vision. With him, seeing was both an art and a science, and it had behind it that love of the common and often overlooked thing, like 'the common rushes', which we find not only in Gilbert White, but in Wordsworth and Constable and Clare, and in an older tradition with its roots in a religious delight in the natural creation, although in the nineteenth century religious observation of nature was often a substitute for orthodox belief. Jefferies' art, though, is not only visual; it also manifests an acute sensitivity to the life of the thing, both its unique identity and its existence as part of nature. He appeals to the sense of touch and the sense of smell as much as to sight, and he emphasizes the relations of the rushes to their surroundings, their drawing of moisture from the earth and sweetness from the air, and their existence in time, their seasonal life. When he likens them to classical columns the image is not stationary or primarily sculptural, but serves to elevate the common plant to its proper importance. Jefferies knew that civilization depends upon nature; his vision of the ditch shows that it is as interesting and at least as important as any place on earth.

Edward Thomas appears to look at the dead leaf as closely as Jefferies looks at the rushes, but whereas Jefferies reveals the life of the plant, Thomas, in spite of making the dead leaf a symbol of winter among the signs of spring, sees it aesthetically, and makes a picture from its colours and sculptural shape. Jefferies' whole intention, the spirit of his seeing, lies behind the image likening the rushes to classical columns, but 'scalloped' and 'semi-cylinder' and 'curving surface' depict the leaf as an object of aesthetic contemplation. Thomas's method here, in fact, is close to Walter Pater's spectatorial stance, which he would describe later with devastating effect. In *The Woodland Life* the aesthetic mode of perception is dominant, but its tension with natural vision, which sees and depicts the life in things, is largely resolved by the joy of the young writer-cum-naturalist in exercising his gifts. The diary included in the book exhibits an art of naming, with a corresponding delight in the thing named, that is closer to Edward Thomas's poetry. Before he could achieve that, though, he had first to undertake a long struggle to relate aesthetic vision and natural vision, instead of obscuring and even betraying the latter with his word-painting.

Recording his response to the nightingale's song in *The South Country* (1909), Edward Thomas says the notes, with their 'inhumanity', convey 'the mysterious sense ... that earth is something more than a human estate'. 'Here for this hour we are remote from the parochialism of humanity. The bird has admitted a larger air. We breathe deeply of it and are made free citizens of eternity.'[3] Thomas, in his writings about nature, often expresses desire for 'a larger air' which is at once physical and spiritual. The words echo the close of Jefferies' *The Amateur Poacher*, which for Thomas as a young man were 'a gospel, an incantation':[4] 'Let us get out of these indoor narrow modern days, whose twelve hours somehow have become shortened, into the sunlight and the pure wind. A something that the ancients called divine can be found and felt there still.'[5] Freedom from 'the parochialism of humanity' is a great theme, but Thomas is rarely able to pursue it with confidence for long. In *In Pursuit of Spring* (1914), for example, he says Salisbury Plain 'makes us feel the age of the earth, the greatness of Time, Space, and Nature; the littleness of man even in an aeroplane, the fact that the earth does not belong to man, but man to the earth'.[6] This is a feeling capable of generating awe, and in the writings of Jefferies it frequently does. The same is true of W. H. Hudson, a friend whose prose style Thomas admired. In *The Country* he quotes a passage from *Hampshire Days* in which Hudson, writing of a time by the barrows on Beaulieu Heath in the New Forest, says: 'The blue sky, the brown soil beneath, the grass, the trees, the animals, the wind, and rain, and sun, and stars, are never strange to me; for I am in and of and am one with them; and my flesh and the soil are one, and the heat in my blood and in the sunshine are one, and the winds and tempests and my passions are one.' Hudson is echoing another writer Thomas admired, Thomas Traherne, whom Hudson has quoted a few pages before: 'You never enjoy the earth aright until the sun itself floweth through your veins, till you are clothed with the heavens and crowned with the stars, and perceive yourself to be the sole heir of the whole world.' Thomas himself sympathized deeply with the feeling of belonging to the earth, which in Traherne expressed his Christian mysticism and in Hudson was a pagan sentiment, but Thomas's distance from them is marked by his awareness that 'cultivation of the instinctive and primitive ... is the fine flower of a self-conscious civilization, turning in disgust upon itself'.[7] And the result, in writing about Salisbury Plain for example, is that he self-consciously turns back upon himself: 'And this feeling, or some variety of it, for most men is accompanied by melancholy, or is held to be the same thing. This is perhaps particularly so with townsmen, and above all with writers, because melancholy is the mood most easily given an appearance of profundity, and, therefore, most easily impressive.' The loss of emotional impetus, the fragmentation of feeling, and the consequent cynicism or self-dislike, give this and similar passages in Thomas's prose a negative and deadening effect. The problem is that his doctrine of Nature, and his feeling that man belongs to the earth, are at odds with the mode of perception which reflects his self-conscious modernity.

In *Richard Jefferies* Thomas calls self-consciousness 'perhaps, the most tragic condition of man's greatness'. 'If the sea-waves were to be self-conscious', he says, 'they would cease to wash the shore; a self-conscious world would fester and stink in a month.'[8] He was one who survived 'the terror', as he calls it; he even made a virtue of it in his poetry, but time and again in his prose,

self-consciousness breaks in, interrupting its rhythmic movement and concentration. It is at the roots of his problems as a
prose writer; as he came to realize, it is a psychological dis-ease
with social origins.

By the time he wrote his book on Walter Pater, Thomas understood the problem in depth:

> men understand now the impossibility of speaking aloud all that is
> within them, and if they do not speak it, they cannot write as they
> speak. The most they can do is to write as they would speak in a
> less solitary world. A man cannot say all that is in his heart to a
> woman or another man. The waters are too deep between us. We
> have not the confidence in what is within us, nor in our voices.[9]

According to Thomas, isolation is the modern condition, which
results in inability to communicate, dividing the individual both
from others and from his own inner depths, so that he has no confidence either in himself or in his voice. Thomas's understanding of
isolation inevitably owed much to his personal history. In *The South
Country*, one of the many *alter egos* that wander in and out of his
writings, the town-bred clerk escaping to the country, says: 'I realize that I belong to the suburbs still.' 'As for myself,' he continues, 'I
am world-conscious, and hence suffer unutterable loneliness.'[10]
Such figures at once express Thomas's situation and sentiments,
and distance him self-critically from the emotional extravagance.

Born and brought up in the London suburbs, Edward Thomas
early identified Wales, his parents' original country, as 'my soul's
native land'.[11] Later, he found in southern England 'a kind of
home, as I think it is more than any other to those modern people
who belong nowhere'.[12] Ironically, but not surprisingly, some of
his most effective prose, in *The Childhood of Edward Thomas* and *The
Happy-Go-Lucky Morgans* (1913), explores the suburbs, while his
descriptions of the country are frequently weakened by the
escapism arising from his lack of a necessary relation to it. For, as
he says in *The Country*: 'only a rarefied conscious appreciation is
made possible by detachment and the severing of all bonds of
necessity'.[13] This is by no means the whole truth of his relation to
nature and rural England, but the social and psychological forces
isolating him were formidable. They were fortified, moreover, by
his strongest, and otherwise opposing, literary influences: Richard
Jefferies and Walter Pater. Jefferies, in the nature mysticism of *The
Story of My Heart*, abstracted himself from the circumstances of his

life and from all relationships, and stood 'bare-headed before the sun, in the presence of the earth and air, in the presence of the immense forces of the universe'.[14] As Jefferies chose to be alone with the elements, Pater elected solipsism, a condition in which experience 'is ringed round for each one of us by that thick wall of personality through which no real voice has ever pierced on its way to us, or from us to that which we can only conjecture to be without'.[15] For Pater, every impression 'is the impression of the individual in his isolation, each mind keeping as a solitary prisoner its own dream of a world'. 'Dream' is one of the deadly words in Thomas's vocabulary, as it was in the Celtic Twilight and in the English pastoral tradition at large in the quarter-century before the First World War. Solipsism and a vague and isolating nature mysticism were both negative influences upon Edward Thomas's prose. In addition, his contempt for his readership, the 'villa residents' that he discusses in *The Country*, exacerbated his lack of confidence and his self-disgust, and increased his uncertainty of tone and focus. Self-consciousness made him his own severest critic, too. 'I rarely see much in the country', he confesses in *The Heart of England* (1906); 'I always carry out into the fields a vast baggage of prejudices from books and strong characters whom I have met.'[16] He then proceeds to condemn in himself 'the egoism of an imitative brain'. Later, after he had begun to write poetry, he spoke to Eleanor Farjeon of the 'rhetoric and formality which left my prose so often with a dead rhythm only'.[17] The curiously unmemorable quality of his prose especially at its 'finest' is due to its lack of a living rhythm. This in turn is due to its exclusively 'written' character, which is a product of the isolated, self-conscious literary mind.

Edward Thomas's strongest description of the imagination occurs in *Richard Jefferies*:

> The clearness of the physical is allied to the penetration of the spiritual vision. For both are nourished to their perfect flowering by the habit of concentration. To see a thing as he saw the sun-painted yellow-hammer in Stewart's Mash is part of the office of the imagination. Imagination is no more than the making of graven images, whether of things on the earth or in the mind. To make them, clear concentrated sight and patient mind are the most necessary things after love, and these two are the children of love.[18]

Thomas is here in process of making a distinction, but has not quite completed it. For clear seeing, which he attributes to Jefferies, is radically different from 'graven images', which Pater made from the life of things. In *Walter Pater* Thomas would describe Pater as 'a spectator. His aim is to see; if he is to become something it is by seeing.'[19] He would describe the style, 'free from traces of experience',[20] in which Pater, in words that are 'anything but living and social words',[21] turns life into art. What he would diagnose in Pater's 'exquisite unnaturalness' is absence of passion, lack of the emotion that commands rhythm and makes an imaginative whole. Pater's 'prose embalms choice things, as seen at choice moments, in choice words'.[22] Pater's transformation of 'animate and inanimate things into words like graven images'[23] is clearly not the kind of seeing or writing that Thomas admires in Jefferies.

Thomas continues his definition of imagination in *Richard Jefferies* by saying that those who have the rare 'power of repeating these images by music or language or carved stone' are 'aware that human life, nature, and art are every moment continuing and augmenting the Creation – making to-day the first day, and this field Eden, annihilating time'. This is a crucial passage for understanding Thomas's own way of seeing: his identification of imagination not with the historical present but with myth, and his vision of Eden. His idea of imagination also contains another meaning, fruitful with possibilities, although it too has a mythical dimension. Thus he mythologizes Jefferies the Wiltshireman, eloquently: 'He ... was the genius, the human expression, of this country, emerging from it, not to be detached from it any more than the curves of some statues from their maternal stone.'[24] He sees Jefferies not only as earth-born, however, but as a man with something 'to rest upon', a man with a people, who 'came to express part of this silence of uncounted generations'. Thomas thus sees Jefferies as fulfilling the conditions of poetry, which is 'a natural growth', with 'roots deep in a substantial past. It springs apparently from an occupation of the land, from long, busy, and quiet tracts of time, wherein a man or a nation may find its own soil. To have a future, it must have had a past.'[25] And Thomas sees Jefferies' writing career much as we may now see his own: as a progressive self-revelation. In Thomas's view, Jefferies, by the time he wrote *The Story of My Heart*, was 'the poet, the larger man who, though exquisitely sensitive, has no mere delicacy and rejected no part of life in man or nature, country or town'.[26] Jefferies had 'the clear vision that saw in all forms of life one commonwealth, one law, one beauty'.[27] He was, therefore, in spite of his loneliness, the opposite of the 'isolated selfconsidering brain',[28] which Thomas felt himself at his worst to be. Jefferies' seeing, then, had nothing in common with that of the spectator, who petrifies life in graven images. Using the bird imagery that would be a crucial element in his poetic vision, Thomas says of Jefferies' style that, 'given an entirely suitable subject, he wrote with a natural fineness and richness and a carelessness, too, like the blackbird's singing'.[29] It was in Jefferies, then, that Thomas first found his ideal of writing that is the natural speech of the whole man. Jefferies dictated his last essays, and it is significantly of these that Thomas says: 'he has found himself; and now it is no longer the sportsman, or the naturalist, or the agriculturalist, or the colourist, or the mystic, that speaks, but a man who has played these parts and been worn and shaped by them, by work and pain'.[30] Thomas found, in different degrees, the style that is the speech of 'the poet, the larger man' in other writers whom he admired, too – in Cobbett and Hudson, for example, and, at a decisive moment, in the poetry of Robert Frost, whose *North of Boston* 'speaks, and it is poetry'.[31] The speech of 'the larger man' is what poetry finally released in Edward Thomas himself, but his prose almost always withheld.

Early in his writing career, Edward Thomas attempted to transcend the limitations of the aesthetic vision by peopling nature with mythological presences. In *Oxford* (1903), he claims that he has 'on several afternoons gone some way towards the beginning of a new mythology'.[32] It is, however, of classical deities, Diana and Apollo, that he thinks in the Oxfordshire countryside. In *Beautiful Wales* (1905), an old abbey provokes a characteristic reverie, in which he says that the reader, too, if properly receptive, may seem in that place 'to be on the edge of a new mythology and to taste the joy of the surmises of him who first saw Pan among the sedges or the olives'.[33] Only in his last prose writings did he cease to superimpose the paraphernalia of classical mythology or the atmosphere of the Celtic Twilight on his descriptions of peopled, historical landscapes, and his poetry is not entirely free of the latter. It is not surprising, though, that a young writer should indulge in fancies and fantasies common to the literature and art of his period, and which we also find in

E. M. Forster and Paul Nash, for example. What is harder to accept is that Edward Thomas's prose, early and late, is marked by the escapism, sentimentality, whimsy and air of unreality for which Georgian poetry at its worst has been criticized. Yet this is less surprising if we reflect that, in the opening decades of the twentieth century, the story of poetry is the story of the struggle of the best poets to close the gap between poetry and experience. The dominance of modernism with its anti-Romantic stance has tended to obscure what the new poetry of poets such as Edward Thomas, W. B. Yeats and Wilfred Owen owed to the influence of Blake and Shelley, and Wordsworth and Keats. It was by developing and deepening Romantic influences, rather than rejecting them, that such poets closed the gap between poetic language and experience of the modern world. But still we do, I believe, sentimentalize Edward Thomas by valuing him exclusively in terms of 'a language not to be betrayed', instead of seeing him as a writer whose natural vision and speech, which he freed at last from the prison of aestheticism, were not untouched by late Romantic decadence.

As the following quotation from 'Hawthornden', in *Light and Twilight* (1911), shows, Edward Thomas both displayed and criticized the aesthetic attitude:

> It was literature, nevertheless, and the stage, that had given him the standard which he unconsciously applied to scenes in life which he thought should have been heroical, for example, and were not. Nor was he shaken from his dim-pinnacled citadel of unreality by his own experience of something near tragedy at home. His wife rushed at him one day, with stiff, drawn, red-spotted face and staring eyes, and a shrill voice he had never heard before, to tell him that one of the children was injured. He drew her head to his breast and kissed her hair, and felt at first a kind of shame, then an instinctive disgust at the stains and rude prints of her grief.[34]

Here Thomas criticizes the spectatorial stance, and at the same time illustrates its capacity for cruelty. Hawthornden is one of his many partial self-portraits, and the passage reveals and analyses the detached, cold, and even cruel vision that is a consequence of excessive literary idealism. Thomas's own detachment made him, at times, an acute psychological realist, and in *The Childhood of Edward Thomas*, in particular, he turns a clinical eye on himself

as well as on other people. The honesty, as in his description of
his relationship with his grandmother, makes for good writing:

> Without her, these holidays would have been impossible, and she
> gave me countless pleasures. But if I loved her it was largely
> because of these things, not instinctively or because she loved me.
> She was marvellously kind and necessary but we were never close
> together; and, when there was any quarrel, contempt mingled with
> my hate of her inheritance from semi-rural Wales of George the
> Fourth's time. She was bigoted, worldly, crafty, narrow-minded,
> and ungenerous, as I very early began to feel.[35]

In contrast to Thomas's reverie, this kind of coldness is bracing;
but it is also rather disturbing, and suggests something missing,
and a lack of generosity on the part of the writer himself.
Thomas's autobiographical writings with their portraits of real
people are honest, but curiously empty of love, or any strong
emotion capable of releasing the writer from his stance as an
onlooker. Only the boy's pleasure in nature provides joy; the
whole man is not engaged, and it has to be said that the prose as
a whole expresses, and partially analyses, an emotionally
retarded condition.

When Edward Thomas applies his aesthetic and mythological
imagination to people, the results can be particularly disturbing.
In 'At a Cottage Door', in *Rest and Unrest* (1910), for example, he
describes old women living in poverty in an industrial town in
south Wales:

> Such creatures, chiefly women, were not uncommon. They were
> small, grey-skinned, with clotted grey hair; they had scarred faces,
> had lost an eye and most of their teeth; they wore soiled print or
> black dresses, bedraggled like the plumage of a dead bird in the
> mud and in colour approaching the foul dust of the pavement and
> the garbage of the gutter. In appearance they were genuine
> autochthons. This earth of flagstone, asphalte, granite, brick, iron,
> and ashes, might have protruded such a monstrous birth on a night
> of frost, to prove that it was not yet barren in its age and ignominy.
> One such crone crawling out into the light, unclean, dull and yet
> surprised, had a look as if she had just been exhumed; she might
> have been buried alive in the foundation of the town for luck, and
> had now emerged to see what had been done.[36]

There is fascination and repulsion rather than compassion or
anger here. There is also a suspect pleasure in arranging and

interpreting the scene, with little more sense of moral responsibility than if it were a landscape. The narrator (whose viewpoint is evidently the author's) combines voyeuristic observation with myth-making, and the most disturbing feature of the description is its unconscious cruelty. Above all, the writing simplifies. This tendency is increased by the perception of people in terms of bird imagery, and contrast between them and the singleness of birds, which, according to a character in the story, 'are not all tangled up and darkened with a number of things'. The combined aestheticism and myth-making produce, at the end, a mystifying vision of humanity as a 'demon', which obscures both the narrator's attitude (which is more complex and interesting than the quotation above reveals), and the town's social and historical formation.

Edward Thomas claimed to have 'no historic sense', but in the same book, *The South Country*, showed his ability to read the historical landscape:

> In some places history has wrought like an earthquake, in others like an ant or mole; everywhere, permanently; so that if we but knew or cared, every swelling of the grass, every wavering line of hedge or path or road were an inscription, brief as an epitaph, in many languages and characters.[37]

He then immediately falls back on myth, claiming we are like Taliesin, the fabulous Welsh poet who was present in many times and places: 'We belong to the days of Wordsworth, of Elizabeth, of Richard Plantagenet, of Harold, of the earliest bards.' This is the belief which would inspire 'Lob'; it is what Raymond Williams calls 'a version of history which succeeds in cancelling history'.[38] Thomas calls experiences resembling Taliesin's 'these many folds in our nature', and says 'the face of the earth reminds us' of them. He speculates that, 'perhaps, even where there are no more marks visible upon the land than there were in Eden, we are aware of the passing of time in ways too difficult and strange for the explanation of historian and zoologist and philosopher. It is this manifold nature that responds with such indescribable depth and variety to the appeals of many landscapes.' It is clear that his imaginative domain is not history but interiority, psychological depth. The idea of a 'manifold nature' marks a stage in his long struggle to transcend the limitations of isolation and subjectivity and to connect himself with others, to bind the self to humanity. The 'difficult and strange ways' in which he was aware of time, personal memory and memory in the landscape, would be an important motif in his poetry.

In the following passage in *The South Country* he describes a coomb that is a passage 'into the heart of the Downs'. This eventually shuts out all signs of human history, but 'is not an end but a beginning'. It is a 'divine' region, 'a region out of space and out of time in which life and thought and physical health are in harmony with sun and earth'. Significantly, Thomas connects the mythological ideal to his modernity, to civilization and its discontents, for he says that 'out of it all arises a vision of the man who will embody this thought, a man whom human infelicity, discontented with the past, has placed in a golden age still farther back'. The coomb 'is one of the countless Edens where we are in contact not with the soldier and ploughman and mason that change the surface of the earth but with prophet and poet who have ever lived to trace to Nature and to the early ages the health and vigour of men'. Here, 'in the midst is the mother Earth, the young mother of the world'. Given Thomas's struggle against depression and nervous strain, it is natural that for him Eden should be a place of 'health and vigour'. In his country books he frequently writes of discovering such places, regions of solitude and safety, of 'peace and purity and simplicity', which he sees as fragments of Eden or the Golden Age. The myth fulfilled a strong, even a desperate, personal need; it also represented a widespread literary preoccupation in England in his time, and Thomas's persistence with it calls to mind John Cowper Powys, who developed the myth into a whole complex imaginative world during a long lifetime. He, too, often found in his south country landscapes 'a region out of place and out of time', a Golden Age or Elysian Fourth Dimension, which combined childhood memories with the idea of paradise. He, too, located 'our mother, the Earth' at the centre of his imaginative world.

The mythological imagination is in part a response to history, to a world drained of a sense of the sacred, and there is far more that needs to be said about it than that it cancels history. But in my view, that does need to be said. Here, for example, is a sentence from *In Pursuit of Spring*: 'I confess I did not think about the lad who was hanged for a hare when I caught sight of the church at Orcheston St. George, but rather of some imaginary, blissful time which at least lacked our tortures, our great men, our shame and conscience.'[39] This is indeed an odd mixture of Thomas the populist, admirer of William Cobbett, and Thomas the world-weary dreamer. It may be easy enough to forget about 'great men' but conscience, surely, is not so easily disposed of. Even after the outbreak of war, Thomas was still capable of finding, in 'The Manor Farm', 'a season of bliss unchangeable' awakened from Merry England. Desire for continuity and permanence is strong in the English poetic tradition stemming from Wordsworth, and stronger in the modern period, in which discontinuity and impermanence are rife. Edward Thomas shared with Powys and others a strong need for an essential English history, a history purged of modernity, which resulted inevitably in their construction of myth.

Writing to Gordon Bottomley in the autumn of 1905 Edward Thomas disclosed his ambition to write fiction: 'I see that I may come to stories of some kind – not plotty cathartics, but episodes ending suddenly & soon; & that a novel is possible, & fine on account of its difficulties. Once or twice, I have thought of a suburban novel to be called *A Suburban Education* but vaguely, & I don't like blocks of autobiography. But stories & novels seem far off & what am I to do?'[40] The idea of 'a suburban novel' prefigures *The Happy-Go-Lucky Morgans* (1913) and *The Childhood of Edward Thomas*, both of which belong to the end of his career as a prose writer, but the stories were not so far off as they seemed. Indeed, they were latent in his earliest work, in the nature sketches in which what is being described is subsidiary to mood, and Thomas is shaping episodes of his spiritual autobiography. But for the storyteller's art there are other requirements, too – an interest in people, or at least the ability to project the self into fictional character, and a capacity to render incidents in which human experience reveals its inner significance. At least two sketches in *The Heart of England* (1906) show that Thomas had what was required.

At the beginning of *The Heart of England* a boy in a suburban street watches an old watercress seller pass by, and the old man becomes for him a figure of mystery and wonder that he invests with all the exotic adventures his imagination conceives. Thomas, as the narrator, sees both man and boy in perspective, but he shares something of the child's wonder. The boy sets out to follow the man but stumbles, and falls, uttering 'his intolerable longing in a fit of grave tears'. The more detached narrator adds: 'I thought to follow him myself',[41] and thus shows his partial identification with the child. The juxtaposition of adult and child, and Thomas's attitude towards the latter, are characteristic of his later fiction.

Another treatment of the motif occurs in *The Heart of England* when Thomas describes how he and his 'companion' (a version of the 'other' that haunts his writings) are out in the woods at dawn on the first of May, and find a welcome:

> And for ourselves – we seemed to be home from a long exile …
> Here, then, was the land to which had fled those children who once
> bore our names, who were our companions in the days when sun-
> shine was more than wine had ever been since, and they left us
> long ago, not suddenly, but so strangely, that we knew not that
> they were far off: hither those children had fled, and their compan-
> ions of that time; here they had been hiding these many years;
> abiding here they had become immortal in the green-fledged
> antique wood, and we had come back to them.[42]

Re-entering childhood by recapturing its joy and peace, Thomas comes 'home'. There are haunting footsteps in the wood, which are reminiscent of Walter de la Mare, rather than the Eliot of 'Burnt Norton': a reminiscence that places Thomas in the literary tradition to which, as a prose writer, he belongs. His preoccupation with the child is with the child in the man, and with a state of being to which the man can sometimes and fleetingly win.

In February 1909 Edward Thomas wrote enthusiastically to Gordon Bottomley that he had been writing character sketches and stories. Although he is uncertain of their quality, he is excited by the venture. Later, he wrote that they had been written 'under a real impulse': 'I feel sure it is better work or in a better direction than all but the best of the old but it is even less profitable.'[43] Creative writing does not pay: this is a familiar lament of Thomas, who has had to suppress his real talents; but here he sees a glimmer of the creativity which newspaper and publishers' deadlines have held in check, and we can see in his fiction, published in *Light and Twilight* and *Rest and Unrest*, a hint of the spiritual renewal which is to come fully with the poems. The fiction is concerned mainly with the paradisal myth, of which Thomas wrote in *The South Country*: 'As mankind has looked back to a golden age, so the individual, repeating the history of the race, looks back and finds one in his own past.'[44]

For Alice Lacking, in 'The First of Spring', spring renews an aspiration, 'a strong but vague and wordless desire to be something other than she was, to do something other than she was doing or had ever done'. Looking back from her present discontent, she recalls her childhood: 'she remembered simply the bliss which she had in those days not recognised'. In her youth she had written poetry, and had carried 'a secret' within her. It was 'her personality, her self, what made her the equal of all men and things'. Then, 'she and her mother possessed the world'. But in growing older she lost the secret, her identity became uncertain and diffused, and the state of whole-hearted being gave way to the divisions and discontents of self-consciousness. Alice's aspiration is now projected on to the spring and her desire to adopt a child, as an unconscious compensation for the child she has lost in growing older. But her wishes are frustrated, and the story ends ironically:

'I think, Alice,' said Colonel Lacking that evening, 'you had better have a sea voyage. We will take one together, I think. Yes. This English spring is too much for us when we are no longer young. You're looking a fright.'

'It's not the spring, father, it's myself.'

'Where shall it be?' he continued, looking at a map of this world.[45]

In spite of the wooden dialogue, the story establishes the significance of the commonplace statement: 'It's not the spring, father, it's myself', and the sense in which the spring is too much for Alice. No place on the map can indicate the lost world of childhood, which is, for her, more real than 'this world'.

'Home'[46] has a similar theme. A young soldier dying in a foreign country returns in his delirium, not to his home in England but to Wales, his father's country, which he once visited with him. This is a real country, where, as his mother reflects, 'they spoke a different language, had queer names, different food, different ways and ... a kind of common life as of one big family'. But it is also the land of his childhood, and 'another country'; it has no geographical location but persists for him as a felt reality, the only one in a world of adult unrealities, such as the war in which he has fallen, and the cause for which he has fought. In death he returns to that other country, away from the dream world of his mature life, back to the only dream that makes life real – the fulness of being once experienced in childhood. It would be cheap to dwell on the ironies of this in view of Edward Thomas's subsequent death in battle – he went to war in order to defend the country he loved. It is however interesting to note his identification of the 'common life' – that Wordsworthian theme – with Wales, and to reflect how much his own idea of 'home' owed to his sense of Wales as 'that other country'.

In addition to these and other stories in *Rest and Unrest* and *Light and Twilight*, the episodic *The Happy-Go-Lucky Morgans* is about the possession, or loss, of a spiritual kingdom, which is usually identified with a period of unselfconscious childhood. The episodes are connected by the Morgans' house in Balham, and by the characters in revolt against suburban constraint who, gathering there, yearn romantically for 'a larger air', which belongs to the past or to exotic legends or dreams. Here, again, is the 'country' of childhood, found by Arthur and Philip in the woods and fields near London, and called by them 'Our Country'. It is a real place, but exists now in Arthur's memory as a state of being, a 'Palace of the Mountain of Clouds', where boys are safe and solitary, 'separated by great distances and great enchantment from the rest of the world'. Another character, Mr Torrance, dwells on 'the real world' in his mind, which is the place where he lived as a child; his writings and his actual life have no connection with it. In this respect, he is one of Edward Thomas's most significant self-projections. So are Aurelius, the 'superfluous man', and David Morgan, a 'mystic' who isolates himself in his 'Folly' in Wales, and dies there. Thomas was well aware of the suicidal potential of a certain form of mysticism, as he shows in his portrait of David Morgan, a man who has severed 'all bonds of necessity', except that with his wife, and crossed all the boundaries of human identity in his search for God. All the characters are 'innocents', and the novel is completely lacking in adult relationships or developed emotions. The Morgans' Abercorran House is a boy's paradise, and a refuge in which the various misfits find a physical and imaginative life that feeds their starved minds and senses; but it is itself a reflection of a more distant ideal, the place in Wales from which it gets its name. Glen Cavaliero, in his introduction to the edition published in 1983,[47] makes a strong case for the novel, which he describes as 'pervaded by a tartness that prevents it from smacking in any way of compensatory fantasy'. It does indeed contain some impressive writing, especially in descriptions of the suburbs and in the chapter called 'The House under the Hill', but while I recognize that Edward Thomas is self-consciously critical of his own romanticism, I see his novel as being far more indulgent towards his escapism than Glen Cavaliero does. *The Happy-Go-Lucky Morgans* does however contain one particularly interesting chapter, which indicates Thomas's subsequent development.

In Chapter XV, Mr Stodham speaks for England:

> 'England made you, and of you is England made ... Having denied England and your father and mother, you may have to deny your own self, and treat it as nothing, a mere conventional boundary, an artifice, by which you are separated from the universe and its creator. To unite yourself with the universe and the creator, you may be tempted to destroy that boundary of your own body and brain, and die. He is a bold man who hopes to do without earth, England, family, and self.'[48]

In *The South Country* Thomas had looked back to 'England, that swan's nest, that island which a man's heart was not too big to love utterly', and contrasted it with present-day 'Great Britain, the British Empire, Britons, Britishers, and the English-speaking world'. In this Empire, 'he is fortunate who can find an ideal England of the past, the present, and the future to worship, and embody it in his native fields and waters or his garden, as in a graven image'.[49] That, of course, was precisely what the politics of wartime patriotism were about, as we see in poems as various as Rupert Brooke's and Ivor Gurney's, and Edward Thomas's own. It was a complex issue, involving tangled emotions and motives, and the retrospective wisdom of those not subject to the tensions of the time scarcely meets the case. The chapter about English pariotism in *The Happy-Go-Lucky Morgans* expresses something of the complexity, especially as it affected a writer who loved Wales as well as England, and who knew he was living in a confused and divided society. Our reaction to it can hardly be unaffected by the fact that Edward Thomas was soon to practise what Mr Stodham affirms. That he would do so is suggested by his wartime essays, (later included in *The Last Sheaf*, 1928), 'England', 'Tipperary', 'It's a Long, Long Way', and 'This England', and in his poems.

Earlier, Thomas had tended either to picture landscape aesthetically, or to dissolve it in evocations of Eden or the Golden Age. His concern had been with atmosphere and essenc_, but now it is with word and thing, and he accepts the 'boundary' marked by 'earth, England, family, and self'. In 'This England', for example, he conveys a sharper sense of a particular corner of the country, in Herefordshire, than he had in earlier voluminous descriptions of landscapes. Now, his mind and mood are concentrated. This is due in part, no doubt, to his friendship with Robert Frost, which both enabled him to communicate freely at a deep level, and confirmed his ideas about the relation between style and speech. But it is also because now, in wartime, as he says in 'England', 'the whole land is suddenly home'.[50] The conclusion of 'This England' shows clearly that the essay originated from the same experience that gave rise to his poem, 'The Sun Used to Shine':

> Then one evening the new moon made a difference. It was the end of a wet day; at least, it had begun wet, had turned warm and muggy, and at last fine but still cloudy. The sky was banded with rough masses in the north-west, but the moon, a stout orange crescent, hung free of cloud near the horizon. At one stroke, I thought, like many other people, what things that same new moon sees eastward about the Meuse in France. Of those who could see it there, not blinded by smoke, pain, or excitement, how many saw it and heeded? I was deluged, in a second stroke, by another thought, or something that over-powered thought. All I can tell is, it seemed to me that either I had never loved England, or I had loved it foolishly, aesthetically, like a slave, not having realized that it was not mine unless I were willing and prepared to die rather than leave it as Belgian women and old men and children had left their country. Something I had omitted. Something, I felt, had to be done before I could look again composedly at English landscape, at the elms and poplars about the houses, at the purple-headed wood-betony with two stiff pairs of dark leaves on a stiff stem, who stood sentinel among the grasses or bracken by hedge-side or wood's-edge. What he stood sentinel for I did not know, any more than what I had got to do.[51]

It would be absurd to make a qualitative comparison between the essay and the poem, but it may be observed that the prose does not have the poem's somewhat conventional ending, where everything fades into memory and a sense of mortality dominates the mood. The prose has mystery, like the poem, and is simultaneously clear-cut with the edge of decision, which both arises from the concentrated mind and confirms it. Thomas 'possesses' both himself and the land, but with a possession that depends upon his willingness to sacrifice his life. He is no longer an isolated sensibility, free of a landscape which he can rearrange aesthetically at will or whim. The moon is not a vaguely mysterious poetic symbol intimating the spectator's solitude. It is 'the same new moon' standing over the battlefield, the moon that will make 'many other people' think of what it sees. 'The purple-headed wood-betony', 'stiff' and 'sentinel', is a masculine image standing at once for sexual potency, protective love, and acceptance of death. It is not, I think, a consciously comprehensive symbol; its meaning arises rather from that 'something that overpowered thought', by which Thomas, moved to his depths, is at once taken out of himself and gathered together, resting his being on the country he is prepared to die for. Written in September 1914, two months before the first poems, 'This England' reveals the whole man in a landscape to which he is decisively, substantially, related, and in which he shares common bonds. Without this reality to rest upon, Edward Thomas could not express himself as a poet, and neither could he voice more than a baseless and incomplete self in his prose.

5

Landscape of history, landscape of myth: Edward Thomas's south country

> Let us get out of these indoor narrow modern days, whose twelve
> hours somehow have become shortened, into the sunlight and the
> pure wind. A something that the ancients called divine can be
> found and felt there still.[1]

Richard Jefferies' words, which to the young Edward Thomas
'were a gospel, an incantation', speak of desire for liberation, for
physical and spiritual enlargement, from a contracted sense of
time and of space. Liberation is represented by the 'divine',
which can be experienced in contact with the elements.

It is a well-known fact of literary and cultural history that with
the withdrawal of 'the sea of faith' in the second half of the nineteenth century, more and more thinkers and writers sought the
divine in Nature instead of in the Christian Church or any other
established religion. For many in England, Wordsworth was the
main evangelist of a religion of Nature. In the words of William
Hale White in *The Autobiography of Mark Rutherford* (1881), for
instance:

> God was brought from that heaven of the books, and dwelt on the
> downs in the far-away distances, and in every cloud-shadow
> which wandered across the valley. Wordsworth unconsciously did
> for me what every religious reformer has done, – he re-created my
> Supreme Divinity.[2]

Edward Thomas's sense of the divine in Nature owed something
to the Romantic poetic tradition: to Wordsworth, but also to
Keats's paganism, Shelley's idealism, Matthew Arnold's pastoral
landscapes, and above all to Jefferies, whom he considered
essentially as 'the poet, the larger man'. Thomas's worship of
Nature expressed the needs of a man from the suburbs, who
sought liberation from its conditions and mentality in 'the South
Country', in Nature which was indeed made 'wilder' by 'the
idea of London', as it was for the woman in 'Up in the Wind'.[3]

It is evident from Thomas's writings, however, that Nature afforded him, at best, an ambiguous liberation from the strains of modern life, and, at worst, conspired with his self-consciousness to isolate and imprison him. He was an incomer to the country-side during a period of agricultural decline, his work as a writer connected him to London and a largely urban readership, rather than to the country people of whom he wrote, and he brought with him the discontents of modern civilization. Stan Smith, in a penetrating study of Edward Thomas, defines Thomas's 'dilemma' as that of 'a middle-class liberal individualism under strain, faced with the prospect of its own redundancy in the changed world of a new era, and struggling, with remarkable intensity and integrity, to understand the flux in which it is to go down'.[4] I agree with Smith that 'it is not only the individual here who is in crisis. Rather it is the age itself.' But my understanding of Thomas is couched in a different terminology, which is reli-gious in the root meaning of the word. It is the loosening or the severing of the bonds of all foundational relationships that con-stitutes Thomas's crisis: the bond between person and person, man and woman, individual and society, language and reality, humanity and the ground of being. I see the specific problems of class allegiance and national identity during a later phase of the British Empire as involved in the breaking of ties that formed the image of man in Western civilization, and the struggle to rede-fine the human that continues to the present. Social and eco-nomic decline, against a background of imperial power, is bound up with a larger crisis of meaning, in all our relationships, which defines the modern condition. 'The flux' Thomas experienced, to use Smith's word, is the flux we are still living in, and it is because he was, in that sense, 'one of us', a man questioned as to the very meaning of his existence, that his work matters now.

The religion of Nature afforded a temporary stay to the chal-lenge of modernism, but was implicated in the decline of sym-bolic power that the language of Nature owed to traditional reli-gious sources. Ruskin in *Modern Painters* diagnosed a sadness in his age, a 'darkness of heart', which he ascribed to 'our want of faith'.[5] Edward Thomas spoke in a memorable phrase of 'the modern sad passion of Nature'.[6] Both writers were prophetically aware of earlier stages of the process that has led in our time to 'the end of nature', which occurs when 'we can no longer imagine that we are part of something larger than ourselves'.[7] Or when, in Edward Thomas's phrase, we are absolutely imprisoned in 'the parochialism of humanity', and shut out from the eternal life of Nature.

In Thomas's view Jefferies ultimately became 'the larger man, who ... rejected no part of life in man or nature, country or town'. But the mysticism of *The Story of My Heart* isolates Jefferies' soul in the universe. It is frequently taken for a religious book, but in fact it is about the breaking of the bonds, between man and Nature, the individual and mankind, and the human mind and the creation, which were the foundations of Wordsworth's religion of Nature. The final result for Jefferies was absolute spiritual isolation, as his last notebooks show.

Edward Thomas went some way along the same road. He knew the terror of extreme self-consciousness, and diagnosed it:

> You see the central evil is self-consciousness carried as far beyond selfishness as selfishness is beyond self-denial ... and now amounting to a disease and all I have got to fight it with is the knowledge that in truth I am not the isolated selfconsidering brain which I have come to seem – the *knowledge* that I am something more, but not the belief that I can reopen the connection between the brain and the rest.[8]

His disease of self-consciousness was a form of inner and outer disconnection: between the brain and his other faculties, and between the self and the world. I have already suggested that this is what deadened the rhythm and clouded the vision in his prose writing about Nature: he was writing with part of himself, and for a class of people he despised. I have also argued that he showed, especially in his criticism, an acute understanding of the condition, which he knew was not peculiar to himself. He analysed the 'solitary world', and expressed the state of isolation succinctly, in words reminiscent of Matthew Arnold: 'The waters are too deep between us.' He read isolation into the history of English poetry, which he interpreted in terms of the separation of poets from their society. Only Chaucer wrote 'about neighbours for neighbours'; even Shakespeare 'stands apart from his age in a kind of inevitable exile'. In his own poetry, Thomas learnt to speak as the larger man, the man who integrated his different faculties and connected himself to the world. To the end, though, he tended to ascribe most meaning to non-human voices, voices of wind and water, and above all voices of birds. In the review[9] from which I have quoted above, he said: 'As for lyric poets, they appear but sudden sharp voices as of birds flying over in a dark night.'

Edward Thomas, the suburban and bookish incomer, the Paterian aesthete and disciple of Richard Jefferies, took with him to the country a sense of emptiness, of loss:

> *There is nothing left for us to rest upon*, nothing great, venerable, or mysterious, which can take us out of ourselves, and give us that more than human tranquillity now to be seen in a few old faces of a disappearing generation.[10]

Finding nothing to rest upon, in a decaying rural culture, and with a language of Nature from which a sense of the sacred was evaporating, Edward Thomas attempted to supply the lack, and played with the idea of beginning 'a new mythology'. It was more than play: Edward Thomas's prose delineates – indeed, dramatizes and elaborates – a myth. This might be described, in the phrase of Peter V. Marinelli, as 'a pastoral of childhood'.[11] In using words such as 'myth' and 'pastoral' in this context, how-ever, it is essential to bear in mind the relation of the phenomena they describe to history. As Bruno Snell says of 'the longing for peace and a home' in Virgil's Arcadia, 'after the disastrous anar-chy of the civil wars the desire for peace was paramount', so that 'Virgil's poetry reflects a genuine political reality'.[12] Something similar has to be said about Edward Thomas's pastoral myth, in which the unselfconscious child lives in a golden age: that it reflects the strains of a divided consciousness, in a time of increasing imperial power, which stimulated a corresponding idea of 'manhood', and masked spiritual emptiness. But this is not all that needs to be said about it. In terms of Mircea Eliade's concept of the 'nostalgia for Paradise',[13] Thomas's mythic aware-ness expresses a universal human aspiration. Though it some-times manifests itself as a fanciful 'dream', it is a real need, a need for wholeness of being, which at once conflicts with the limitations of his historical situation and judges those limitations by standards based on a larger sense of human potential.

The fullest treatment of the myth in Edward Thomas's prose is *The Happy-Go-Lucky Morgans*. But elements of the myth, and especially the spiritual and emotional needs it is designed to meet, appear in the landscape of the poetry, a landscape in which history and myth interact, and come into conflict. Thomas's overt use of religious language – heaven and hell, for instance, or earth and heaven – similarly describes, in mythic terms, a spiritual and psychological drama, but without the traditional Christian connotations. The principal literary sources of his pastoral of childhood were Wordsworth's 'Intimations of Immortality from Recollections of Early Childhood' and Jefferies' *Bevis*, but he also drew upon his considerable knowledge of Celtic Otherworld stories. The myth originated, however, in his own childhood visits to Wales, which he described in 1899 as his soul's *'matria,* a home with the warm sweetness of a mother's love, and with her influence, too'.[14] Edward Thomas's idea of the imagination was closely associated with his awareness 'that human life, nature, and art are every moment continuing and augmenting the Creation – making to-day the first day, and this field Eden, annihilating time'.[15] Indeed, the idea ascribed the same power to the imagination as to human life, and Nature. It was an idea that linked the recovery of Eden to the child's possession of the golden age, and it both inspired Thomas and was a source of the quarrel with himself dramatized in his poetry. Two other crucial terms of his landscape of myth were 'Wales' and 'home'.

It is commonly accepted that Thomas's idea of Wales was closely associated with his sense of a lost or unobtainable home:

> This is my grief. That land,
> My home, I have never seen;
> No traveller tells of it,
> However far he has been. ('Home', 39)

The effect of Thomas's Welshness upon his vision of southern England, however, has not received due emphasis. It should be seen in the light of his well-known statement about the south country: 'Yet is this country, though I am mainly Welsh, a kind of home, as I think it is more than any other to those modern people who belong nowhere.'[16] The affirmation of belonging is qualified, 'though I am mainly Welsh', and is made in the context of a definition of modernity as a state of radical dislocation: 'those modern people who belong nowhere'. It was with an imagination nourished by his reading of Celtic stories, with their magical sense of another world existing parallel to this world, and with the hunger for home of a spiritual exile, that Thomas looked at the southern English landscapes which he transformed into the world of his poetry.

The following passage from Thomas's prose is one of those that make one wonder how he ever became a real poet:

> The little old house rippled over by creeper was beautiful then – the lime tree and the creeper trembling in the gusty moonlight, and the windows and doorway hollow and dark and romantic as if a poet had made them to sting men's hearts with beauty and with regret.[17]

This is indeed the twilight of Romanticism. What principally survived from it in Thomas's poetry were the words, which he often links, 'dark' and 'hollow'. In 'The Gypsy', for instance:

> That night he peopled for me the hollow wooded land,
> More dark and wild than stormiest heavens, that I searched
>   and scanned
> Like a ghost new-arrived. The gradations of the dark
> Were like an underworld of death, but for the spark
> In the Gypsy boy's black eyes as he played and stamped his
>   tune,
> 'Over the hills and far away', and a crescent moon.   (33)

The 'dark and wild' land, 'the hollow wooded land', is recognizably a south country landscape (probably the country near Petersfield in Hampshire). But it is transfigured by the gypsy's tune, which introduces into the familiar land a sense of the supernatural, an underlying reality, 'an underworld of death'. Here Thomas remakes the landscape in terms of pagan myth, which is not exclusively Celtic (the boy plays 'a rascally Bacchanal dance'), although it is reminiscent of Annwn, the Welsh Otherworld. The enchanted land of the poem is not necessarily to be identified with physical death, but rather, through imagery of dark and storm and wildness, with the revelation of a transformative magical power. A sense of distance, of transcendence, and of a dangerous subterranean or subconscious energy, instils in the poet an awareness of vast unrealized potential, present in the land itself, and existing over against his disembodied state.

Edward Thomas's landscapes are as haunted as Thomas Hardy's by the dead, but with a difference. Hardy lived on ancestral ground and had a sense of kinship with the dead. In 'Poems of 1912–13' a whole landscape aches with the absence of his dead wife, and is haunted by their original happiness. Things in Hardy's Wessex speak with the voices of the dead, who were actual people known to him or his family, or recorded in books or on tombstones. For Thomas, by contrast, the dead were more a metaphor than 'friends beyond', and they carried other meanings. In 'Two Houses' he wrote: 'the hollow past/Half yields the dead that never/More than half hidden lie'. The landscape that at first seems the abode of the dead is rather the place where they manifest their continuing life, and coexist with the living. Their life, though, tends to be symbolic of something in the poet himself, as distinct from representative of the community of the generations. It is not just his mortality that the dead symbolize, but also his buried potential for a larger existence.

Nevertheless, if 'the hollow wooded land' symbolizes a source of hidden energy for Thomas, it is also a place under the shadow of war. All Thomas's poems are, in a sense, war poems. He is preoccupied by his personal mortality, and he shares the death-obsession of the national psyche in wartime. The coomb is 'far more ancient and dark' because it is where 'they killed the badger', 'That most ancient Briton of English beasts' (21). The badger, like some imaginative power, or spirit of place representing the original Britons, has been killed. But, paradoxically, the war gives new life to ancient symbols; the woods attract yet oppress the poet with a 'darkness' that threatens (or promises) loss of the self; the land renews its early character as a necropolis, haunted by the tragic mystery. Yet all is held in a curious suspension; the war is both here and not here; the poet is imaginatively more alive than he has ever been; he is discovering his powers as a poet, in part through his newly real awareness of death. As in the Celtic stories he loved, there are – in the words of John Cowper Powys – 'all manner of magical *mixings* up'; life is mixed with death and death with life. As in the Celtic stories, life appears 'even from the lap of death',[18] so Edward Thomas's poems are born not of the war alone, but of the dying rural culture of which he is at once celebrant and elegist. As I shall later show, his landscape of the dead was not a static symbol, but underwent a change with the continuation of the war.

The beginning of 'Wind and Mist' (50)

> They met inside the gateway that gives the view,
> A hollow land as vast as heaven

describes Thomas's south country under two of its main aspects: hollow and vast, insubstantial and paradisal. One of the two voices (the poet's) says of the South Downs, 'Sometimes a man feels proud of them, as if/He had just created them with one mighty thought.' In this poem, however, Thomas expresses what we might call the other side of his paradisal myth, in which the mind continues the Creation. From the house with the view, 'the eye watching … saw,

> Many a day, day after day, mist – mist
> Like chaos surging back – and felt itself
> Alone in all the world, marooned alone.
> We lived in clouds, on a cliff's edge almost
> (You see), and if clouds went, the visible earth
> Lay too far off beneath and like a cloud.' (51)

Loss of the god-like power of thought reduces the poet to 'the eye watching', and to the state of an outcast facing the return of chaos. The next three lines make one of the central statements of Thomas's poetry:

> 'I did not know it was the earth I loved
> Until I tried to live there in the clouds
> And the earth turned to cloud.'

What the poem establishes is that belief in the mind's creative autonomy, in isolation from the Creation, dissolves the earth, and reduces it to chaos.

Thomas both uses and criticizes the mythopoeic imagination. It would be a useful simplification to describe his poetry as a quarrel between the dreamer and the larger man, and between myth and history. It would be wrong, though, to historicize myth, and reduce it to a dream-world with no purchase upon reality. The larger man is the man who seeks wholeness and integration; his need is to resolve contraries, in a way that is well known to mythologists:

'The wall of Paradise,' says Nicholas of Cusa, 'is built of contraries, nor is there any way to enter but for one who has overcome the highest spirit of reason who guards the gate.' It is a function of mythology to confound this guardian spirit of reason so that finite man may glimpse the infinity which lies beyond the confines of the cosmos. Coincidences of opposites and of other irreconcilables give a shock to the understanding and transport the spirit to the gateway of the Other World.[19]

Thomas's south country, the landscape of his poetry, is where, through coincidences of opposites, he glimpses the infinite, or, in Jefferies' terms, his mind is liberated from 'narrow modern days' by 'something that the ancients called divine'. The landscape is not only this, however; it is also a kind of battleground, in which the actual war affects the interaction in his mind between history and myth, and between the dreamer and the larger man.

Edward Thomas associated lyric poetry with the song of birds: 'As for lyric poets, they appear but sudden sharp voices as of birds flying over in a dark night.' He found in Jefferies' mature writing 'a natural fineness and richness and a carelessness, too, like the blackbird's singing'.[20] It is a way of thinking typical of Jefferies himself, who wrote, in 'Hours of Spring': 'The bird upon the tree utters the meaning of the wind – a voice of the grass and wild flower, words of the green leaf; they speak through that slender tone.'[21] The bird's voice transcends human self-consciousness: 'Genius is nature, and his lay, like the sap in the bough from which he sings, rises without thought.'

This way of thinking clearly has religious implications. For Thomas, 'The Word' is 'a pure thrush word' (73). In 'March the 3rd', he says that when the 'singing day' falls on Sunday, 'the birds' songs have/The holiness gone from the bells' (46). Both 'The Glory' and 'March' contain a note of religious ecstasy. In the latter, for instance:

> The sun filled earth and heaven with a great light
> And a tenderness, almost warmth, where the hail dripped,
> As if the mighty sun wept tears of joy. (7)

Sun, earth and heaven are divine, though it is not the divinity of organized religion. The evangel in Thomas's world is that of the birds. 'What did the thrushes know?' he asks.

> Something they knew – I also, while they sang
> And after. Not till night had half its stars
> And never a cloud, was I aware of silence
> Stained with all that hour's songs, a silence
> Saying that Spring returns, perhaps tomorrow.[22]

It would be crude to reduce Thomas's religious sense to a determinate meaning. What can be said without being reductive is that he identifies birdsong with a spirit in nature that transcends time, and with the coincidence of contraries that opens the gate

of Paradise – here, 'silence/Stained with all that hour's songs'.
The contradictions implicit in Thomas's thinking about the relation of birdsong to poetry may be better understood by reference to the passage in *The South Country* about the nightingale's song, the song which conveys 'the mysterious sense ... that the earth is something more than a human estate'.

> Here for this hour we are remote from the parochialism of humanity. The bird has admitted a larger air. We breathe deeply of it and are made free citizens of eternity. We hear voices that were not dreamed of before, the voices of those spirits that live in minute forms of life, the spirits that weave the frost flower on the fallen branch, the gnomes of underground, those who care for the fungus on the beech root, the lichen on the trunk, the algae on the grave-stone. This hazel lane is a palace of strange pomp in an empire of which we suddenly find ourselves guests, not wholly alien nor ill at ease, though the language is new. Drink but a little draught of this air and no need is there to fear the ways of men, their mockery, their cruelty, their foreignness.[23]

It is hard not to see an unintended irony in the political terms Thomas uses here. Humanity is parochial; Nature is 'an empire'. In fact, it is the writer who is a refugee from the historical empire who finds himself a citizen of eternity in a Nature on to which he projects both his spiritual needs and his anthropomorphic fancies. What he has escaped from is time, and the parish of the human. In this place, a place out of time created by the nightingale's song, it is men with their mockery and their cruelty who are the foreigners. How then is the poet to use this 'new' language if he wishes to speak as a human being to other men and women? Rather than being a solution to the problem of how to speak as 'the poet, the larger man', the idea of a language of Nature may compound it.

I think we should bear this possibility in mind when considering what is probably Thomas's most admired statement of his poetic aspiration. 'I never saw that land before' (104) is set in an actual landscape, which is described in loving detail. This, however, is assimilated to the landscape of myth, not only by the opening lines, but also by the contraries implicit in 'blackthorns down along the brook/With wounds yellow as crocuses', in which the wounds become flowers. Here the voices of nature are enigmatic, paradoxical: 'the breeze/... hinted all and nothing spoke'.

> I neither expected anything
> Nor yet remembered: but some goal
> I touched then; and if I could sing
> What would not even whisper my soul
> As I went on my journeying,
>
> I should use, as the trees and birds did,
> A language not to be betrayed;
> And what was hid should still be hid
> Excepting from those like me made
> Who answer when such whispers bid.

It is tempting to isolate the line, 'A language not to be betrayed', and let it stand for Edward Thomas's honesty and integrity. While I do not wish to deny the validity of this, I do want to ask what the lines actually mean. What they seem to be saying is that, if 'I' (Edward Thomas) could sing, it would be as a voice of Nature that 'would not even whisper my soul'. The soul is a term Thomas uses, like Jefferies, to mean the inner man, the essential being, so that he seems to be saying that it is not possible to utter the soul in human speech, and therefore not possible at all. I do not intend this reading as any kind of judgement on the poem, let alone the poet. My aim is to suggest that what the poem expresses is an acute sense of the poet's aloneness, of his distance from human kind, and that this is an inevitable outcome of identifying the poetic voice as a voice of Nature. This is a partial reading, however, for it should also be borne in mind that birdsong intimated for Thomas a mystical or mythic state in which contraries such as singularity and unity are somehow resolved.

In order to carry this discussion further I would like at this point to broaden the perspective from the native English tradition, in which the Welsh Edward Thomas may appear both ambiguous and parochial, to European Romanticism, and then to make a brief comparison between Thomas's poetic landscape and the painted landscape of his friend, Paul Nash.

In defining 'the Faustian soul', Oswald Spengler[24] quotes the Easter scene from *Faust*, Part 1, in which Faust, 'dispossessed' of faith, recalls the past:

> A longing pure and not to be described
> drove me to wander over woods and fields,
> and in a mist of hot abundant tears
> I felt a world arise and live for me.

The wandering, the salvation from despair through joy in Nature, and the return via childhood memory to being 'earth's child' again, are all characteristic not only of Richard Jefferies and Edward Thomas, but of the Romantic movement to which they ultimately belong. Goethe's *Faust* was one of Jefferies' favourite books, and its importance for him may be gauged from his character as a solitary wanderer, and his idea of himself as an explorer, a discoverer in the realm of ideas. Jefferies' notebook entries, made when he was dying, show his preoccupation with the soul and the Beyond, and his fascination with the mechanics of flight, a practical matter, but with spiritual implications. In a broad sense, Spengler's definition of the Faustian applies suggestively to both Jefferies and Thomas. Spengler asked, rhetorically: 'To fly, to free one's self from earth, to lose one's self in the expanse of the universe – is not this ambition Faustian in the highest degree? Is it not in fact the fulfilment of our dreams?' He saw in Western religious art 'transfigurations of this motive', 'emblems of soul-flight'. One may find this suggestive without assenting to Spengler's ideology. He describes 'the Faustian craving – to be *alone* with endless space', and defines Western lyric poetry as monologue, a poetry of 'immense *inner* distance' between persons. The latter, in particular, calls to mind Thomas's idea of poets who 'appear but sudden sharp voices as of birds flying over in a dark night'. Aloneness, though, is not necessarily what the poet craves. On the contrary, it may be with regret, and with the desire to bridge them, that he says 'The waters are too deep between us.' And in 'endless space' he may seek not a 'home' in 'infinite solitude' but 'a larger air': liberation from time, from his specific temporal and historical situation, and the freedom of eternity. Nor is it certain that the poet can achieve such freedom, although to be more whole, a 'larger man', he must have the desire.

This, I think, is what birdsong intimates, and the coincidence of opposites symbolizes: the infinite lying behind the finite, eternity annihilating time, and the reality of life and death and renewal which mundane existence conceals. The words themselves are clumsy, too programmatic. What I am referring to is an experience, aesthetic and metaphysical, which may be seen in Paul Nash's landscapes, for example, in his transformation and transfiguration of southern English places: Wittenham Clumps,

Dymchurch, Avebury, Dorset and so on. Nash himself spoke in mathematical terms of his vision:

> Last summer, I walked in a field near Avebury where two rough monoliths stand up, sixteen feet high, miraculously patterned with black and orange lichen, remnants of the avenue of stones which led to the Great Circle. A mile away, a green pyramid casts a gigantic shadow. In the hedge, at hand, the white trumpet of a convolvulus turns from its spiral stem, following the sun. In my art I would solve such an equation.[25]

His landscapes 'equate' the near and the far, the 'at hand' and the universal powers, the aerial and the earthbound, the female hollow or rondure and the male upright, the animate and the inorganic, the living and the dead. They are landscapes which, as in the description above, symbolize not just inner states of the painter, but his apprehension of an order informing the cosmos, which he sees in particular places and which he makes visible in his art. Seen in their historical context, Nash's landscapes are both a lyrical celebration of English country, and a search for wholeness, for integration, by a man who knew the obverse of this landscape, in the broken trees and gouged out earth of the Western Front, and knew ill health and mass death, and sought to understand death and what might lie beyond it. Anthony Bertram saw in his war drawings 'the presence of the absent', and said that in the most desolate, we are 'made tragically aware of man by the mark of his passage – his terrible footprint'.[26] Unlike Edward Thomas, Paul Nash survived the First World War, and was a war artist in the Second. All his work, too, reflects the experience of war, in the sense that it is born of awareness of death, and quickened by the need to see meaning in and beyond the cycle of life and death.

Birds are usually the only creatures in Nash's landscapes, which show his fascination with flight and aerial perspectives. Roger Cardinal lists the 'things he envied in birds – the exhilaration of flight, the possession of a medium of unsurpassable fluency, the sense of liberation from all that is earthly'.[27] The soaring bird, for Nash, was what Cardinal calls 'euphoric master of space'.

Nash was influenced by Sir Thomas Browne's reference in *Urne Buriall* to the soul visiting the Mansions of the Dead. In a late writing, 'Aerial Flowers',[28] he described 'the essence of the virtue of flying' as 'the escape into vast lonely spaces in complete freedom of bodily action and, above everything, in silence'. At the end of the essay, written in wartime and at the end of his life, Nash says that what he has been writing about in describing his lifetime's preoccupation is death: 'Death, about which we are all thinking, death, I believe, is the only solution to this problem of how to be able to fly. Personally, I feel that if death can give us that, death will be good.'

His writings provide verbal images of his vision. In 'The Face of Dorset', for example, he records 'the tradition that King Arthur's soul inhabited a raven's body which nested' in Badbury Rings, and says of the Rings: 'A magic bird in a haunted wood, an ancient cliff washed by a sea changed into earth. There is scarcely anything lacking...'[29] The magic of transformation, and the mystery of the soul, are both equally part of Nash's landscapes.

The preoccupation with death might be described as Romantic, but is better described, I think, as universally human, and integral to any understanding of life. Death is, as it were, the absence that inhabits Nash's landscapes, an absence heavily underscored by the fact that the actual places are burial grounds. But death also manifests itself in other forms: in the midst of life, and inseparable from it, and as a specific, existential question, as well as negatively – nothingness, the end to all creative tension. For Nash, it was both a question and integral to his vision.

For Edward Thomas, the nightingale's song 'admitted a larger air'. 'We breathe deeply of it and are made free citizens of eternity'; he says 'we' but he means himself – like Jefferies, Thomas the writer usually wanders alone. In 'The Unknown Bird' (28–9) the song accentuates and somehow confirms his aloneness: 'I alone could hear him/Though many listened.' The bird, like the gypsy boy with his tune, creates a kind of 'distance' in the enclosed landscape, so that within 'the great beech-wood' its notes were 'seeming far-off –/As if a cock crowed past the edge of the world,/As if the bird or I were in a dream.' Which, then, is in the real world, poet or bird? And is the real world not the world of waking sense? The poet certainly hears and knows something: 'I never knew a voice,/Man, beast, or bird, better than this.' The knowledge, however, is ambiguous:

> Sad more than joyful it was, if I must say
> That it was one or other, but if sad
> 'Twas sad only with joy too, too far off

> For me to taste it. But I cannot tell
> If truly never anything but fair
> The days were when he sang, as now they seem.

The bird unsettles the poet's sense of time, and creates uncertainty about what 'truly' was in the light of present seeming. It opens a distance between this world and another world, that is, in some sense, this one: more deeply known, but unshareable. Yet the poem does communicate what the poet seems unable to share. The bird is an agent of transformation, turning 'A heavy body and a heavy heart' to lightness. As its voice was 'bodiless sweet', so the poet when he thinks of it, becomes 'Light as that bird wandering beyond my shore'. Is the bird, therefore, a symbol of death? Death is 'unknown'; yet the poet knows this voice better than any other. Is it the attraction of death that he knows? Or is the poem about his inmost being, the core of subjectivity, that cannot be shared? It is surely significant that 'the edge of the world' becomes 'my shore', which suggests an image of the poet himself as an island. The poem may be about all these things. If Edward Thomas knew exactly what he wanted to say, he would not have written the poem. Further insight may be gained however if we hold in mind Nash's 'a magic bird in a haunted wood', and juxtapose it with a passage from Thomas's retelling of 'Branwen Daughter of Llŷr' from *The Mabinogion*. The men of the Island of the Mighty, bearing the head of Brân to the White Mount in London, rested at Harlech.

> As they sat eating and drinking, the three birds of Rhiannon flitted up to the darkness of the rafters and began singing. All other songs were unpleasant compared to theirs. The birds seemed to be very far away, as it were across a wide sea, yet their notes were distinct. They were seven years sitting at this repast and listening to the birds of Rhiannon, and the seven years were no longer than a day.[30]

Rhiannon's birds are magic birds belonging to the Otherworld, and their songs bring those who hear them to paradise, and annihilate time. Like the notes of the bird in the poem, 'their notes were distinct', yet they 'seemed to be very far away'.

The parallels between the birds of Rhiannon and the unknown bird are suggestive, but I do not want to make out that they are more. Thomas is a poet of the perplexity of experience; as in 'Lights Out', he rhymes 'alone' and 'unknown', and his explorations begin and end with the uncertain and the unutterable.

His feelings are ambivalent, and the landscape of the poem – a beech-wood which contains the bird which is somehow at the edge of the world – creates in words a symbolism that is at once mysterious and multivalent, as Paul Nash in his painted landscapes, with birds or the powers of sun and moon in the sky, symbolizes the bodiless and the invisible, at the border of human understanding, between life and death. That, it seems to me, is the 'place' that Nash and Thomas share: a 'place' wrought from the materials of southern landscapes, under pressures of their personal and historical situations, but expressing a quest for integral being that transcends any particular time, though it always manifests itself differently.

It is time now, though, to return from this excursion into the Faustian life-feeling and the landscapes with their shadows of death to a specific historical moment. Edward Thomas published 'Haymaking' and 'The Manor Farm' in his 1915 anthology, *This England*, and placed them immediately after Coleridge's 'Fears in Solitude'. In his poem, 'Written in April 1798, during the Alarm of an Invasion', Coleridge agonized over the 'tyrannous' offenses of his nation, but finally affirmed his 'bonds of natural love' to his 'Mother Isle'. Mr Stodham quotes the poem in Chapter XV of *The Happy-Go-Lucky Morgans*, 'Mr Stodham Speaks for England – Fog Supervenes'. He also quotes Wordsworth's 'To a Skylark':

> Type of the wise who soar, but never roam;
> True to the kindred points of Heaven and Home!

In his speech, part of which I have quoted in the previous chapter, Mr Stodham affirms that 'England is home and heaven too', and proceeds to describe the 'boundary' that *connects* 'earth, England, family, and self'. Another character in the novel, David Morgan, had died as a result of destroying his human bonds in attempting to unite himself with the universe. He is one of Thomas's self-portraits – a portrait of the partial man, the man whose 'mysticism' isolated him from his kind.

Edward Thomas found his voice as a poet, with the help of Robert Frost, in the process of affirming the bonds binding together earth, England, family, and self. *In the process*; not as the result of one decisive act that miraculously integrated his diverse and contrary impulses. The poetry constitutes not a system of thought, but an emotional and spiritual and intellectual drama, in which the landscape of myth and the landscape of history play a crucial part.

Myth predominates in 'The Manor Farm' and 'Haymaking'. In the former Thomas ignores the historical, social world of Manor Farm and church, and perceives instead 'a season of bliss unchangeable'. The concluding line, 'This England, Old already, was called Merry' (18), reverses the meaning of 'The Owl', in which Shakespeare's owl – 'no merry note, nor cause of merriment' – tells him plainly that he is escaping the plight of 'soldiers and poor' (40).[31] 'Haymaking', too, mythologizes the English rural scene, which it assimilates to stillness and silence, and an immortality which is identified, as in 'The Manor Farm', with great age. Writers and painters – in fact, fairly recent ones, 'Clare and Cobbett, Morland and Crome' – are drawn into the picture.

> Under the heavens that know not what years be
> The men, the beasts, the trees, the implements
> Uttered even what they will in times far hence –
> All of us gone out of the reach of change –
> Immortal in a picture of an old grange.[32]

The vision of the poem is, indeed, picturesque – carefully composed, stilled, mythic. It begins outside time, before change: 'in the perfect blue the clouds uncurled,/Like the first gods before they made the world/And misery.' 'And misery' is true to the actuality of human life; but in this scene man's violence is aestheticized, made into a graven image:

> The swift with wings and tail as sharp and narrow
> As if the bow had flown off with the arrow.

The poem paints a vivid and memorable picture; but in my view it represents the Edward Thomas who appeals to our nostalgia for an England that never existed. And in doing so, in obscuring England now and then, and in betraying the poet's own truer vision, it acts like a poison. This will seem a harsh judgement, and I should explain that I use the word as Thomas does in 'Sedge-Warblers' (69), where he speaks of being rid of his 'dream' of 'a time/Long past and irrecoverable', bearing 'Another beauty, divine and feminine', and draining its 'poison'. It is the venom of dreaming that, to borrow a phrase from Yeats, feeds the heart on fantasies in Edward Thomas's writings – the heart of the poet, and the heart of the reader (I do not except myself) tempted by the idea of an essential pastoral England. This is not always to be distinguished from myth in Thomas's landscapes, but we should discriminate between the fantasy of a poem such as 'Haymaking' and poems in which a conjunction of opposites expresses both a personal and an age-old spiritual need for harmony and integration.

In 'Ambition' (33–4), by contrast, Thomas both uses and criticizes his mythological imagination, and it is consequently a more interesting poem than 'Haymaking', a poem with greater intellectual tension, and a more troubled and questioning spirit:

> Unless it was that day I never knew
> Ambition. After a night of frost, before
> The March sun brightened and the South-West blew,
> Jackdaws began to shout and float and soar
> Already, and one was racing straight and high
> Alone, shouting like a black warrior
> Challenges and menaces to the wide sky.
> With loud long laughter then a woodpecker
> Ridiculed the sadness of the owl's last cry.
> And through the valley where all the folk astir
> Made only plumes of pearly smoke to tower
> Over dark trees and white meadows happier
> Than was Elysium in that happy hour,
> A train that roared along raised after it
> And carried with it a motionless white bower
> Of purest cloud, from end to end close-knit,
> So fair it touched the roar with silence. Time
> Was powerless while that lasted. I could sit
> And think I had made the loveliness of prime,
> Breathed its life into it and were its lord,
> And no mind lived save this 'twixt clouds and rime.
> Omnipotent I was, nor even deplored
> That I did nothing. But the end fell like a bell:
> The bower was scattered; far off the train roared.
> But if this was ambition I cannot tell:
> What 'twas ambition for I know not well.

Here once again we hear the voices of birds: jackdaws, one of them 'shouting like a black warrior/Challenges and menaces to the sky', which is a more disturbing war-like image than that depicting the swifts in 'Haymaking'; a woodpecker that 'Ridiculed the sadness of the owl's last cry'. This is not a merry note, and it is the poet who hears the sadness, and is ridiculed. Then the landscape becomes a landscape of myth: it is 'folk' who are astir through the valley, not men with 'their mockery, their cruelty, their foreignness', but folk, the creatures of song and legend and myth; and the landscape is composed of contraries: 'dark trees'/'white meadows', time/eternity, motion/stillness, silence/sound, open/closed. In this powerless Time the poet could sit 'And think I had made the loveliness of prime,/Breathed its life into it and were its lord,/And no mind lived save this 'twixt clouds and rime./Omnipotent I was...' For its materials the god-like mind has taken not only the earth, but also the train, that means of communication and social change. This is what Alun Lewis, a poet close to Edward Thomas in spirit, called 'The old temptation to remould the world'.[33] In fact, it is a profoundly isolating use of the imagination, and it creates not vision, but illusion. Elysium is the abode of the blessed after death, and this 'happy hour' is a deathly one, and death sounds in the re-entry into time: 'But the end fell like a bell:/The bower was scattered; far off the train roared.'

Sometimes it can be a relief to turn from Edward Thomas's landscapes of myth to the realism of

> And when the war began
> To turn young men to dung ('Blenheim Oranges', 118)

or the conversation with the ploughman about the war in 'As the Team's Head-Brass', or his sense of keeping company with the dead:

> Now all roads lead to France
> And heavy is the tread
> Of the living; but the dead
> Returning lightly dance:
>
> Whatever the road bring
> To me or take from me,
> They keep me company
> With their pattering,
>
> Crowding the solitude
> On the loops over the downs,
> Hushing the roar of towns
> And their brief multitudes. ('Roads', 90)

Paradoxically, for all their lightness, there is a solid feel about this 'company'. They crowd the solitude surrounding the poet, which is partly the solitude of the primeval landscape, but is also the poet's existential isolation, his lack of 'bonds of necessity' in a countryside which for several decades had been suffering depopulation, as long-settled labourers became migrants, and their places were sometimes taken by intellectuals and writers, such as Edward Thomas himself, looking for a meaning that they did not find in their urban civilization. Now, he has forged bonds with the dead, with those who have died for 'This England'.

The keyword is 'Now', as it is in 'In Memoriam (Easter 1915)', too:

> The flowers left thick at nightfall in the wood
> This Eastertide call into mind the men,
> Now far from home, who, with their sweethearts, should
> Have gathered them and will do never again.   (58)

This is not the landscape of myth, in which a song of the moment may open upon eternity. The men 'Now far from home' are not exiles from the golden age. Now, in the historical present, they are dead, the men who should have gathered flowers from the local wood – flowers growing thick with the indifference of nature to man, but also because they have not been picked. This is not 'the poet's Spring', as Thomas calls it in *The Happy-Go-Lucky Morgans*: spring with youth's sense of infinite possibility. This is 'Eastertide', a word which cannot help but remind us of another death – death and resurrection. It would be wrong, though, to draw too much from the traditional associations. If there is renewal for Thomas at Easter 1915 it is not *now; now* the flowers 'call into mind the men', their home, their sweethearts, and the fact that they 'should/Have gathered them and will do never again'. It is a poem about the bonds that bind us to the earth, and it speaks humanly, with the voice of the larger man. So do many of Edward Thomas's poems, but they often do so through conflict with a strong contrary impulse, which draws upon a language of Nature that is losing its religious significance, and replacing it with a 'mysticism' that threatens to isolate the poet from his kind.

6

Thomas Hardy, John Cowper Powys and Wessex

With the serialization of *Far from the Madding Crowd* in 1874, Thomas Hardy adopted 'Wessex', the ancient name for part of the south-west region of England, and used it to define the scene of his fiction. His was 'a partly real, partly dream country'(48):[1] an imaginative world based upon an actual region, subject to social and historical change. John Cowper Powys, in a number of 'Romances' published between 1916 and 1936, set his stories within the same geographical area. Powys was influenced by Hardy, but the differences between his Wessex and Hardy's are considerable. Hardy was a Victorian novelist, Powys was a modern writer. This, however, is already to simplify. Hardy, especially in his later novels, *Tess of the d'Urbervilles* and *Jude the Obscure*, was concerned with modern experience; Powys, who was born in 1872 and lived into the second half of the twentieth century, was both a traditional storyteller and a sophisticated modernist. Both Hardy and Powys were interpreters of modernity, and both were concerned with tradition, and with the relation between the present and the past. It is consequently in terms of their common concerns that the differences as well as the affinities between them can be most usefully explored. In this respect, the contrast between their visions of Wessex is crucial. They imagined the same places differently, and looked at them with different eyes.

Thomas Hardy's way of seeing may be illustrated by a passage from *The Return of the Native* (1878). In the second chapter of the fourth book, Clym Yeobright, the 'man from Paris', who has rejected his outwardly successful life abroad and come home, is shown working as a furze-cutter in summer on his native Egdon Heath. Since his eyesight was impaired, 'his daily life was of a curious microscopic sort, his whole world being limited to a circuit of a few feet from his person' (312).

His familiars were creeping and winged things, and they seemed to enroll him in their band. Bees hummed around his ears with an intimate air, and tugged at the heath and furze-flowers at his side in such numbers as to weigh them down to the sod. The strange amber-coloured butterflies which Egdon produced, and which were never seen elsewhere, quivered in the breath of his lips, alighted upon his bowed back, and sported with the glittering point of his hook as he flourished it up and down. Tribes of emerald-green grasshoppers leaped over his feet, falling awkwardly on their backs, heads, or hips, like unskilful acrobats, as chance might rule; or engaged themselves in noisy flirtations under the fernfronds with silent ones of homely hue. Huge flies, ignorant of larders and wire-netting, and quite in a savage state, buzzed about him without knowing that he was a man. In and out of the ferndells snakes glided in their most brilliant blue and yellow guise, it being the season immediately following the shedding of their old skins, when their colours are brightest. Litters of young rabbits came out from their forms to sun themselves upon hillocks, the hot beams blazing through the delicate tissue of each thin-fleshed ear, and firing it to a blood-red transparency in which the veins could be seen. None of them feared him.   (312)

The microscopic eye is ascribed to Clym, but it is, of course, Hardy's also. It is Hardy's eye as both poet and naturalist, and as the child who was father to the man. As Robert Gittings[2] has said, Hardy recreated his childhood world in writing *The Return of the Native*. One result of his recovery of childhood vision was the immensity of the Heath as depicted in the novel. Even in the nineteenth century, the Dorset heathland on which Hardy based Egdon would have been truly immense only to a child. This was the wilderness which stretched away behind Hardy's birthplace, and which, as his earliest surviving poem, 'Domicilium', shows, reminded him of a past when the home plot was won from the wild, and established his sense of the precarious human situation between wilderness and cultivation. Moreover, as John Cowper Powys says in *Autobiography* (1934), a child has a magical power, the 'power of finding the infinitely great in the materially small'.[3] The Dorset heaths could not be described as materially small in the nineteenth century, even after the beginning of modern transport and communications, but the Egdon of Hardy's novel has the 'ecstasy of the unbounded' which Powys ascribed to the child's imaginative power. The word may also usefully remind us of

Hardy's description of himself as a child: 'He was of ecstatic temperament.'[4]

In depicting Egdon Heath in *The Return of the Native*, Hardy
revived the sense of immensity he had experienced as a child –
immensity in space, immensity of geological and prehistoric
time, and immensity in the mind which it filled with awe. His
labour of love in thus recreating the child's-eye view fortunately
coincided with his use of the Heath for philosophical and moral
purposes, as a landscape corresponding to the spirit of the times:

> Fair prospects wed happily with fair times; but alas, if times be not
> fair! Men have oftener suffered from the mockery of a place too
> smiling for their reason than from the oppression of surroundings
> oversadly tinged. Haggard Egdon appealed to a subtler and
> scarcer instinct, to a more recently learnt emotion, than that which
> responds to the sort of beauty called charming and fair.   (54)

The times are not 'fair': they are not beautiful, they are not just.
This is the view of Hardy the thinker, and it shapes his didactic
aim in the novel. However, love of the Heath's physical ground-
work, and of its weathers and seasons and creatures, sometimes
works against the indifference or unfairness which its elemental
features are meant to express. Dogmatism and willed pattern are
consequently undermined, and we have instead the presence of
a place that stimulated the depths of Hardy's imagination, and
moved him to love and fear. But it was not only the child in
Hardy who responded to the Heath. In the passage describing
Clym in his immediate environment, love of the wild coincides
with adult awareness of the terrors of natural law, and Hardy
sees with a mind schooled by Darwin.

Hardy has special knowledge of the Heath; he describes
'strange amber-coloured butterflies which Egdon produced, and
which were never seen elsewhere'. He has an inwardness with
the life of the Heath, a tenderness in his observation, as when he
notices the young rabbits, sun 'beams blazing through the delicate tissue of each thin-fleshed ear'. But this is not only sensitive
and vivid descriptive writing; it also defines Clym's place in
relation to natural law. The creatures are his 'familiars'; 'they
seemed to enroll him in their band'; butterflies 'quivered in the
breath of his lips' – a curiously haunting image, which seems to
make Clym's soul visible, but only as the breath which he shares
with the butterflies. Comic and rather touching flirtations of

emerald-green grasshoppers 'with silent ones of homely hue' are akin to the flirtations of humans on the Heath. The place is a Hardyan Eden, where man is not feared – perhaps because not known, for the flies 'buzzed about him without knowing that he was a man'. Indeed, Clym with his hook is an image of death. But death is not now – now is the plenitude of seasonal life. The place, however, is an Eden after Darwin, an Eden where all creatures are equal before the same natural law. All life comprises a web of relationships, but also a struggle for survival which is ruled by chance. The Heath is Eden in its richness and colours, and also because Hardy recovers a child's eye for the oneness of all life. There are actual snakes here, but the invisible one at the centre of the scene – the snake through which man loses Eden – is what the adult knows: oneness of life, but not as the child sees it. What the adult knows are 'the defects of natural laws' and 'the quandary that man is in by their operation' (225). In the world subject to these laws men and women are like the grasshoppers 'falling awkwardly on their backs, heads, or hips, as chance might rule'. The survivors are those who adapt themselves, inwardly and outwardly, to their environment. They are not the vivid and aspiring, like Eustacia Vye, but those resembling the female grasshoppers, 'silent ones of homely hue'.

In the perspective in which Clym appears as 'a brown spot' on Egdon, we see that nature levels all its creatures to a universal equality of insignificance. Clym himself feels in the Heath's 'oppressive horizontality' something 'which too much reminded him of the arena of life; it gave him a sense of bare equality with, and no superiority to, a single living thing under the sun' (267). In this world, suffering is shared by all creatures. Indeed, in his perception of the universality of suffering, Hardy combines 'the defects of natural laws' with St Paul's 'For we know that the whole creation groaneth and travaileth in pain together until now' (Romans 8:22). In this Hardy is like Clym, who says 'I get up every morning and see the whole creation groaning and travailing in pain' (233). John Cowper Powys said of Hardy: 'He flings gibe after gibe at "God", but across his anger falls the shadow of the Cross.'[5] Hardy's reading in Shakespeare and the Greek dramatists influenced the structure of his tragedies, but the spirit of his tragic vision was a compassionate, hyper-sensitive awareness of suffering, but without a corresponding belief that it has any meaning.

Hardy's great power of evoking human feeling, and of moving
us, owes much to the power with which he conceives the non-
human world. In 'At Castle Boterel', for example:

> It filled but a minute. But was there ever
> A time of such quality, since or before,
> In that hill's story? To one mind never,
> Though it has been climbed, foot-swift, foot-sore,
> By thousands more.
>
> Primaeval rocks form the road's steep border,
> And much have they faced there, first and last,
> Of the transitory in Earth's long order;
> But what they record in colour and cast
> Is – that we two passed.[6]

The ecstatic note – 'that we two passed' – affirms the minute
filled with human emotion, 'a time of such quality', that depends
for its effect on being transient, essentially human, set against
'primaeval rocks' and 'Earth's long order'. Hardy's sense of the
unfeelingness of things, of the natural law that indifferently creates and destroys life, made him a great writer of human feeling
– the quality that is alone in the universe and different from
everything surrounding it.

Herein lies one of Hardy's fundamental differences from John
Cowper Powys. In *Tess of the d'Urbervilles*, Hardy wrote: 'the
world is only a psychological phenomenon' (134). But this was
only true in a limited sense, for Tess or for Hardy. She is deceived
by her fancies, which create 'a cloud of moral hobgoblins'. Her
fancies arise from the working of social law on her conscience;
but the underlying reality of natural law is entirely different.
Social law is a human construct which punishes the individual
who transgresses it. Nature uses and discards human life regard-
less of social or individual interests. Hardy's realism is consequently grounded on a belief in laws which the human mind,
with its faculties of will and imagination, cannot change, and
which destroy those who do not adapt themselves to them. As
Necessity dominates the cosmic stage of *The Dynasts*, in which,
through cloud-curtains, we look down through transparent
human masses at the Will blindly working their destruction, so
Necessity dominates Hardy's Victorian society, leaving no scope
for individual freedom.

John Cowper Powys, by contrast, came to believe that 'person-

ality is the only permanent thing in life'.[7] He was of a different
generation from Hardy's – when Hardy was writing *The Mayor of
Casterbridge*, Powys was a boy living in Dorchester; he was from
a different social background, and he had a different cast of
mind. Powys opposed 'the soul of man, that supreme magician',[8]
to all 'behaviouristic, mechanistic' systems. His philosophy was
one of personal struggle. He believed that 'the ultimate nature of
the world is found to be unfathomably dualistic. A sharp dividing line of irreconcilable duality intersects every living soul; and
the secret of life turns out to be the relatively victorious struggle
of personality with the thing that in itself resists its fuller life.'[9]
While Hardy's fundamental theme is necessity, Powys's is the
realization of personal freedom.

In writing *The Return of the Native* Hardy himself was a native
returning home. But not like Clym Yeobright. Clym, in accordance with the pattern of *King Lear*, has his sight impaired, and
his partial-sightedness symbolizes his blindness to himself and
to others. He sees the Heath microscopically, but he does not see
its truth. Hardy, unlike Clym, is both acutely near-seeing and far-
seeing. He has qualities of vision that belong only to the insider
looking in from the outside, or the native who comes home from
a wider world. Hardy's special relation to Egdon represents the
relation to Wessex which made his achievement as a writer possible, and enabled him to come nearer than any other English
novelist to expressing the total life of place.

As well as seeing with a child's eye, microscopically and poeti-
cally, in *The Return of the Native*, Hardy sees as a naturalist, a geo-
grapher and a geologist; and he reads the life on the Heath in its
weathers and seasons, and in its physical nature and forms. He
sees, too, as an historian and an archaeologist, and his vision
suggests the mythic without being irrational, and the preternatural without being credulous. Hence the more than natural presence of Rainbarrow with its Celtic dead, and the living tradition
of lighting a fire against the dark. Hardy combines science and
imagination, describing survivals of ancient tradition, old customs and social habits, and evoking their magic. Unlike Powys,
though, he sees the mythological from a rational and historical
point of view. There are accordingly two contrasting ways of
experiencing time in his novels.

Buzzford's apprehension of time, in *The Mayor of Casterbridge*

(1886), characterizes the way of the uneducated, rooted labourers:

> 'Casterbridge is a old, hoary place o' wickedness, by all account. 'Tis recorded in history that we rebelled against the King one or two hundred years ago, in the time of the Romans, and that lots of us was hanged on Gallows Hill, and quartered, and our different jints sent about the country like butcher's meat.'   (121)

Buzzford's conflation of historical events is both amusing and significant. For history is concertinaed in this way only for those who have a sense of continuity which arises from their ancestral belonging to one place. 'We rebelled against the King one or two hundred years ago, in the time of the Romans,' says Buzzford; 'lots of us was hanged on Gallows Hill.' The instinctive, unconscious claim of 'we' and 'us' is that he is one with his ancestors in Casterbridge: it makes no difference whether they fought at Sedgemoor or lived in the time of the Romans. Nor does it matter whether Buzzford's people really did live in Roman Casterbridge. What is at issue here is a feeling about time, and the space it occupies in the mind. With a sense of belonging like Buzzford's, the difference between one and two hundred years, or between two hundred and two thousand years, is of no account. In fact, his apprehension of the past is a sense of timelessness – historical time does not exist for those who do not think of themselves as being in any way different from past generations, but of one family with them.

The folklore and superstitions richly depicted in Hardy's novels belong to the people with no sense of historical time. But Hardy himself is not one of them. His sense of time is historical; he sees as a man who feels 'the ache of modernism',[10] and knows 'the mind adrift on change, and harassed by the irrepressible New'.[11] This acute awareness of living in history involves a sharp social sense. Hardy consequently sees the people of Egdon as they, with the exception of Clym, could scarcely begin to see themselves: as belonging to England's class society, and suffering its conflicts, at a particular time of social change. Hardy does not emphasize change in *The Return of the Native* as much as he does in later novels, but it nevertheless affects the action; social distinctions are marked and carefully observed by the people of Egdon, and conflicting social aspirations are the basic cause of the individual tragedies.

John Cowper Powys dedicated his first romance, *Wood and Stone* (1915), 'with devoted admiration to the greatest poet and novelist of our age Thomas Hardy'. He was on friendly terms with Hardy, and met him on occasions over more than thirty years. Late in life, he wrote to Louis Wilkinson: 'from T. Hardy I learnt, long long ago, to see all human feelings, gestures, actions, & everything else! – my own & everybody's – against the Inanimate Background of Nature.'[12] In his Preface to *Wood and Stone* Powys said that he did not 'regard his eccentric story as in any sense an attempted imitation' of Hardy. The dedication 'is no more than a humble salutation addressed to the monarch of that particular country [Wessex], by a wayward nomad, lighting a bivouac-fire, for a brief moment, in the heart of a land that is not his'.[13] In fact, Hardy's influence on Powys was extensive, and appears in numerous passages in Powys's romances, as well as in his treatment of 'the Inanimate Background of Nature'. Imitation, however, is not the right word for it, since Powys was a great absorber and assimilator of literary influences. He once wrote that 'mythologizing of one's own identity and its projection upon reality ... makes the essence of every writer's imaginative world'.[14] This was certainly true in his case, and in consequence the most Hardyan passages of his work show, paradoxically, the distance between his fiction and Hardy's, for Powys assimilates everything to his particular form of mythologizing.

Powys was in his early twenties when he addressed a poem in his *Odes and other Poems* (1896) to Thomas Hardy and was subsequently invited by Hardy to visit him at Max Gate. Powys recalls the visit, and Hardy's return call at his father's vicarage at Montacute, in *Autobiography*. He remembers telling Hardy 'how I detected in his work that same portentous and solemn power of dealing with those abstract-concrete phenomena, such as dawn, and noon, and twilight, and midnight, that Wordsworth displayed in his poetry'. Following a hint from Hardy Powys read Edgar Allan Poe's 'Ulalume', and 'drew from it a formidable influence in the direction of the romantically bizarre'. On Hardy's visit to Montacute, as they emerged from the churchyard, Powys pointed out 'the house where the most beautiful girl in our village lived'. Hardy's response was 'a curious little start'.

'We get back to humanity, back, back to humanity, Powys!' he chuckled.

It happened that there were imperceptible frost-marks that day in the road, making those odd little creases and criss-cross wrinkles in the mud that my father always loved to see, and these minute tokens of the processes he knew so well, were not missed, though I had missed them, by the hawk's eye of this other Dorset-born noticer of such things.[15]

The recollections tell us more about Powys than Hardy, and their main importance in this context is for the three things to which I have drawn attention. First, Powys shared the 'solemn power' which he perceived in Hardy and Wordsworth; but in his treatment of 'abstract-concrete phenomena', such as the two twilights, the intimation of mystery, of a Fourth Dimension, was central. Second, Hardy's hint about 'Ulalume' pointed Powys towards 'the romantically bizarre', a phrase which well describes the Wessex of his romances, in contrast to Hardy's 'partly real, partly dream-country'. In both imaginative worlds, however, we are constantly brought 'back to humanity', since, for all their differences, both writers were intimately concerned with emotional and sexual relationships. Third, Powys made a close connection between Hardy and his own father, who, like Tess Durbeyfield, was born in Blackmore Vale. Both men were, in the words of Hardy's 'Afterwards' to which Powys here alludes, noticers of such things as 'minute tokens' of natural processes.

John Cowper Powys knew parts of Dorset and Somerset intimately. As mentioned earlier, he lived as a boy in Dorchester while Hardy also was living there, though Powys did not even hear of Hardy until after he had left Cambridge, in 1894. From early on, he knew Weymouth and the adjacent coast. Montacute, where his father became vicar at St Catherine's, in 1885, was another centre of John Cowper's early life-experience. He was at Sherborne School from 1885 to 1891, and the area of West Dorset and East Somerset, with its geographical and atmospheric divisions, became one of his primary landscapes. Free from school on Sunday afternoons, he and his brother Littleton 'used to wander to every point of the compass till for miles round we knew that countryside with the knowledge of poachers and gamekeepers'.[16] Like Hardy in his novels, Powys developed his imaginative powers by the consecutive use in his romances of the West

Country landscapes and places he first knew in childhood and youth.

Yet in Powys almost everything he shared with Hardy was changed, by differences of class, history, psychology and philosophy. Powys knew the West Country as a boy who was hypersensitive to nature and atmosphere. He knew Dorset and Somerset society as a vicar's son, seeing it from within a large and remarkable family which was virtually self-sufficient, and which deeply influenced his creation of a fictional world based upon personal contrasts and peculiarities. In relation to his ecclesiastical and upper-middle-class background, his position as a university extension lecturer in England, and later as an itinerant lecturer in America, was socially ambiguous. He described *Autobiography* as 'the history of the "de-classing" of a bourgeois-born personality'.[17] He also described himself as 'a tatterdemalion Taliessin', in reference to his Welsh ancestry and his passionate advocacy of 'the magical view of life', which he identified with the Welsh. Behind Powys's Wessex, so to speak, was his idea of Wales as a magical realm associated with the powers of the imagination.

John Cowper Powys knew the West Country from books, too, including Thomas Hardy's. And it is evident that he assimilated Hardy's writings, like everything else, to his life-illusion. His adoption of this idea from Ibsen and frequent use of it are profoundly significant. In *The Wild Duck* Dr Relling keeps his 'patients' alive by feeding their life-illusions – the term is also translated as 'life-lie': the idea or ambition or self-image that makes their lives enjoyable or endurable, as opposed to the limitations that would otherwise humiliate or destroy them. It is an idea that has behind it a great weight of intellectual and cultural history, which may be briefly summarized as the dissolution of absolutes and the triumph of relativism, with the consequent destabilization of the generally accepted idea of reality, and blurring of the distinction between the fictional and the real. It is an idea born of disillusion with established values and beliefs, but instead of producing despair, it validates illusion, empowering the mind to tell itself life-enhancing stories. It is in this context that Powys's 'dominant life-illusion', that he was 'a magician', should be understood. The idea is not negated by being an illusion; on the contrary, it thereby affirms the power of the individual soul to create and to destroy its own world. The crucial connection in Powys's thought between scepticism and the sense of possibility stems from this idea.

In *Autobiography* Powys describes his first experience of reading a Hardy novel as entering 'a stone circle of monoliths and trilithons, grey with the lichen of centuries'. To him, these were 'not pages of a book at all, but wind-shaken oak-leaves in some oracular grove of Dodona!'[18] Later, reading Hardy during his travels as a university extension lecturer in England, when tormented by his 'demon' – Powys graphically describes his neurotic sufferings and his nympholepticism in *Autobiography* – 'the genius of Hardy would drive my demon away and some formidable Spirit from Stonehenge would come rushing out of the Magic West'. Powys would then 'feel myself to be what the great Magician Merlin was'.[19] It is evident, then, that for Powys Hardy became became part of his dominant life-illusion, supporting his idea of himself as a magician, and a prophet of the magical view of life. Moreover, what Powys drew from Hardy strengthened what he had already drawn from his father as 'a man who used to notice such things', and from the romance with which his father coloured every thing, every person and every place associated with his experience. So, Powys tells us, through his father's stories, 'long before I had seen anything of the Weymouth coast except the wet and dry sand by the bathing-machines, all the well-known sea-marks there ... were imprinted on my imagination through a mythological haze of enchanted wonder'.[20] It would be untrue, of course, to say that Hardy did not mythologize *his* Wessex, but the Hardy novel, even at its most ballad-like, espouses an idea of the individual in society that belongs to the tradition of the realist novel, while the Powysian romance harks back to an earlier tradition of storytelling, which is best known in Europe through Arthurian Romance, with its settings in 'the Magic West'.

Powys's experience of Wessex places was like Magnus Muir's experience of Weymouth in *Weymouth Sands* (1934). Magnus's father 'had endowed each separate one of the material phenomena of the place of his earthly sojourn with a curious mythological identity for his son's mind'. Every one of the characteristic objects of Weymouth 'was seen by Magnus in a different way from the way others saw it. *It was a piece of his father's life.*'[21] Magnus is peculiarly passive – he does not see every object, every object was 'seen by' him, as if its presence were stronger than his identity as an active agent. A similar passivity typifies a line of Powys's male characters. This had, no doubt, a psychological cause, and one may speculate that it stemmed from John Cowper's relationship with his father, which was a loving one, but which was probably marked on John Cowper's part by some degree of guilt, arising from what must have felt like a fundamental disobedience, since he rejected his father's morality and religion. Whether or not this was so, however, the point I want to make here is a simpler one: the kind of psychological and emotional understanding, which identifies things in the world with people's sense of themselves and of others, is partly what makes Powys a great writer of place.

Late in life, Powys described *Wolf Solent* (1929) as 'a book of Nostalgia, written in a foreign country with the pen of a traveller and the ink-blood of his home'.[22] *Wolf Solent* was largely written in hotels and trains in America, as Powys travelled between lecture engagements. The description of *Wolf Solent* could also be applied to *Autobiography, A Glastonbury Romance* (1933) and *Weymouth Sands*, which were written in upstate New York. There is consequently a great deal in Powys himself, and in his characters, his landscapes and his appeal, that relates to the condition of exile, and to nostalgia as a specifically modern emotion, arising not only from deracination, geographical displacement or social mobility, but also from the unsettling of traditional beliefs and relationships. The evocation of place is less vivid in *Maiden Castle* (1937) than in the other Wessex Romances. This was partly due, no doubt, to Powys's fear of being prosecuted for libel, which his setting of fictional characters in real places in *A Glastonbury Romance* had drawn upon him. But I think it owed more to the fact that *Maiden Castle*, unlike the books 'written in a foreign country with the pen of a traveller and the ink-blood of his home', was largely written on home ground, in Dorchester itself. Moreover, Powys wrote the romance while in transit to Wales, his mind preoccupied by Welsh mythology. He completed *Maiden Castle* in Wales, and its spirit of place is imbued with Welsh mythology, which is more important in his fictional Dorchester than the town's actual history.

Hardy had returned to Egdon Heath with a child's microscopic vision, but he understood Egdon society in terms of the problems of Victorian morality and the conflicts generated by historical change. Powys's engagement with his landscape was different. From the beginning, in *Wood and Stone*, he had used the history and physical properties of place for mythological purposes, which served to reunite him imaginatively with his childhood world. Living in Dorset in the present had the effect of partially drying up the spring of nostalgia which had re-vivified his early impressions. He had returned in story after story to the Wessex of his childhood, partially identifying himself with characters who were returning to their native ground, such as Richard Storm, Wolf Solent, John Crow and Dud No-man. All embody his deracinated spirit, which does not seek a specific social settlement or return to a known world – to use Raymond Williams's terms, which refer to something centrally important in Hardy, but can only be used to misunderstand Powys. It would be quite untrue, however, to say that Powys did not respond deeply to his times. His response, too, was to the mind adrift on change, indeed, the mind driven mad in a cruel and increasingly mechanistic world. What he shares with his heroes is a spirit that seeks to lose – and find – itself in the continuity of life. It is a Wordsworthian quest, a quest that marks Powys as a late successor to the Romantic poets, but it is conducted in modern circumstances of cultural and psychological breakdown.

A crucial book for understanding this is *After My Fashion*, which Powys wrote after the First World War, probably in 1920,[23] but which remained unpublished until 1980. The novel starts with the return of Richard Storm, after twenty years abroad, to the place in southern England associated with his family. It is set partly in Sussex and partly in New York, and contrasts Storm's vision of rural England with his experience of the modern city. In Sussex, he feels 'the continuity of the generations', and 'the presence … of earth-rooted things'.[24] He craves to write a new kind of poetry, 'to find expression, expression that he and others, bewildered and chance-driven as himself, might hold to and live by, for this mysterious undertone of the earth's gathered experience, moving through generation after generation of human subconsciousness and binding the ages together'.[25] Storm fails in his endeavour, but his ideas adumbrate the poetic vision that Powys himself would express most successfully in his prose romances. This is especially true of Storm's feeling of 'a strange marginal purlieu, lying midway between the loneliness of solitary human beings and the loneliness of inanimate things', which he experiences just before leaving England again, and which affords him a glimpse 'into the very secret of his native soil'.[26] *After My Fashion* reveals, more nakedly than any of Powys's other books, the part played by displacement in forming his idea of place. It is a novel that probes the English psyche wounded by the War, and posits, but also questions and criticizes, an essential Englishness. It shows how Powys's own displacement, his wandering life and his exile's nostalgia, combined with the upheaval of the War to influence his idea of continuity. In its way, *After My Fashion* deals with the deep and widely felt sense of a modern spiritual and cultural crisis, and it is to this that Powys's quest for continuity is a response.

Powys said of Hardy, 'the continuity of life is his theme and the long, piteous "ascent of man", from those queer fossils in the Portland quarries to what we see today'.[27] Hardy's Wessex gives some substance to this view, in the geological age of its landscapes, in the prehistory of Egdon Heath and Stonehenge and Cranborne Chase, in the influence of ancestry on families such as the Durbeyfields. For the most part, though, Hardy's sense of the past is affected by his awareness of a break in the continuity of Victorian cultural tradition, and radical social change. Contrary to Powys, it would be truer to say that discontinuity is Hardy's theme. In his Author's Preface to *Far from the Madding Crowd* (1874), looking back from 1912, Hardy described the disappearance of the traditional Wessex of which he had written:

> The change at the root of this has been the recent supplanting of the class of stationary cottagers, who carried on the local traditions and humours, by a population of more or less migratory labourers, which has led to a break of continuity in local history, more fatal than any other thing to the preservation of legend, folk-lore, close inter-social relations, and eccentric individualities. For these the indispensable conditions of existence are attachment to the soil of one particular spot by generation after generation.   (48–9)

In the Wessex of the major novels long-settled communities are disintegrating and the protagonists are migrants, leaving behind them a broken tradition which once sustained folklore and legend. Consequently it would not be an exaggeration to say that in Hardy's Wessex history drives out myth.

The continuity Hardy does see, moreover, is a continuity of suffering and cruelty, as in 'the leering mask' over the door in *The Mayor of Casterbridge*, or the symbolic link between Tess and the white hart brutally killed by the Norman, or the 'tragic sadness' of marriage in *Jude the Obscure*. Hardy was increasingly concerned in his novels with the problems caused by a specific 'civilization', rather than with 'the continuity of life' in Powys's sense. And Hardy, looking at the past, sees it with a rationality that knows where to draw the line between fellow feeling and indifference. It is he, with his interests in archaeology and architecture, not Buzzford, who sees 'old Rome' everywhere in Casterbridge, and looks with fascination at a skeleton of 'some tall soldier or other of the Empire'. Unlike Buzzford, Hardy sees the discontinuity between past and present:

> Imaginative inhabitants, who would have felt an unpleasantness at the discovery of a comparatively modern skeleton in their gardens, were quite unmoved by these hoary shapes. They had lived so long ago, their time was so unlike the present, their hopes and motives were so widely removed from ours, that between them and the living there seemed to stretch a gulf too wide for even a spirit to pass.
> (140)

If a writer with an historical imagination recognizes some kind of continuity in human affairs, he will also see the unlikeness of different times, which distinguishes the 'modern'; he will see the presentness of the present, as well as the pastness of the past. And if he sees essence, he will also see identity, the unique integrity of person and historical period, which resists the sameness that would melt and merge every outline and every form. It is however essence that the person with a mythological imagination sees. Thus Dud No-man, as he surveys the Dorchester landmarks, from the prison to 'the sacred clump of trees ... that hid the house built for himself in his early days by the great Wessex novelist', defends his way of seeing the past:

> It was this stream of life flowing down the ages, with its magical overtones and undertones, that he had come to seek in a thousand chance-given groupings of things and people. This was the purer, the less personal element in his subjective life. This was the reverse side of the shield to his cerebral sensuality ...
>
> He was no historian in a scientific sense ... History to him was life *at one remove*, life purged and winnowed of its grosser impact![28]

Dud No-man is thinking about what Powys in *Mortal Strife* would call 'the poetry of the life of the generations'.[29] It is the 'stream of life flowing down the ages', the stream in which he and the characters resembling him seek again and again to immerse themselves. It is a continuity which extends far beyond historical time and links the individual soul with life's primordial beginnings, and the powers of the mind with the creativity of Nature. Powys's landscapes and places are frequently a source of descriptions, metaphors, and images which reveal his characters using their sensations to draw upon or immerse themselves in this stream.

Overemphasis on Powys the 'magician' may suggest that he was preoccupied with a 'romantically bizarre' idea of the self communing with nature. This is indeed an element within his fiction, but Powys the storyteller is also the creator of worlds in which his characters interact. The aloneness of the individual soul, and the fundamental duality of male and female, determine the shape of his vision. In *Wolf Solent*, as Wolf lay beside Gerda, one of his last thoughts before falling asleep 'was of the vast tracts of unknown country that every human consciousness includes in its scope. Here to the superficial eye, were two skulls, lying side by side; but, in reality, here were two far-extending continents, each with its own sky, its own land and water, its own strange-blowing winds.'[30] This 'unknown country' is the domain in which Powys's characters exercise their freedom; but it is also special to each, dividing even those who are most intimately related, so that their ultimate aloneness is a condition of their freedom. But Powys does not confine imagination, the creative and destructive power within the individual soul, to human beings. He sees all our fellow creatures as fellow creators. All create a world of their own out of external reality. He does not see a static universe but an active multiverse: 'a congeries of these personally created worlds wherein animals and birds and fish and plants and insects all contribute a fresh, vital element of change, as they carry the whole teeming caravan forward, into an indetermined, unpredictable, and perhaps not even irreversible future.'[31] The Powysian fictional world accordingly develops into a multiverse in which not only is every human character a 'far-extending continent', but both the animate and inanimate creations are endowed with individual consciousness.

The result is aṣ humbling for the human individual as is Clym's
sense of 'bare equality' with every 'single living thing under the
sun'. But the Powysian world is 'indetermined', and minutely
and multifariously alive with possibilities of creative freedom.

Places in Powys's Wessex are reshaped by individual minds,
becoming criss-crossing streams of psychic phenomena, in which
the same landmarks play many different parts. An everyday
instance in *Weymouth Sands* has Jobber Skald, who is thinking
about Perdita Wane, teleporting the statue of George III from its
pedestal 'so that its location in space might be used ... as a material support for his psychic evocations'.[32] A more elaborate
instance of Powys's psychological realism occurs when Magnus
Muir is squeezed between the Jobber and a youth reading
Hardy's *The Well-Beloved* on a seafront seat:

> As Magnus glanced down at this book he caught the word 'oolite',
> and the word seemed to dance before him. A baby, somewhere on
> their crowded seat ... was holding by a string a rose-coloured toy
> balloon, an object which kept tapping the shoulders of the prome-
> naders, and was indeed once tossed back by a spiteful old man
> with a vicious flick that sent it rebounding against its owner's
> head. It was upon this rosy toy that the word 'oolite' now fixed
> itself, like a label on the surface of a red moon, and although the
> Jobber's stony island was hidden from their eyes at that spot by
> Weymouth Pier, the tutor had the sensation that the whole of Port-
> land, with all its people and all their passions, was no more solid
> than this airy, floating ephemeral balloon.[33]

Extreme subjective transformation of external reality belongs in
the age of Proust and Joyce, Woolf and Dorothy Richardson, but is
also an element within the realist tradition. It occurs in Hardy, in
characters under stress or under the influence of strong emotion.
In *The Well-Beloved* (1897), for example, for Pierston, who is attend-
ing a dinner party after hearing of Avice Caro's death, the dining
room and his fellow guests are gradually transformed into scenes
inseparable from Avice, until the marchioness 'in geranium-red
and diamonds' became a sunset over Deadman's Bay, her 'cran-
nied features ... shaped themselves to the dusty quarries', and the
plants and lights in the room 'were transmuted into the ivies of the
cliff-built Castle, the tufts of seaweed, and the lighthouses on the
isle'. Salt airs 'killed' the smell of the food, and instead of voices
Pierston heard 'the monologue of the tide off the Beal'.[34]

But while such transformation is an element in Hardy, in Powys it is one of his principal modes. In Hardy, moreover, the subjectivity of his characters is set in the context of their 'real' conditions, according to nature and social laws. Powys though, has a magician's sense of the malleable and soluble nature of external reality, as the stuff which the soul exercising its primordial freedom transforms into its inner world. The tendency in his stories of the solid globe to dissolve or become insubstantial as a balloon expresses his Prospero-like vision of the astronomical universe, which to him is not all there is. At his best, however, Powys combines this vision with a strong sense of the world outside the mind – both Nature, the elemental *matter*, or aboriginal Mother, and social behaviour. Thus, in the passage quoted above, psychological realism is congruous with the sharply observed spiteful old man. Powys also humorously brings together Hardy's novel about the pursuit of the ideal and the Jobber and Magnus Muir, men obsessed by *their* ideal girls, and connects them all with the stone symbolism of the novel. Powys has, in fact, a good deal of traditional literary sophistication. At his best, he is one of the most delightful of all great storytellers. In *Weymouth Sands*, for example, he moves, with seeming effortlessness, from mind to mind, and between different levels of reality, combining psychological realism with a sense of both the elemental substance and the magical livingness of place, and combining symbolism and imagery with generous humour.

Weymouth Sands is one of John Cowper Powys's best novels, partly because Weymouth was his special place, recovered in nostalgia's transfiguring light, yet also a place where people live and work, a place known through different kinds of experience. Writing of Weymouth in *Autobiography* Powys speaks of the 'transubstantiating magic' with which 'every aspect of the Weymouth coast' sank into his mind so 'that when I think now of certain things I think *with* St John's spire and the Nothe', and other features of the place – backwater, bridge, groynes, pier-posts, dead seaweed, flotsam, star-fish. 'Yes, it is through the medium of these things that I envisage all the experiences of my life; and so it will be till the end.'[35] Thinking *with* the things of place, seeing through the medium of the things: this is what makes Powys and Hardy, in their different ways, great writers of place. In *Weymouth Sands* 'psychic evocations' and 'material support' work together harmoniously, because Powys is thinking, seeing and feeling with the landmarks and seamarks. The result is a most entertaining novel, which is also a great metaphor for its author's dual personality, for the elementalist and the magus with his transubstantiating magic. The world of *Weymouth Sands* has the substance of oolitic limestone and is as airy as a child's balloon.

Powys has noted how, in early unsympathetic reviews of *Jude the Obscure*, 'poor little Sue's attitude to intellectual matters, and even Jude's own, were held up to scorn as branded with the unscholarly brand of "University Extension"'.[36] Powys himself was a university extension lecturer in England, and later lectured in the same spirit in America. He expended a great deal of his time and energy, over many years, sharing his knowledge and enthusiasm with audiences drawn largely from the working and lower-middle classes; he regarded no theory or idea or experience, whether literary or philosophical or religious or psychological, as too recondite or esoteric to share with people on equal terms. He was an actor, and a compelling lecturer, with a rhetoric which influenced his style of storytelling, not always to its advantage. He was a great teacher, who practised his fundamental belief in what he called 'the profoundest of all the great Christian dogmas ... the startling doctrine of the immeasurable and equal value of every living human soul'.[37] In his art he was a modernist, but with a difference; there are, for example, parallels between his depictions of consciousness and the experiments of Dorothy Richardson, and between his use of myth and that of James Joyce. Unlike most modernists, he was consistently a democrat in spirit and behaviour. It is worth emphasizing the public expression of his thought, in lectures and books and essays spanning the period of two world wars, and the consistency of his stand on issues of freedom and toleration. He was a lifelong spokesman for freedom who opposed all forms of tyranny – political, religious, social, intellectual – and he had a passion for helping the pariah, the ill-conditioned, the persecuted minority. The spirit of the man informs the fiction, and determines the kind of spacious world it is.

Powys associated Hardy with 'the large free horizons of humour and poetry', with his view that art 'must keep the horizons open', and have 'a certain spirit of *liberation*, and the pres-

ence of large tolerant after-thoughts'.[38] Certainly Powys is close
to Hardy's generosity of spirit, to the radical Hardy who champi-
oned those whom Victorian morality condemned or bourgeois
superiority overlooked, and to Hardy's identification with the
Pities and their hope in 'tendermercy' and loving-kindness'. Yet
here, too, their different expressions of a common quality mark
the distance between their worlds.

Powys's ultimate object in his romances was liberation, imaginative enlargement, for himself, his characters and his readers. One
expression of this is Wolf's vision towards the end of *Wolf Solent*:

> Then, as he turned eastward, and the yellowness of the buttercups
> changed from Byzantine gold to Cimmerian gold, he visualised the
> whole earthly solidity of this fragment of the West Country, this
> segment of astronomical clay, stretching from Glastonbury to Mel-
> bury Bub and from Ramsgard to Blacksod, as if it were itself one of
> the living personalities of his life. 'It is a god!' he cried in his heart;
> and he felt as if titanic hands, from the horizon of this 'field of Sat-
> urn', were being lifted up to salute the mystery of life and the mys-
> tery of death!
>
> What he longed to do was to plunge his own hands into this Sat-
> urnian gold, and to pour it out, over Mr Urquhart, over Mattie,
> over Miss Gault, over Jason, over all the nameless little desolations
> – broken twigs, tortured branches, wounded reptiles, injured birds,
> slaughtered beasts ... All ... all ... all would reveal some unspeak-
> able beauty, if only this Saturnian gold were sprinkled upon
> them![39]

It is with a Hardyan noticing of little things – the buttercups –
that Wolf's vision begins, and the spirit of pity informing it
would not have been alien to Hardy. What would have been
alien to him is the apparent assumption of preternatural powers,
in the land conceived as a god, and in 'Saturnian gold'. These
bespeak the mythological imagination, with which Powys forged
his idea of a golden age which might be actually recoverable.
Hardy, though, was a rationalist, who based his meliorism on
what he believed to be realizable in real social and historical
terms. His Henchard is fetishistic and superstitious; Hardy himself was not. Powys's heroes are fetishists, polytheists, animists,
'deboshed' magicians; and so was he. It was how he expressed
his sense of the sacred.

Yet Powys was also fundamentally sceptical – the 'as if' con-

struction or an equivalent occurs in his stories wherever there are
wonders and marvels, or a suggestion of occult powers
(here, for example, Wolf visualizes the place 'as if it were itself one
of the living personalities of his life'). Nevertheless, Powys allowed
his characters, or some of them, to find methods of escape or liberation that to Hardy would have been impossible, simply incredible,
fantastic. But Powys's sense of possibility was not achieved without a struggle on his part: a struggle whose great personal cost may
be measured by comparing what he reveals of himself in *Autobiography* with the rawer experience of the Powys-hero in his first five
novels. His fiction up to and including *Wolf Solent* is about learning
how, under certain conditions, to survive. The conditions are those
experienced by characters whose personal needs are contrary to the
conventional wisdom of the modern world, and who struggle both
against what is considered natural and what is considered socially
desirable. In *Wood and Stone*, *Rodmoor* (1916), *After My Fashion*, and
Ducdame (1925), the tragic strain kills the heroes. Wolf Solent is the
first to learn to use his imaginative freedom to enjoy or endure life.
Not that this is all there is in the early Powys, or that the Powys-hero
completely dominates the fictional interest; but the stories do show
an increasing 'enlargement', as the tragic strain is released. The
romances are, among other things, the story of Powys's spiritual
quest. It should be obvious from reading them that the sanity which
his admirers value in him was won from a prolonged struggle with
the angels of madness and destruction. Not the least modern quality of his writing is its expression and resolution of the problems of
the mind adrift on change.

As Hardy's novels developed it was not freedom that
increased, but the grip of necessity, and, while he feels with his
characters, his historical and social realism determines that Tess
and Jude do not escape their fates. In this context, his imaginative use of Stonehenge provides an interesting contrast to
Powys's. Tess sleeping on the Altar Stone is a sacrifice to natural
law – the power that makes her both love Angel and murder her
seducer, who frustrates that love – and to the social laws which
regulate, limit and judge the expressions of nature. It is a pattern
of iron necessity that binds her to the Altar Stone with invisible
bonds, and directs the judgement executed in Wintoncester, the
legal centre of Wessex.

In *A Glastonbury Romance* Stonehenge is the focus of John

Crow's stone-worship. More mysteriously, it is a magnet within the field of magical force extending from south Wales deep into Wessex, and of which Glastonbury is the centre. It is where in the chapter called 'Nature Seems Dead' the dream-laden wind from Glastonbury and Wales deposits, on the Altar Stone, 'the more psychic portion' of its 'aerial cargo'.[40] The wind blows from 'the Magic West', and, like Saturnian gold, it symbolizes the large acceptance of Nature, which is never dead, and from which the imagination draws its power to create and to destroy. Stonehenge is not a locus of historical necessity, bound to a sacrificial meaning, but a lodestone of the soul's creative freedom, which is the shaping force of Powys's mature imaginative world. Hardy employed a pattern suggested by Greek tragedy and even played with the idea of malevolent gods, but it was his sense of Victorian social law and morality and of the prevailing historical conditions that determined what is possible in his novels, and frustrated or destroyed his heroes and heroines. In his Wessex, there is no escape from history and social law; to him, Powys's symbols of liberation would surely have seemed whimsical and extravagant fancies. Hardy, with his recognition of Necessity, is a great tragic novelist. Powys, with his sense of Freedom, had an essentially comic genius; Saturnian gold and the dream-laden west wind are functions of the imaginative enlargement he claimed and exercised.

7

'Masks of Life': *The Mayor of Casterbridge* and *Maiden Castle*

In Chapter XXI of *The Mayor of Casterbridge*, Elizabeth-Jane contemplates the exterior of High-Place Hall, the house in which her new friend, Lucetta, has just taken up residence. Thomas Hardy is at some pains to describe the house and to suggest its social history. His knowledge of architecture is especially important in *The Mayor of Casterbridge*, where he uses it both to establish the physical structure of the town and to describe the meaning of buildings in terms of social status. High-Place Hall is 'an example of dignity', and the only residence like a country mansion situated 'so near the centre of the town'. Some of its rooms overlook the market-place.

Elizabeth-Jane goes in through the open front door, and nervously slips back out by a side door which opens into an alley:

> The door was studded, and the keystone of the arch was a mask. Originally the mask had exhibited a comic leer, as could still be discerned; but generations of Casterbridge boys had thrown stones at the mask, aiming at its open mouth; and the blows thereon had chipped off the lips and jaws as if they had been eaten away by disease. The appearance was so ghastly by the weakly lamp-glimmer that she could not bear to look at it – the first unpleasant feature of her visit.
>
> The position of the queer old door and the odd presence of the leering mask suggested one thing above all others as appertaining to the mansion's past history – intrigue. By the alley it had been possible to come unseen from all sorts of quarters in the town – the old play-house, the old bull-stake, the old cock-pit, the pool wherein nameless infants had been used to disappear. High-Place Hall could boast of its conveniences undoubtedly.   (211–12)

Elizabeth-Jane 'could not bear to look at it', but Hardy looks closely at the mask, as befits its importance to the novel. The mask symbolizes a cruel and barbarous history, in which the wealthy have been implicated with the poor. 'High-Place Hall could boast of its conveniences undoubtedly', as Hardy ironically comments.

The history is not past, however. It is not clear from this description whether 'the old play-house, the old bull-stake, the old cock-pit' have gone; but in the present of the novel, in the years before the repeal of the Corn Laws in 1846, primitive customs still survive, and crime, vice and disease flourish in certain areas. The skimmington ride is an example of the first, Mixen Lane of the second. Now, too, a man sells his wife and child at a country fair, and, with the same obstinate will, uses his freedom and prodigious energy to become a man of wealth and substance, and Mayor of Casterbridge. Intrigue, too, continues to thrive. Lucetta has been the mistress of Henchard, whom Elizabeth-Jane believes to be her father, because he has lied to her. Without being seen by her, because she is wishing to escape notice, he enters the doorway with the mask, on a secret visit to Lucetta. It is another step towards his tragic end.

The ghastly mask, with cruelly damaged lips and jaws, is Hardy's symbol of a comic, yet ultimately tragic, history, in which people intrigue with or against each other, exploit each other, fail to communicate, refuse to understand. As the mask had once exhibited a comic leer, so grotesque or absurd incidents contribute to the tragedy. The lips of the mask have been chipped off; it is with our lips that we kiss and speak, it is in our faces that we show our humanity and our personal identity. The mask symbolizes not only the history of Casterbridge but also Hardy's tragic vision of the human condition. It accords with the story of a man who sells those nearest to him in order to gain the world, and ends with nothing, his humanity defaced.

Fifty years after the first publication of *The Mayor of Casterbridge*, the mask appears again in a novel. In John Cowper Powys's *Maiden Castle*,[1] Enoch Quirm calls the attention of his son, Dud No-man, 'to a curious water-spout or gargoyle head that had been placed above the old brick entrance to what looked to our friend like a Quaker meeting house. He had come upon a mention of this head in Hardy's book, but apparently it occupied in poor Trenchard's time a different position from what it did now' (256). Is it Dud or Powys who gets Henchard's name wrong? Ultimately, it may not matter which one it is, since both are imaginative transformers of external reality. In the overcast light the stone face 'wore a most ambiguous expression':

'Well? What about it, lad? What about it?' chuckled the Glymes
man grimly.

'I don't – know – what – to think,' hesitated the son. 'Doesn't it
look – rather – as if – as if it hid some terrible world-joke behind
that skull, some joke that nothing could –'

His father gave him a most sardonic glance from under his eye-
brows. 'Joke, do you say? He's grinning at his own mental pain –
that's what he's grinning at. He's the face in God's backside – that's
what he is. You've got to walk round your precious world, my lad,
and see *the other side*, before you can talk about *his* little joke. It's a
joke all right, but it's a deep one! It's the deepest, my good boy.
He's the original Momus, lad, that's what he is: the face that
peeped out of God's backside when He found His creation
"good".'   (256)

Neither man identifies the face with the history of the town, as
Hardy does. Enoch identifies it with his desire to break through
to 'the other side' of reality. Dud associates it with Enoch, and
receives 'an uneasy impression that Mr Quirm would have
exactly that same grimace on his own majestic physiognomy
when he came to die'. Enoch's desire is connected with the
power of frustrated sex, and might be described as religious. He
defines it in terms of Welsh mythology and the old gods of Mai-
Dun, the prehistoric earthworks known as Maiden Castle; he
believes himself to be a reincarnation of Urien, the corpse-god.
Hence the 'ambiguous expression' of the stone face: it symbolizes the fundamental duality of life and death with which the
story is concerned. Enoch's mental pain is caused by his effort to
penetrate to the state in which the opposites, such as life and
death, good and evil, male and female, are reconciled. The image
of the mask, especially in the form of a gargoyle or water-spout,
is central to the novel.

As I have already shown, there are aspects of Powys's fiction
that resemble Hardy's because Hardy influenced him, but the
resemblances are almost entirely superficial, and the Powys
world is quite different from the Hardy world. This is most
remarkable in their novels set in the same place – if it can be said
to be the same place. Hardy's Preface to *The Mayor of Casterbridge*
informs us that 'the incidents narrated arise mainly out of three
events ... in the real history of the town called Casterbridge and

the neighbouring country' (67). His Casterbridge belongs to his 'partly real, partly dream-country', and is as much an individual creation as Powys's Dorchester. But Hardy in his novel responds to 'the real history of the town' and to its social and commercial structure, as Powys in *Maiden Castle* does not.

Hardy's novel includes footnotes such as the following: 'Most of these old houses have now been pulled down (1912)' (96). Powys incorporates apparently similar items of information in his text. For example, 'Readers of this meticulous chronicle who know the district will look in vain today for any relic of Glymes, for not only has the plough passed over the spot, but ashes have been sprinkled where the two cottages stood' (32). The similarity is superficial, however. Hardy's note, separated from his text, refers to a place that exists outside the novel, and has been affected by the process of historical change which is one of the novel's major themes. Powys's comment is part of the tissue of his fiction, and belongs to the imaginary world he has made, and is free to unmake. Such comments also have the practical effect of protecting him from the risk of libel. They have, too, a playful quality, which is consistent with his mode of storytelling. By the end of *Maiden Castle* we learn that none of the houses in which his characters live still exists in Dorchester. This is quite inconsistent with the time scale of his novel. But we know that the world of *Maiden Castle* only exists in Powys's mind, in the minds of his characters, in his readers' minds, and has no reference to the real history of Dorchester, despite the fact that Dud No-man is described as a historical novelist who is writing the story of the real Mary Channing.

From the outset *Maiden Castle* resolves the 'long history' of Dorchester into the idea of 'a familiar continuity of unbroken tradition'. Time itself seems to partake of this resolution:

> The homely sense of a recurrent satisfaction of old human necessities found another expression in the pleasant chiming of the clock in the tower of the Corn-Exchange situated at the head of the street, a chiming that seemed in its perennial cheerfulness to purge the very mystery of time of its tragic burden and divide the hours to the tune of some secret knowledge of its own that good hope, in spite of all evidence to the contrary, still abode at the bottom.   (1)

Use of the subjunctive mood – 'seemed … to purge' – is, as I have said, one of Powys's persistent stylistic strategies, by which he simultaneously allows for scepticism by incorporating it into the text, and suggests the possibility of what is being proposed or intimated. That sense of possibility is the beginning and the end of his mature fiction: it stems from his concept of the imagination, and aims at imaginative enlargement. The clock whose chiming 'seemed in its perennial cheerfulness to purge the very mystery of time of its tragic burden' is in profound accord with the Powysian spirit informing the story, and with his faith – he calls it 'secret knowledge' – 'that good hope, in spite of all evidence to the contrary, still abode at the bottom'. The social function of time, the fact that it is the Corn Exchange clock that chimes, is irrelevant.

Hardy's Casterbridge depends for its existence upon 'the agricultural and pastoral character of the people'. In describing the town Hardy gives priority to nature and commerce at the expense of organized religion:

> They came to a grizzled church, whose massive square tower rose unbroken into the darkening sky, the lower parts being illuminated by the nearest lamps sufficiently to show how completely the mortar from the joints of the stonework had been nibbled out by time and weather, which had planted in the crevices thus made little tufts of stone-crop and grass almost as far up as the very battlements. From this tower the clock struck eight, and thereupon a bell began to toll with a peremptory clang. The curfew was still rung in Casterbridge, and it was utilized by the inhabitants as a signal for shutting their shops. No sooner did the deep notes of the bell throb between the house-fronts than a clatter of shutters arose through the whole length of the High Street. In a few minutes business at Casterbridge was ended for the day.   (96)

The life of the place depends ultimately upon nature, and nature in the form of stone-crop and grass, aided by nature's conditioning factors, time and weather, is consuming the very fabric of the church. Here, time is the time of the seasons, and the time of social change; at the outset, at Weydon Priors, we are in a changing society where, as the old man tells Henchard, houses are being pulled down. Daytime is business time, too. The striking of the church clock, at 8 p.m., is the sign for the curfew, which ends the business day. The agricultural and pastoral life depends upon nature, business ultimately depends upon nature, and time in one of its aspects is, in Casterbridge, an adjunct to buying and selling.

A later description, of the purlieu called Durnover, reinforces the impression that the church is overshadowed by commerce:

> Here wheat-ricks overhung the old Roman street, and thrust their eaves against the church tower; green-thatched barns, with doorways as high as the gates of Solomon's temple, opened directly upon the main thoroughfare. Barns indeed were so numerous as to alternate with every half-dozen houses along the way. Here lived burgesses who daily walked the fallow; shepherds in an intramural squeeze. A street of farmers' homesteads – a street ruled by a mayor and corporation, yet echoing with the thump of the flail, the flutter of the winnowing-fan, and the purr of the milk into the pails – a street which had nothing urban in it whatever – this was the Durnover end of Casterbridge.   (162)

Wheat-ricks 'thrust' against the church, and the barns have 'doorways as high as the gates of Solomon's temple'. The image implies that they are Casterbridge's temples, where citizens worship, and where their fates are decided. The town is not only 'the complement of the rural life around'; it is dominated by that life. This is a situation that will change – the repeal of the Corn Laws, the coming of the railway, the increase in the class of migrant labourers, these and other factors will transform the society of which Hardy is writing in the novel. The change is already occurring in Casterbridge, through the agency of the methodical, innovative Donald Farfrae. Henchard is a massive character, integral as a bull. His tragedy is the more poignant in that he represents a doomed way of life.

Casterbridge is a centre of commerce; that is a major theme of the novel. It is dependent on the agricultural surroundings, and especially on the production of wheat. Here in Durnover is 'a street of farmers' homesteads – a street ruled by a mayor and corporation, yet echoing with the thump of the flail, the flutter of the winnowing-fan, and the purr of the milk into the pails'. The street is ruled by a mayor and corporation, but they depend for their very existence on corn and milk. The mayor – Henchard, and after him, Farfrae – is also the corn-factor, the mediator between raw material (corn) and end product (bread); between the agricultural world and the town life. His position is as vulnerable as it is important, since so much depends on his successful service of his function. Henchard and Farfrae are intermediaries between the land and the urban world; to a significant extent, the stability of the community rests on them.

The Mayor of Casterbridge depicts a whole way of life which is about to change almost completely. For now, though, Casterbridge is a place of 'legend, folk-lore, close inter-social relations, and eccentric individualities'. Hardy recognized that these depend on 'attachment to the soil of one particular spot by generation after generation'. This, as I have suggested, is the root cause of the differences between Hardy's and Powys's Wessex. The latter, too, is rich in 'eccentric individualities', but they do not arise from a society bound, generation after generation, to the soil. Powys's major characters are all deracinated modern individuals, and in place of myth that is culturally based, springing from long human occupation of one spot, he uses myth that is a function of the individual imagination: his own, which he ascribes to his protagonists. It is important, then, to realize that Hardy and Powys write in quite different modes, which accord with their radically different senses of possibility, and that these were shaped by their responses to distinct 'moments' in the history of their culture. Unlike *Maiden Castle*, *The Mayor of Casterbridge* observes the tragic necessity according to which Character is Fate, and the flawed hero brings about his own downfall. Henchard's world offers chances of social advancement but, like that of Oedipus or that of Hamlet, is one of strictly limited moral and imaginative possibilities. Hardy's realism was both a product of his time and a form of fidelity, which curbed what he permitted himself to imagine; Powys felt himself to be under no such constraint.

Henchard, when we first meet him, is preoccupied with money and status: 'I'd challenge England to beat me in the fodder business; and if I were a free man again I'd be worth a thousand pound before I'd done o't' (74). But the price of his freedom to succeed – the sale of his wife and child – is the downpayment on his tragedy, and finally costs him his identity as a human being. Nance Mockridge remarks of him when he is mayor, ''a was a poor 'parish 'prentice, that began life wi' no more belonging to 'en than a carrion crow'. Solomon Longways responds. 'And now he's worth ever so much a minute … When a man is said to be worth so much a minute, he's a man to be considered' (154–5). The argument from wealth to worth is characteristic of Casterbridge, and Henchard himself accepts it without question, although he knows the vicissitudes of fortune as well as the labourers do. He knows 'that a man might gamble upon the square green areas of fields as readily as upon those of a card game'. He has been a labourer himself, and he retains the fatalism which Hardy ascribes to the class.

Henchard is a man of rectitude. Declared bankrupt, he wishes to give his creditors all he possesses, including his gold watch and the money in his pocket. When they refuse his offer he sells the watch and takes the proceeds to a poor cottager, 'one among the smaller of his creditors'. 'Now you have all I've got in the world', (292) he declares to his creditors. The expression is commonplace but, in the circumstances, terribly poignant. For Henchard's money and possessions *are* all he has got. Love and affection, human relationships – all that even the poorest and humblest may have – are lost to him: Farfrae, whom he once thought of as a brother, he now regards as an enemy; Susan is dead; Lucetta is Donald's wife; and he knows Elizabeth-Jane to be Newson's child. For all Hardy's use of chance, his story has a stark moral outline; it begins appropriately, with Henchard reading a ballad sheet. His fortunes begin with his betrayal of his closest bonds; what he subsequently gains, and then loses, costs him all that makes life worth living. Hence, when he says 'now you have all I've got in the world', the declaration is terrible because it is true.

The truth illuminates his state of mind in writing his will:

> 'That Elizabeth-Jane Farfrae be not told of my death, or made to grieve on account of me.
> '& that I be not bury'd in consecrated ground.
> '& that no sexton be asked to toll the bell.
> '& that nobody is wished to see my dead body.
> '& that no murners walk behind me at my funeral.
> '& that no flours be planted on my grave.
> '& that no man remember me.
> 'To this I put my name.
>
> 'Michael Henchard.' (409)

When she sees the paper, Elizabeth-Jane exclaims, 'What bitterness lies there!' It is certainly a painful document, but even she does not fully comprehend it. The will contains bitterness, but is also a work of pride, demonic in its intensity, as though Henchard in proclaiming his nothingness were claiming another kind of distinction at the last, and putting his name to it in a passionate affirmation of identity.

A will bequeaths the possessions of the dead to the living. But
Henchard has nothing to leave, and has become a stranger to all
human relationships (except, finally, that with Abel Whittle). His
will, therefore, can be seen as his final comment, savage and
despairing, on the materialistic values that corrupted him. With
its negatives, it is a bitter parody of the idea of a will. It is not
nothing, however, but an image of Henchard, as material as his
effigy used in the skimmington ride. By the effigy he was known
publicly, in life; in the will he has made an image by which the
world shall know him after his death. But who was the 'real'
Michael Henchard? In the materialistic world which Hardy
describes in *The Mayor of Casterbridge* people are not known apart
from what they do and what they own. The face by which we
ultimately know Henchard is symbolized by the mask in the
doorway, its human features all but destroyed.

Despite its affinities with classical tragedy, *The Mayor of Casterbridge*, like all Hardy's tragic novels, is about the pressure of life
in Victorian society: the power and influence of money; social
advancement and decline; the effects of social and economic
inequalities on love relations between men and women; the double threat of natural law and social law to human happiness.
Casterbridge constitutes a world of rigid social structures, in
which the various buildings and areas represent differences of
status and function. It is physically a world of doors and high
walls, which bear their public meaning on the outside. Powys's
Dorchester differs not least from Hardy's Casterbridge in being
fluid, like the water with which it is associated. It is a mental
rather than a social phenomenon, consisting of his characters'
differing philosophies, life-illusions, versions of reality. Powys
moves, 'as we all have to do, in the midst of a flickering cat's-
cradle of erotic currents' (359). The drama of the novel is in the
struggle of individual souls for fulfilment, the clash of different
life-illusions and the conflict of opposites: life and death, male
and female, sensuality and mysticism, egoism and altruism,
science and nature. Powys recognizes the possible criticism
that his concerns are 'outside the real pressure of life' (258) by
incorporating the objection in the novel. The words express
Dud No-man's 'uncomfortable feeling' but Claudius Cask is the
character who most vigorously assaults the evasion of social
reality:

'I tell you, No-man, it costs money to live a simple life. A simple life's the luxury of the comfortable. Your benevolent poetical gentleman feeds on the poverty of others.'   (402)

Powys differs from Hardy in being a novelist of ideas, and, more importantly, a novelist who dramatizes different philosophies and contrasting life-illusions. But his fundamental difference from Hardy, and the basis of his special kind of modernity, lies in his concern with religion, with the psychology of religious obsession, and with the connection between religious and sexual experience. This may be seen in the following passage, in which Dud is thinking about his father's seeming madness in identifying with the Welsh god, Urien:

> 'Our age,' he thought, 'just as Spengler says, is full of rumours and intimations of the occult; and who can tell whence or when some new religion may arise? If it *does*, isn't it likely enough that it'll draw its symbols, though not its *life*, from the prehistoric past? It's not absolutely impossible' – so his erratic imagination concluded – 'that in a few hundred years some devoted, mystical group of people will actually be invoking you, you old arch-humbug. Yes, and I dare say claiming *me* as your first convertite!'   (246)

Once again, Powys is working, as it were, through a double layer of scepticism: that of the character towards the claim he is making, and that of the narrative voice, which describes Dud's imagination as 'erratic'. But this method of doubling scepticism is one that Powys persistently uses in order to overcome our disbelief, and to make the 'darker' passages of his thought acceptable. *His* thought, because Powys, like D. H. Lawrence, is an exploratory thinker and novelist, a writer who uses his characters to think with, dramatizing ideas and testing them against experience. Powys's philosophical books treat the same ideas in an expository and polemical manner. In *In Defence of Sensuality* (1930), for example, he writes about the sub-human and super-human 'margins' of human life; and these are the margins he explores in his fiction. In the same book, he delineates what he calls 'a new Culture, a new Religion', which 'liberates ... that magnetic life-sap in the depths of our being which has been sterilised by the industrial system and by society'.[2] Elsewhere I have described Powys as 'the novelist of margins, the poet, philosopher and psychologist of margins', and 'pre-eminently, the explorer of the border between the human and non-human constituents of human nature'.[3] Initially, the imaginative terms he adopts from mythology may seem strange, but the religious concern has affinities with Dostoevsky's view of the human situation between angel and beast, with Prospero's kinship to Caliban and Ariel, and with what Hardy perceived as 'a deadly war waged between flesh and spirit'.[4] Powys's aim is to explore the animal and spiritual capacity of human nature, in opposition to scientific and psychological determinism with its narrow and destructive ideas.

In my view, a full understanding of Powys's fiction depends upon our taking seriously his use of character and setting to explore the possibilities of a new religion, which works through sub-human and super-human margins to liberate the 'magnetic life-sap'. This is partly what *Maiden Castle* is about, and it is not only certain characters who are preoccupied with symbols drawn from the prehistoric past. This is one of Powys's own main concerns, and his use of ancient symbols and images is among his most distinctively modern traits. However, his interest in the sub-human and the super-human does not prevent him being one of the most human of novelists, especially in his depiction of what men and women think and feel about each other. We may consider, for example, Wizzie's exasperated observation of Dud's boots:

> How well she knew the expression of those two thick-soled objects! They seemed to say to her, 'We shall walk steadily on; we shall be still walking round Poundbury, still walking round Maumbury Rings, when a silly little girl like you has learnt at last to give up all hope of your Glymes man, all hope of your circus triumphs, all hope of your little house with the rosy porch! A quiet self-satisfied man's *boots* can outlast the most spirited girl's fancies!'   (403)

As Powys's male characters are usually creatures of habit ruled by fixed ideas, so his female characters frequently subvert their self-importance, as well as having needs – to work creatively, for example – to which their besotted male lovers are blind. As in this instance, both the humour and the pathos of Powys's stories spring in large measure from the difference between the desires and expectations that his male and female characters entertain towards one another. Sexual difference is also the main source of ecstasy in the Powysian world. In *Porius*, he would describe 'elemental depths of planetary substance ... into which, beyond and beneath the living substance of flesh, extended the great para-disic division of male and female'.[5]

Powys contrived several parallels between his story set in Dorchester and Hardy's. *The Mayor of Casterbridge* is about a man who, like the stone mask, ultimately loses his human identity. *Maiden Castle* is partly about a man without a name, who is reborn, and gains an identity. Hardy is referred to in *Maiden Castle* as 'the great Wessex author', and 'the great Wessex novelist'. Here and elsewhere, Powys's regard for Hardy and sense of indebtedness to him are evident. There is however no doubt in my mind that Powys is intent on doing to Hardy's world what he did with all the places, actual or imagined, that were impor-tant to him: remaking it in his own image. Even the inaccuracy of references to Hardy's novel in Powys's is part of this process. For example, in view of the cenotaph, Dud reflects:

> 'How like a figure in Hardy ... poor Nance looked that day stag-gering against those rails! It's funny how I began my life in Dorch-ester just as the Mayor began his, only Trenchard *sold* his woman and I *bought* mine!'
>
> (255)

The Powysian male character is a storyteller who assimilates other people's fictions to his own. It seems to me that Powys, through Dud, is doing the same. Henchard, not Trenchard, sold his wife and child, not his woman, at Weydon Priors, not Caster-bridge. Twenty years elapse after the sale, before we see Hen-chard in the town.

Earlier, the statue of Hardy has been for Dud 'but a negligible framework' to a certain look in Thuella's eyes. He thinks, as his father does: 'It's all in my mind, all, *all*!' (213). But the two out-standing scenes in which Powys makes use of Hardy in *Maiden Castle* are the scene concerning the 'curious water-spout or gar-goyle head' and the scene at Hardy's statue, after the excursion to Mai-Dun on Midsummer's Eve.

The latter begins with a description of the statue:

> Straight towards the barracks, as if he were acting as umpire in some invisible aerial tournament, gazed with fixed stare the great sculptor in words. His bronze legs in their serviceable stockings were crossed restfully at the knee, and his compact head, poised above his upright shoulders, was held as alert and as raptorial

towards the cunning masks of the Immanent Will as it had been
held in life for the best part of a century.   (389)

The associations of the word 'umpire' produce a slightly ridicu-
lous effect. It is evident, however, that Powys is enlisting Hardy
as a fellow elementalist, a writer concerned with the conflict
between good and evil on a cosmic scale. Thus Hardy's idea of
the Immanent Will is made to harmonize with Powys's idea of
the First Cause (though of course Hardy uses that name too).
Powys's First Cause is both good and evil, and the source from
which the opposites constituting life ultimately proceed. 'The
cunning masks of the Immanent Will' is a particularly significant
image, as I shall shortly attempt to show.

No-man then cries to his friends: 'You look as if you were all
gathered round the figure-head of a ship!' Wizzie takes up the
fancy in her mind, feeling 'as if the old town lying round them
were actually and indeed some huge phantasmal ship, loaded to
the bulkheads with the perilous cargoes of the generations, and
voyaging to its unknown port behind that forward-gazing
bronze figure'. In that he was a meliorist, and a man who looked
to the future, Hardy can be reasonably described as 'forward-
gazing'. But in fact the complex image of him as figure-head of
the ship of the town represents a typically Powysian mode of
perception, which his characters frequently share. The water
image is one of its constituent parts – indeed water is, so to
speak, the element of Powys's vision, his imaginative matrix, the
womb of life's absolute possibility. Among its several meanings
in *Maiden Castle* are a sense of Heraclitean flux, and a sense of the
essentially fluid nature of reality, to which minds constructing
their life-illusions give form. It is also time purged of its tragic
burden, that 'stream of life' down the generations which Dud in
particular values, but which for Powys himself is the essence of
poetic truth. In accordance with the multiple meanings of the
water imagery, identified with Dorchester, 'the Camp upon the
Waters', the unknown towards which the Hardy figure-head
gazes is not the future but the 'mystic Past', the Elysian Fourth
Dimension, the secret of the Golden Age – the object of Powys's
quest, which Hardy would surely have equated with 'belief in
witches of Endor'.[6]

The scene continues with Dumbell, the Fascist, sketching, on a blank page from one of his Blackshirt tracts, an image which they have just seen at the Mai-Dun excavations, and which Enoch Quirm identifies with the great goddess Caridwen. To make the sketch Dumbell leans the fly-leaf on the bronze back of the Hardy statue. We see all this through the mind of Wizzie, who feels herself 'wading through water ... and being aware of this demon beast [the prehistoric image] as a great slippery fish-head swimming between her knees' (390). What happens next we see through her uncertainty, which, like Powys's scepticism, enables us to think the incident may be occult. Dud takes the pencil from Dumbell to make some alteration to the sketch. But what gets written across it – not, Dud swears, by him – is 'Mona', the name of Dud's dead wife, 'whose spiritual body he had embraced in his amorous fidelity every night for ten years' (9), in the bed with the heraldic bedpost, which resembles the prehistoric image. He has come to Dorchester with 'a longing to solve ... the ultimate meaning of death itself' (5). It is possible, therefore, for us to think that he has, at this moment, solved it, since Mona, in some form, survives. It is equally possible for us to think that Dud himself has scrawled the name, unconsciously, thereby revealing his continuing obsession with his dead wife. What is certain is that the incident is connected with the psychic magnetism of concrete images. It is associated with the Hardy statue, figure-head of the 'phantasmal ship' carrying the generations 'to its unknown port', and it involves a trinity of votive offerings excavated from Mai-Dun – Caridwen, 'the headless unknown', and 'the eyeless, earless beast snout'.

Powys shares his use of primitive images and symbols with other modern writers and artists. Their attraction for him, as for others, is their association with pre-rational or irrational modes of cognition, and with integrated ways of being, not subjected to modern fragmentation. In this respect, he has affinities with the Lawrence of *Women in Love*, in which African figurines play an important part. Unlike Lawrence, though, Powys is not concerned with conflict between creative and destructive forces, but with their balance or union. One major difference between Powys and Lawrence is that Powys has a far greater tolerance for sexual and other kinds of ambiguity, and for cerebral eroticism and inter-personal behaviour that Lawrence would have regarded as decadent. It may be observed in this context that

Powys *knew*'he was decàdent, and welcomed it: 'decadence', he said in an essay on Anatole France, is the opposite of popular false ideas, and 'simply wisdom'.[7] His wisdom included a large acceptance of aberrations from socially constructed sexual and behavioural norms, and a special sensitivity towards repressed and victimized aspects of female experience. Release of female sexuality from masculinist ideas and patriarchal attitudes is a central motif of Powys's mature fiction. Ironically Dud No-man, whose relationships with women are a fiasco, is writing a novel about Mary Channing, the woman found guilty of murdering her husband, and burnt at the stake in Maumbury Rings in 1706. But while there are aspects of Powys's thinking congruent with Feminism, it should be understood that his primary concern is with male and female opposites as manifestations of Nature. His prehistoric images consequently have fetishistic and even totemic qualities, and symbolize the human, with its extensions into sub-human and super-human realms, as a locus of different possibilities of being and of relating, alternatives to the ways of 'that *anti-nature rebel*, the male-animal'.[8]

The point about Dud's bed-post head is its ambiguity:

> For the thousandth time he asked himself to what conceivable body could that extraordinary head have been attached. Was it a lion's head, a bird's head, a dragon's head, or a human head? Or had it, as happens sometimes with ecclesiastical gargoyles, elements of each one of these natures, of the bird's, of the beast's, and of the man's?   (3)

Man, beast, bird (which traditionally symbolizes the human soul): the ambiguous symbol intimates an enlargement of human life by means of embracing the elements, and extending into sub-human and super-human dimensions of being. It is an enlargement that involves upsetting received ideas of nature and of reason, so that in this respect Powys is developing a line of Romantic thought which connects him to Nietzsche and Goethe, as well as Wordsworth and Blake. But the subject that the author of *In Defence of Sensuality* and other philosophical books treats didactically, the storyteller treats experimentally and imaginatively, through character and psychic experience, relationships, dramatic situations, and with image and symbol. Powys was a more sophisticated novelist, and a more cunning artist, than he may initially seem, but he was also a writer 'torn and rent by the

Demon within'.[9] For Dud No-man in his writing, 'the aura' of Dorchester, 'with its layers upon layers of human memories, semi-historic and prehistoric, seemed to have a magical power' over his imagination. Powys, too, is like Dud in 'tapping levels in his consciousness that he had not known he possessed', and sometimes writing 'so fast – especially when his more analytic faculties were in abeyance – that it was as if he became a medium, writing he scarce knew what, under some unknown control' (91). But while Dud is of course under control, under the control of his author, Powys's exploratory mode, which included his trust in inspiration, ensured that his stories have the capacity to surprise the storyteller, and to question the philosopher.

The mask which is a gargoyle or water-spout is a primary image in *Maiden Castle*, and is particularly but not exclusively associated with Enoch Quirm:

> Mr Quirm's features were indeed nothing less than tremendous. Brow, nose, mouth, chin, all were modelled on a scale of majestic massiveness that would have been awe-inspiring if the man's eyes had been different. But Mr Quirm's eyes were dull, lifeless, colourless, opaque. They were empty of every gleam of human response. They neither softened nor warmed; they neither lightened nor darkened; they were simply *there*, as if someone had found a great antique mask with empty eye-sockets, and had inserted a couple of glass marbles into the holes. (33)

The lifelessness of his eyes may reflect his self-proclaimed character as the incarnation of a corpse-god; the resemblance of his face to 'a great antique mask with empty eye-sockets' suggests that another face – or another mask, or some other power – may exist behind and manifest itself through it; that Enoch is a medium.

In chapter 4, he describes a figure excavated at Maiden Castle the previous summer:

> Urien's massive features composed themselves like a dark stream on the surface of which an unknown animal has been swimming, leaving curious ripples. 'It's a three-horned bull,' he said, 'with two human torsos impaled on its horns and another one transfixed on its up-curving tail. It is one of those things,' he said, 'that go deeper into life than anything in ... Plato. *You've* had, Mr No-man, haven't you ... visions of life that suggest our being impaled on the horns and tail of darkness? ... Well! it's not classical symbolism anyway;

it goes back further. And when you talk of science, you must remember that these things are like dark-finned fish embedded in ice. *They have life in them that can be revived ...'* (154)

The description of Urien's features relates him to the image of the gargoyle or water-spout. But if he is a medium, what is he a medium for? What he believes is that ancient symbols *'have life in them that can be revived'*, and that he, as Urien, is an incarnation of the god. He believes he has 'been the power that's older than all this damned sunshine, the power that's older than all these new gods, the power that's deepest of all, for it's got death in it as well as life'. It is the power which he calls 'the old magic of the mind', and he claims the Welsh preserved its secret by hiding it. Urien, then, claims to be a god – one among many:

'I tell you *we*, I and others like me, are the gods of Mai-Dun – the same, yesterday, today, and forever. There's no one god, lad. Lay *that* up in your heart. Things are as they are because there are so many of us; and as fast as some create, others destroy: and a good thing too, as the Son of Chaos cries out in *Faust*. Certain masks of life *ought* to be destroyed, to make room for others, to make room sometimes for those that have lain beneath them for ten thousand years.' (241)

Maiden Castle does not endorse Enoch Quirm's belief that he is an incarnation of Urien; indeed, he may be seen as a tragic figure, who destroys himself by publicizing his life-illusion. But nor does it simply discredit it. What it demonstrates is the storytelling power of the human mind, and the capacity of the imagination to create and destroy forms of identity. As Lovie, the little girl, can cause the miracle by which a bit of paper becomes 'a person with a past and a future', so Enoch can tell himself a story in which he becomes a god; and so Powys with his story creates all the worlds that constitute the novel.

If the novel does not endorse Enoch's belief, it does, I think, express Powys's faith that it is possible to destroy 'certain masks of life', in order 'to make room for others, to make room sometimes for those that have lain beneath them for ten thousand years'. Powys's stories themselves subvert 'the cunning masks of the Immanent Will', the fixed ideas of determinism, which largely shaped the intellectual universe of Hardy and other Victorians. In Powys's multiverse, the energy of life itself feeds the mind, which has the capacity to create or destroy identity, and to revive masks worn in the ancient days of the gods. Character in Powys's world is not Fate, but Imagination.

The primitive images in *Maiden Castle* are fetishes, and 'exteriorized souls'. For those who use them imaginatively, they are channels of power. Like the gargoyle which spouts water, the images mediate a renewing and transformative force. Powys's primitivism is identified particularly with Welsh mythology and the Welsh language. Dud conceives the latter as 'the most primitive of all tongues', as a voice of the elements. This seems to be Powys's view as well, so that for him Welsh is conveniently a language without social or cultural determinants or functions, and therefore entirely at the disposal of the individual imagination. Powys completed the novel in Wales, in the land that was the source of his own life-illusion, of his idea of himself as a magician, by which he shaped his identity as a man, a thinker, and a writer. It is partly because of his identification with Wales that Powys's primitivism differs from that of other modernists, but it does not differ essentially in function from the primitivism of Ezra Pound or T. S. Eliot, for example, both of whom used ancient traditions as part of their own making (and unmaking) of cultural and personal identity. They too constructed new (or old) world-pictures as alternatives to what they saw as the disintegrated culture of the West, and invented roles for themselves in accordance with their constructed traditions. Self-making on such a scale is rather the norm than the exception among modernists, from whom Powys differs mainly on account of his Romantic affinities. Instead of inclining to ideas of classical discipline, and to the hardness and clarity of imagist aesthetics, he developed lines from Rousseau and Goethe, and from Wordsworth, Blake and Keats; he worshipped Nature and prized sensation; he emphasized the part played by the mind in the creation of 'reality'; and his literary and philosophical tradition exalted the freedom of the imagination, rather than appealing to any external authority, whether human or divine.

Maiden Castle is set at the beginning of the Aquarian age. Dorchester, as Dud reflected, 'meant "the Camp upon the Waters", and its psychic as well as its physical life seemed connected with the absolutely inexhaustible subterranean river that fed its water-tower' (186). The 'consecrated-looking erection' (Powys, like Hardy, uses the word with appealing innocence!)

reminds Dud of a print of a temple of Vesta. In *The Mayor of Casterbridge* the barns are the temples, and upon them, or upon
nature and commerce, which they represent, both the life of the
community and the fate of individuals depend. In *Maiden Castle*
the water-tower is a temple, and symbolizes an inexhaustible
source of psychic and physical life. It is a source of transforming
imaginative energy, on which each character draws in constructing his or her vision of reality. The caretaker at the cemetery
sums up Powys's Dorchester when he says: ''Tis a fancy-world,
sir, look at 'un as us may' (13). In order that the imagination
should have, as it were, the freedom of the town, Powys has
simultaneously to dissolve its modern society and its actual history, and to transform their chief imaginative representative,
Thomas Hardy, into a Powysian figure-head. I have already suggested how he effects the latter. He achieves the former by
emphasizing, largely through his characters' minds, 'the insub-
stantiality of all reality', and replacing history with an idea of
continuity, the 'stream of life flowing down the ages'.

It is in looking at cuckoo-flowers that Dud No-man escapes
into 'this reality behind reality', and dips into 'those pure springs
where each generation washes away its brutality, its blood, its
guilt, its executions in Maumbury Rings!' It is into a similar
'place' out of time, a 'green dimness', evoked by the sound of the
wind, that he wishes to carry the soul of Mary Channing:

> 'That's what I must do in my book! I must collect the shreds and
> patches of her poor substance that were dissolved among the ele-
> ments, and comfort them, and give them pardon and peace. I must
> wash away every memory of our accurst justice from them and
> bathe them in this healing greenness.'   (254)

'Pardon and peace' was surely also what Powys in his books
sought ultimately to bestow upon us, and I find that in reading
him a phrase from Coventry Patmore (which Seamus Heaney
quotes in 'The Harvest Bow') comes frequently to my mind: 'the
end of art is peace'. Fortunately, though, the novel itself does not
bathe all in 'healing greenness', thus imposing upon all suffering
and injustice a resolution that no human being has the right to
make. The play of Powys's scepticism in his best romances subverts even his own fixed ideas, which his philosophical writings
tend to harden and overstate. In the bonding and in the war

between the sexes, and in the vicissitudes of his characters' daily lives, all is not in the mind, and much is provisional and incomplete, neither sub-human nor super-human, but only human. Powys's scepticism allows us to believe what his mystics and magicians believe, if we want to, but does not require us to do so, or suggest that it is all there is. His is not a tragic vision, but happily he is not too certain that life is a comedy, either. Like the chiming of the Corn Exchange clock, *Maiden Castle* may seem to purge time of its tragic burden and affirm that good hope, in spite of all, still abides at the bottom, but it does not require us to believe that it does.

It is not only through their relationships with one another but also – indeed, especially – in their aloneness that Powys's characters have access to a sense of possibility that is unknown in Hardy's socially circumscribed world. Aloneness in Powys's view of life is an infinite space connecting the individual mind to the First Cause, and is to be enjoyed. In Hardy, by contrast, aloneness is a determining factor of the tragic human condition. In *The Mayor of Casterbridge* it is not only Henchard who ends with nothing, his identity defaced, like the mask that is the keystone of the arch. Mrs Cuxsom, describing Susan Henchard after her death, says she was a woman who 'minded every little thing that wanted tending'. She describes, by hearsay, Susan's preparation for her death: her coffin clothes, and four ounce pennies, two for each eye, which she directs to be buried after use, and not spent. She then describes how Christopher Coney dug up the pennies, and spent them at The Three Mariners, justifying himself by saying, 'Why should death rob life o' fourpence?' Mrs Cuxsom's listeners exclaim: ''Twas a cannibal deed!', but Solomon Longways repeats, with emphasis: 'Why *should* death rob life o' fourpence? I say there was no treason in it.' It is then that Mrs Cuxsom speaks her elegy for Susan:

> 'Well, poor soul; she's helpless to hinder that or anything now ...
> And all her shining keys will be took from her, and her cupboards
> opened; and little things 'a didn't wish seen, anybody will see; and
> her wishes and ways will all be as nothing!'   (191)

There is a zest for life in Hardy's labourers, as has often been remarked. But for those like Susan, careworn by minding little things and anxious about personal dignity, there is no such zest but only, at the last, a pathetic wish to look respectable. Now, 'her wishes and ways will be as nothing'. She has invested her identity in details, and their disclosure will negate her. Such ultimate loneliness is a condition of the Hardy tragedy, in which personality is defaced. But in Powys's story the aloneness of each character is a condition of his or her capacity to destroy 'masks of life', in order 'to make room for others'. The keystone of Powys's house of fiction comprises no one mask, expressive of human limitations; in his world, there are many changing masks, and many possible faces.

8

In the shadow of a dying god: *The Enigma of Arrival* and *The Spire*

> Land is not land alone, something that simply is itself. Land partakes of what we breathe into it, is touched by our moods and memories.[1]

V. S. Naipaul's words are true for the individual who experiences the land personally, and creates from it an imaginative world. And they are true of the cultural making of the land, which is not Nature, but Nature shaped to human needs over a long period of time. In 'Walks in the Wheat-fields' (1887), Richard Jefferies described the wheat-fields as 'the battle-fields of the world'.[2] He was thinking not only of the agricultural depression of his own time and 'the struggle between nations ... for the ownership or for the control of corn', but of the constructive and destructive acts of the Romans and of subsequent invaders, Saxons, Danes and Normans, by whom the land had been possessed and settled. He knew the common history of toil as well, and described it memorably in his tribute to John Brown, the labourer, for example:

> If a man's work that he has done all the days of his life could be collected and piled up around him in visible shape, what a vast mound there would be beside some! If each act or stroke was represented, say by a brick, John Brown would have stood the day before his ending by the side of a monument as high as a pyramid. Then if in front of him could be placed the sum and product of his labour, the profit to himself, he could have held it in his clenched hand like a nut, and no one would have seen it.[3]

Jefferies, more than most writers, was aware of the cost of the making of the land: 'The wheat is beautiful, but human life is labour.' But 'Jefferies' Land' is still an imaginative realm, personal and aesthetic, a place of beauty as well as labour; a land into which Jefferies breathed his spirit, a land touched by his moods and memories.

According to Raymond Williams:

A working country is hardly ever a landscape. The very idea of landscape implies separation and observation. It is possible and useful to trace the internal histories of landscape painting, landscape writing, landscape gardening and landscape architecture, but in any final analysis we must relate these histories to the common history of a land and its society.[4]

Emphasis upon 'the common history' is a useful check to merely wilful fantasy, but it may also cause us to overlook not only the uncommon achievements of creative individuals but also the part played by the imagination in shaping the way we see and feel about a country. The land is a historical and social phenomenon, but it is also a ground of vision, a ground seen and interpreted differently over time, or by different individuals and groups at the same time. There is a complex relationship between, say, Jefferies' Liddington Hill, or Paul Nash's Wittenham Clumps, or Edward Thomas's 'hollow land as vast as heaven', and the historical landscape on which the image is based. In what sense are the imagined landscapes less real than the working country? They too contribute to an idea of England, to a country of the imagination. Such places are lived in, invested with meaning, as necessary as dreams to the life of the mind.

As my discussion of writers who have set their work in southern England has shown, seeing the land is not simply a matter of opening the eyes and looking, but a complex imaginative process involving both mythic and historical awareness, personal responses, and religious and cultural influences of which the writer may be only partially conscious. Some writers emphasize the historical nature of the land. Thus in *Tess of the d'Urbervilles* Thomas Hardy places his heroine in a Wessex shaped by historical forces; he stresses her Norman ancestry, and the history of male (but also female) depredations committed upon Nature and the weak, which are symbolized by the white hart. But history is not only the past; it is also change in the present, and Tess is driven to wander in a Wessex which is undergoing transformations, and where she is victimized by Victorian morality and law, and suffers from the mechanization of agriculture, as well as from exposure to the weather and to traditional forms of labour. Hardy is not concerned with external change only, but with his characters' experience of an 'ache' at the roots of being, which leads them to question the meaning of existence. Religion plays a significant and mainly negative role in their society and in forming their minds.

In his poetry, Hardy treats the land as a historical and ancestral domain, but also as a psychological phenomenon. For both Edward Thomas and Richard Jefferies, too, the land is at least partly the scene on which they project their psychological and spiritual autobiography. This is also true of John Cowper Powys and the characters that resemble him. Nature worship is an insistent but problematic impulse in Jefferies and Thomas and Powys, as well as in many other Victorian and modern writers. Love of Nature, but not Nature worship, is strong in the rational Hardy who is critical of Wordsworthian optimism as well as of anything smacking of the supernatural, and Nature worship is strongest in Powys with his animistic and magical propensities. Near the beginning of *Wolf Solent* Wolf sees a cow ruminating in a churchyard, with 'such an inviolable placidity that its feet seemed planted in a green pool of quietness that was older than life itself'. It then seemed to him 'as though all the religions in the world were nothing but so many creaking and splashing barges, whereon the souls of men ferried themselves over the lakes of primal silence'. He has the idea that, one night, from church tower to church tower, 'there might be sent ... the real death-cry of a god'.[5] Wolf's landscape is emptied of orthodox Christian belief, but, towards the end of the novel, he sees part of the West Country itself as a god. Idolatry on this scale is rare, but a tendency to substitute the land, or Nature, for God, as the ultimate ground to rest on, is apparent in other writers of the late Victorian and modern periods, including Jefferies and Thomas. Hardy avoids it by virtue of his rationalism, and his Darwinian perspective, but also because his concern is with emotional relationships between men and women, rather than with the solitary mind communing with Nature. The typical locus of the Hardy poem is a place which the poet visits alone, but which is pervaded for him by the absence of the beloved. But Hardy was of course far from indifferent to religion, which he depicts as a force influencing his changing society, and intimately affecting human behaviour and relationships. His Wessex, no less than John Cowper Powys's, lies under the shadow of the dying god. This, indeed, is an inextricable part of the *history* that defines the modernity of the writers with whom I am concerned in this book. Their landscapes figure in a search for ultimate meaning, expressed in a religious vocabulary – 'soul', 'mystery', 'eternity', 'divine' and so on – which they translate to meet the needs of their unorthodox thought. Their quest is not secondary to a history of imperial politics, class conflict and social change, but integral to lived experience.

It is a mistake to see these writers in terms of a 'Southern Metaphor, or English Dream',[6] or as seeking a haven from the modern world in landscapes that have somehow remained miraculously untouched by historical change. Their modernity is evident even in the most archaic or mythological elements of their work, or perhaps especially there, since the need to seek wholeness through alternative vision is itself a response to deterministic modes of thought, fragmentation, and loss of a sense of the sacred. It would also be a mistake to think that the serious imaginative use of southern English landscapes ended with the death of Thomas Hardy, or the shift of John Cowper Powys's attention from Wessex to Wales. I want in the rest of this chapter to consider aspects of two more recent novels, by William Golding and V. S. Naipaul respectively, and to relate them to concerns of the earlier writers discussed in this book.

In his article, 'An Affection for Cathedrals', William Golding describes the building of Salisbury Cathedral spire in the thirteenth century as 'a technological gamble which makes space travel seem child's play'. Under the enormous weight of material, the cathedral might well have collapsed. 'Yet the whole building still stands. It leans. It totters. It bends. But it still stands.'[7] Golding's space-age novel, *The Spire*, first published in 1964, and based imaginatively on medieval Salisbury, shows a fascination with the greater achievement of the medieval builders, but interprets the creative act in terms of modern psychology.

In the article, Golding images the effect of Salibury Cathedral spire on the surrounding landscape: 'So it stands, a perpetual delight, a perpetual wonder, with the whole of our little body politic shrugged into shape about it.' This is similar to what Jocelin sees from the tower of the fictional cathedral in the novel: 'The rivers glittered towards the tower; and you could see that all those places which had been separate to feet and only joined by an act of reason, were indeed part of a whole' (105–6).[8] The tower has changed the nature of the world, making more of it visible, but also bringing it into a unity; and it will influence the future:

> In a flash of vision he saw how other feet would cut their track arrowstraight towards the city, understood how the tower was laying a hand on the whole landscape, altering it, dominating it, enforcing a pattern that reached wherever the tower could be seen, by sheer force of its being there. He swung round the horizon and saw how true his vision was. There were new tracks, people in parties, making their way sturdily between bushes and through heather. The countryside was shrugging itself obediently into a new shape. (107–8)

Jocelin is a man of 'vision'. But he is also blind to himself and to the roots of his obsession, which drives him, in creating, to destroy himself and others. The novel is a modern treatment of medieval religious faith: it is based on a psychological interpretation of human creativity, which emphasizes its sexual and unconscious dynamics. It begins with blinding vision, which is phrased to imply both the violence of the creative act, and that natural and human causes determine sacred effects; and as it develops, Jocelin learns the complications of his vision, and its great cost, and how little he knows. If at last he achieves wisdom, it is because he knows that he does not know himself.

Yet the spire is built, and stands, against all reason. Jocelin's vision is vindicated, though it was not what he thought: a simple vision of a man chosen by God. The spire stands, and changes the world; as space exploration was changing the world at the time that the novel was written – and was it changing it as its architects predicted? And was it being conducted in terms of their conscious motivation? Or does man always create in his blindness, and produce results that he did not foresee? The questions are not explicit in *The Spire*, but they are implied.

Golding is, above all, a novelist who explores the human mind:

> What man *is*, whatever man is under the eye of heaven, that I burn to know and that – I do not say this lightly – I would endure knowing. The themes closest to my purpose, to my imagination have stemmed from that preoccupation, have been of such a sort that they might move me a little nearer that knowledge. They have

been themes of man at an extremity, man tested like building
material, taken into the laboratory and used to destruction; man
isolated, man obsessed, man drowning in a literal sea or in the sea
of his own ignorance.[9]

Man 'tested like a building material': the symbolic connection
between man and the cathedral, and the cathedral as a metaphor
for its human creator, are evident in *The Spire*. Jocelin describes
himself as 'a building with a vast cellarage where the rats live'
(210). He asks the Mason the question that preoccupies his
author: 'What's a man's mind Roger? Is it the whole building,
cellarage and all?' (213).

In both the talk and the novel we may note the use of the word
'man'. It might be considered generic in the former; but Golding's concern in *The Spire* is with a man, and with men, and the
women characters are defined by the mind and needs of men.
The women could be described as stereotypes, or, more gener-
ously, archetypes; at any rate, as symbolic representatives of
male needs and obsessions. They are identified, in particular,
with Nature – the opposite and the antagonist of Jocelin's vision.
Or so he feels and believes, true to the opposition between the
spiritual and the material. What the novel shows, however, is
that spiritual vision is rooted in Nature, and has Nature woven
into it.

Early in the novel, Jocelin reflects of the cathedral: 'I could
think this was some sort of pagan temple' (10). And so it is – for
the workmen who are devil-worshippers and light fires at Stonehenge on Midsummer Night, and who murder Pangall and bury
him in the pit, a sacrificial victim with a sprig of mistletoe
through his heart, to appease the powers of darkness seething
underground, which would otherwise cause the tower to fall.
And so it is for Jocelin, for the whole man as distinct from the
visionary.

When Jocelin looks into the pit and sees what the cathedral is
founded on – in fact a marsh on which the original builders laid
a brushwood raft – he sees corruption: 'the darkness under the
earth', Doomsday, hell, 'or the living, pagan earth, unbound at
last and waking, Dia Mater' (80). Mother Earth, Nature, woman:
that is what Jocelin, as a man of vision and faith, fears; which is
also to say that he fears himself, as a sexual being, a whole man.
When he looks from the tower he sees 'the rounded downlands

that rose to a wooded and notched edge. They were soft and warm and smooth as a young body' (106). He sees the landscape in the image of his desire; the downs are one nature with Goody, whom he loves but cannot admit he desires. And his response is to pray:

I bring my essential wickedness even here into thy air. For the world is not like that. The earth is a huddle of noseless men grinning upward, there are gallows everywhere, the blood of childbirth never ceases to flow, nor sweat in the furrow, the brothels are down there and drunk men lie in the gutter. There is no good thing in all this circle but the great house, the ark, the refuge, a ship to contain all these people and now fitted with a mast. Forgive me.   (106–7)

This is Jocelin's orthodox medieval vision: 'no good thing' in the world but the Church, the ark of salvation; God is the Lord of air and light, and the earth belongs to death, Nature and evil. But even as he prays, Jocelin's imagery betrays him. What he calls 'essential wickedness' – sexual desire – is an integral part of his creativity, and the spire, which he envisages as the mast of a ship, is a phallic symbol.

In his vision of God Jocelin takes the part for the whole, making a sharp and absolute distinction between the holy and the unholy, heaven and earth, soul and body. What he comes to wish for is a wholeness that abolishes the distinction, and in which all is holy: 'there ought to be some mode of life where all love is good, where one love can't compete with another but adds to it' (214). And, as he lies dying he thinks: 'If I could go back, I would take God as lying between people and to be found there. But now witchcraft hides Him' (220).

The first statement sounds like a modern theological concept: God is to be found in the relation between I and Thou. The reference to witchcraft is medieval. But the connotation has now undergone a reversal. Jocelin has identified witchcraft with woman, with sexual desire and love. Now he seems to realize that what has bewitched him is that way of seeing, which makes love an ugly thing.

Golding uses his southern places and landscapes to explore religious themes. *The Spire* may, as Mark Kinkead-Weekes and Ian Gregor claim, reverse 'the psalmist's cry', and make the straight 'crooked and the plain places rough', but in describing it in terms of 'ambiguity, paradox, reversal'[10] they indicate its concern with the disturbing and unsettling nature of the sacred. Like John Cowper Powys, Golding probes the connection between religion and sexuality, spirit and Nature. Both are modern, but neither is reductive, as Marxism and psychoanalysis are. Golding's novel as a mode of thinking bears out his self-description, in 1980, as a novelist 'floundering in all the complexities of twentieth century living, all the muddle of part beliefs'.[11]

There are two kinds of vision in the novel, both of which Jocelin experiences: the vision of light, in which the man sees with part of himself, and a whole seeing, which is more complex, more difficult, for the novelist as well as the character. The latter involves Nature, and woman, and imagery of trees, and the symbol of The Tree, which complement the symbolism of spire and phallus. Goody is associated with Nature, and Jocelin comes to realize that she is 'woven' into his vision. But it is not the girl alone that complicates what was initially 'clear and explicit'. Rather, 'A single green shoot at first, then clinging tendrils, then branches, then at last a riotous confusion' (168). Later, speaking to Father Adam, Jocelin elaborates the image:

> 'Growth of a plant with strange flowers and fruit, complex, twining, engulfing, destroying, strangling.'
>   And immediately the plant was visible to him, a riot of foliage and flowers and overripe, bursting fruit. There was no tracing its complications back to the root, no disentangling the anguished faces that cried out from among it.   (194)

It is indeed a 'complex' image, which calls to mind the modern psychological meaning of the word, but also Gothic tracery; imagery of the Tree of the Knowledge of Good and Evil, from among which appear 'the anguished faces' of those he has destroyed, including his own, like faces of the damned in medieval iconography. But the image also evokes the other Tree in the Garden, the Tree of Life, which is an image of wholeness and integration. And this, perhaps, is what Jocelin sees in his vision of the appletree:

> There was a cloud of angels flashing in the sunlight, they were pink and gold and white; and they were uttering this sweet scent for joy of the light and the air. They brought with them a scatter of clear leaves, and among the leaves a long, black springing thing. His head swam with the angels, and suddenly he understood there was more to the appletree than one branch. It was there beyond the

wall, bursting up with cloud and scatter, laying hold of the earth and the air, a fountain, a marvel, an appletree; and this made him weep in a childish way so that he could not tell whether he was glad or sorry. (204–5)

Jocelin has seen the 'thing' as the root of evil: the snake, Satan, the phallus. But it is as much part of the tree as the blossom, which he sees as 'a cloud of angels'. The tree is both an appletree and a symbol, 'laying hold of the earth and the air, a fountain, a marvel'; the Tree of Life which connects heaven and earth. The experience awakes the child in the man, and his response is ambivalent, as human responses to the sacred usually are. And through the vision, and part of it, flies the kingfisher: 'all the blue of the sky condensed to a winged sapphire, that flashed once' (205). It is what Golding in 'A Moving Target' calls 'the descent into this world of beauty's mystery and irradiation, flame, explosion'.[12] And it is made possible by Jocelin's state of enlarged consciousness, in which man and child, and maker and sinner, are open to the revelatory moment.

The vision is comprehensive; it is a vision of wholeness, of creation and the creative act, in which 'light' and 'dark' elements work together, and Nature and sexuality partake of the sacred. If Jocelin is deceived in his 'angel', which is in fact the disease that is killing him, Golding does not reduce human creativity to a disease of body or mind; his aim is rather to explore the integration of spiritual and material forces in the act of creation. The meaning is not that of the medieval Church, but nor is it merely a reduction of creativity to sublimated or inhibited sexual instinct. The novel does not explain away evil, but rather attempts to comprehend the whole complex structure of profane and sacred elements that constitute what 'man is under the eye of heaven'.

V. S. Naipaul's *The Enigma of Arrival* is also centrally concerned with seeing, and with 'the past, the sacred earth, the gods' (310), but it is a quite different kind of book from Golding's. It is an autobiographical novel, set in the ancient landscape of Wiltshire, in a river valley between Salisbury and Stonehenge, and in the grounds of an Edwardian manor, a house built in the security and on the wealth of empire. Its protagonist is the writer himself, a man from Trinidad but who is ultimately of Indian extraction, since his grandparents had been brought from India to work in the plantations. His family and personal history, therefore, has been shaped by empire. The situation is fraught with historical

ironies, the chief of which is the fact that the writer is making a
new life in the old world, exploring Wiltshire and the English
social experience much as English explorers in the heyday of
empire observed 'exotic' and 'native' peoples and places.
Naipaul shows considerable knowledge of the English literary
and artistic rural tradition – Wordsworth, Constable, Cobbett,
Hardy, Borrow and so on. He does not mention Jefferies, but we
may be aware of the irony that Jefferies, Wiltshire-born in the
nineteenth century, explored his own country by analogy with
the imperialist explorers and pioneers in Africa and the new
world. To juxtapose the wild England of *After London* with the
Wiltshire of *The Enigma of Arrival* is to experience an almost ver-
tiginous sense of the ironies of history and empire. Yet there is,
too, a kinship between the fictions, in which lonely figures bearing a close resemblance to their creators, seek in a fearful time,
and in a world largely divested of a sense of the sacred, for some
kind of sustaining structure of ritual and belief.

Another irony is that the writer feels himself blessed with a
new life during his years in a cottage in the grounds of the
manor, at the same time that the manor itself, and its English
owner, in the aftermath of imperial decline, are falling into decay.
There are many ironies in the situation, but it seems to me that
Naipaul is not concerned only or even primarily with making an
ironic critique of empire, but has an aim that is both more and
less ambitious than that. Less ambitious in that it is to understand himself, to make sense of his own experience as man and
writer. More ambitious in that his experience is that of the changing world, in which many people are on the move, deracinated,
alienated from traditional cultures, communities and religious
rites, and facing great problems, but with new creative possibilities, too. The enigma of arrival is his enigma; but it is also that of
many others in the second half of the twentieth century, and the
novel set in Wiltshire, with memories of journeys from Trinidad
to New York and London, and of other journeys to India and
Africa, is thus a novel about the post-colonial modern world. It is
not only about geographical displacement and social change,
however; it is also about religion, about the fundamental meanings people give their lives, and the loss or breakdown of those
meanings, and what if anything replaces them. None of the writers whose work I have discussed had a simple relation to his

subject, the relation of a 'native' celebrating his 'roots'. The intimacy of John Cowper Powys's Dorset and Somerset landscapes, for example, was a reconstruction based largely on childhood impressions. '*Wolf Solent* is a book of Nostalgia, written in a foreign country with the pen of a traveller and the ink-blood of his home.'[13] Even Hardy of Wessex, identified by contemporary readers with the 'partly real, partly dream-country'[14] which seemed to have a stability their society lacked, was a mythical figure created by those who preferred romance to reality. The Hardy who speaks to us is a man who wrote from his experience of social instability and change, and who is aware not only of injustice, social tensions, and conflict between the sexes, but of failure in individuals of the very will to live. The lineaments of a longer lasting, but not unchanging, social pattern may be discerned in his Wessex, and he depicts the survival of pre-modern ways of enjoying and enduring life, but the modern experience with which he is centrally concerned is discontinuous with the past, and expresses 'the mind adrift on change, and harassed by the irrepressible New'.[15] Dislocation, in one form or another, and varying degrees of alienation, characterize all English 'writers of place' from John Clare to the present, with the exception of those with a vested interest in depicting an England that never existed. Naipaul's novel does not romanticize a settled rural order in any of the places with which it is concerned, but expresses and analyses complications of seeing, which arise from his complex relation to his two 'homes', his original home in Trinidad, and his home in Wiltshire.

The Enigma of Arrival is about moral and physical perception, as the opening paragraph indicates:

> For the first four days it rained. I could hardly see where I was. Then it stopped raining and beyond the lawn and outbuildings in front of my cottage I saw fields with stripped trees on the boundaries of each field; and far away, depending on the light, glints of a little river, glints which sometimes appeared, oddly, to be above the level of the land. (11)

It is not the rain alone that obscures the writer's vision. Initially it is because the place has little meaning for him, or false meanings based on romantic expectations, that 'I could hardly see where I was'. 'Later', he goes on to say, 'the land had more meaning, when it had absorbed more of my life than the tropical

street where I had grown up.' Seeing the land means relating to
it, and knowing his manifold experience that partakes of the
relationship. At first we simply do not know what is making the
country 'a blur' to him. Only later do we learn that in his early
days in Wiltshire he was writing a story set in Africa, 'a book
about fear': 'And the mist that hung over the valley where I was
writing; the darkness that came early, the absence of knowledge
of where I was – all this uncertainty emanating from the valley I
transferred to my Africa' (93). The African story about a journey
is one of several versions of 'The Enigma of Arrival'. There are
hints at the beginning of what will be revealed as Naipaul
explores the land and discloses what he has breathed into it – in
the word 'stripped', for example, in the 'glints', and above all in
the implied 'darkness' that obscures his vision. There is an image
not quoted in the novel that haunts it, nevertheless: Marlow's, in
Heart of Darkness (1902), when, in a yawl in the Thames estuary,
he says: 'And this also has been one of the dark places of the
earth'.[16] Naipaul, like Conrad, has been heavily criticized[17] for
his perception of what are now referred to as Third World soci-
eties from a 'centrist' (or Western) viewpoint, and in terms of an
ideology fed by metaphors of primitive 'darkness', as distinct
from the 'light' of civilization and enlightenment. It is not my
aim to enter the critical debate, or to consider Naipaul's other
writings here. My concern is with his treatment of the land in *The
Enigma of Arrival*, and in this context, it may be observed that,
just as Conrad's 'dark places of the earth' include London and
Brussels as well as the Belgian Congo, so *The Enigma of Arrival* is
about a darkness that is universal, and in which the author himself, in his 'book of fear', is at least partly shrouded.

The writer's neighbour, Jack, with his garden, is not so much a
character as one of the main subjects of the novel. Initially his
view of him may suggest a mythical figure, and remind us of a
Wordsworthian solitary, or Edward Thomas's view of Richard
Jefferies as one who 'emerged from the womb of the Wiltshire
earth',[18] or of Thomas's other essential Englishman, Lob, a man
'of old Jack's blood,/Young Jack perhaps, and now a Wiltshire-
man/As he has oft been since his days began'.[19] At first the
writer's perception of Jack is coloured, and distorted, by his
sense of himself as 'an oddity', and 'unanchored and strange', so
that he sees Jack as his opposite: 'part of the view', his life 'gen-

uine, rooted, fitting: man fitting the landscape' (19) Through Jack's garden he comes to know the seasons, which form a vital part of his new life in the valley. But as he comes to know the place so he comes to understand Jack differently:

> I had seen Jack as solid, rooted in his earth. But I had also seen him as something from the past, a remnant, something that would be swept away before my camera would get the pictures. My ideas about Jack were wrong. He was not exactly a remnant; he had created his own life, his own world, almost his own continent.   (87)

The writer has seen Jack in the light of his own insecurity, and thus created an image of Jack as what he himself is not: a man 'rooted in his earth'. This is a familiar literary and psychological process, which constructs ideas of security out of the observer's insecurity. We see it in the pastoral tradition, in images of a golden age produced by troubled urban minds; in John Cowper Powys, travelling across America in trains and staying in hotel rooms, constructing his dream of Wolf Solent's West Country; in Edward Thomas, looking for an essential permanence, a Lob or a Merry England, even as he experiences a rural world on the verge of extinction; in Hardy's contemporary readers, fashioning the image of their author as the archetypal 'countryman' rooted in an unchanging way of life. Hardy avoided stereotypes of Hodge, but under extreme pressure, in 'In Time of "The Breaking of Nations" ', imaged human figures emblematic of continuity in the English countryside, even after the culture based on the land had broken down.

The writer in Naipaul's novel sees the tenuous hold of people on the land, and acknowledges that 'My ideas about Jack were wrong'. Jack, disregarding that tenuousness, 'had created a garden on the edge of a swamp and a ruined farmyard: had responded to and found glory in the seasons' (87). Now he sees Jack as heroic, and as a man who celebrated life. He was not a remnant but a creator, and consequently he becomes for the writer a model, and his counterpart: a man who creates among ruins. At the end of the novel he links Jack with the experience of his own people, the Indians in Trinidad. He has described Jack as having 'sensed that life and man were the true mysteries; and he had asserted the primacy of these with something like religion' (87). In the final sentences of the novel he writes that his sister's death 'showed me life and man as the mystery, the true religion

of men, the grief and the glory'. 'And that was when', he concludes, 'faced with a real death, and with this new wonder about
men, I laid aside my drafts and hesitations and began to write
very fast about Jack and his garden' (318). Earlier he has said:
'Death was the motif ... Death and the way of handling it – that
was the motif of the story of Jack' (309).

The setting of *The Enigma of Arrival* is appropriate to the motif.
Dud No-man in *Maiden Castle* had sought to solve, 'on the spot
where his own dead lay, the ultimate meaning of death itself'.[20] It
was one of the primary concerns of his author, an ageing man
returning in story after story to the land once secured in the
image of his father's religion, and still haunted by the dying god.
The primeval landscapes of Wessex are especially appropriate to
the idea of such a search. This is not only because they are vast
burial grounds, denoting a continuity of life and death from the
origins of man to the present, but also because they are, or have
been, sacred landscapes, rich in religious sites. In the words of
the writer in *The Enigma of Arrival*:

> As much as any comparable area of Egypt or India, the region
> (once a vast burial place) was full of sacred sites: the circles of
> wood or stone, the great burial mounds, the medieval cathedrals
> and abbeys, and the churches that were often no less grand. And
> faith hadn't stopped there. Scattered about these monuments, cul-
> tural shrines, and side by side with them sometimes, were relics of
> more recent ways of worship.   (270)

The writer shows that 'faith hadn't stopped there', but he also
writes sceptically about 'the historical feeling' behind church
'restoration', and distinguishes between the medieval 'sense of
an arbitrary world, full of terrors, where men were naked and
helpless and only God gave protection', and the renovated
parish church, which 'celebrated a culture, a national pride, a
power, men very much in control of their destinies' (271). His
view of Victorian-Edwardian restoration recalls Hardy's depiction, in *Jude the Obscure*, of the building that replaces the demol-
ished original church at Marygreen:

> In place of it a tall new building of modern Gothic design, unfamil-
> iar to English eyes, had been erected on a new piece of ground by a
> certain obliterator of historic records who had run down from Lon-
> don and back in a day. The site whereon so long had stood the
> ancient temple to the Christian divinities was not even recorded on

the green and level grass-plot that had immemorially been the church-yard, the obliterated graves being commemorated by eighteenpenny cast-iron crosses warranted to last five years.[21]

Hardy too depicts a new power, destructive and utilitarian; his emotional sympathy is obviously with 'the ancient temple to the Christian divinities', which recalls Golding's way of seeing the cathedral. It is a description which relates the original church to the land, with its integration of pagan and Christian elements, and contrasts it with the new forces, centred on the metropolis, which are obliterating both community, with its links between the generations and its settled adaptations to life and death, and place itself. Already in Hardy's late novels, 'immemorial' religion with its rituals is dead. It is Jack's distinction, in the eyes of the writer in *The Enigma of Arrival*, that he restored meaning to 'the earth stripped finally of its sanctity', and the cottage 'stripped of its atmosphere of home' (58). His is not 'the religion of constriction and discipline' (272) – the religion, in fact, which ruled in the Wessex of Tess and Jude; instead he 'had celebrated the seasons with rituals of his own' (51), and 'in his way of dying ... he had asserted, at the very end, the primacy not of what was beyond life, but life itself' (87). He was thus like the writer's own people, of whom he says at the end of the novel: 'our sacred world had vanished. Every generation now was to take us further away from those sanctities. But we remade the world for ourselves' (318).

This may sound like an idealization of Jack, the construction of another static image to fit over him. But the writer acknowledges that his vision of Jack is incomplete. There is always 'something new' to learn, something which affects his way of seeing. This is even more true for the reader, as Naipaul uses his art of progressive disclosure to complicate our vision of reality.

In the course of his experience the writer rejects an idea of decay and replaces it with an idea of change. The former idea implies a past perfection. Thus both the manor and his landlord stand for an idea of the perfect state, at the height of imperial wealth and security, and in consequence both are decaying, the building and grounds physically, and the man spiritually. But for the writer the time of their decay is the time of his new life; and this is because he accepts the idea of change. Seeing is never complete in a world of change; there is always something new to see, and always something new to make. Decay implies creative exhaustion: there was once a perfect time, nothing people do can bring it back, and therefore they do nothing, they only mourn the past. Change, despite or because of all the problems it brings, implies creative possibility.

All the themes of the novel – seeing, learning, writing, change, religion – are closely linked. The writer has found that 'To become a writer it was necessary to shed many of the early ideas that went with the ambition, and the concept my half-education had given me of the writer' (221). Despite the radical difference of their 'places' in the world, it is implied that he has been educated to conceive of himself as a writer in the same way that his landlord has of himself. But while the writer was educated, 'the man was in the profoundest way – as a social being – untutored' (103). A writer's 'greatest discovery', he says, is that 'man and writer were the same person'; but it took him 'time – and how much writing! – to arrive at that synthesis' (102).

The idea he received from his 'half-English education' was 'that the writer was a person possessed of sensibility' (134), a special kind of person, 'someone who recorded or displayed an inward development'. He ascribes the ideas to the aesthetic movement and to Bloomsbury, and says they were 'bred essentially out of empire, wealth and imperial security'. The argument and the connections are forced: there are *other* ideas in the English tradition of the writer, ideas of the writer as a social being, rather than a person of sensibility; and as for Bloomsbury, Virginia Woolf expresses rather the insecurity of empire, and E. M. Forster forges its critique; but Naipaul is intent on making the connection between the writer's sensibility and empire, and simplifies literary history in order to do so.

The protagonist describes an alternative idea of the writer as coming to him as a revelation: 'vision was granted me'. Writing 'very simply and fast of the simplest things in my memory', he defined himself through the work, 'and saw that my subject was not my sensibility, my inward development, but the worlds I contained within myself, the worlds I lived in' (135). His writing, then, comes from his experience as a social being: the Indian from Trinidad who has participated in the great mid-century upheaval of peoples and patterns of existence; the man of voyages and enigmatic arrivals, who sums up in his own person a large part of the modern historical experience; the man who has lived different ideas – of change and decay, of writing – as an inner conflict affecting his nervous system.

His landlord's story has been quite different: a story of privilege, leading, in early middle age, to 'a disturbance of some sort, a morbid, lasting depression, almost an illness, resulting in withdrawal, hiding, a retreat to the manor, complicated after a while by physical disorders and – finally – age'. (173–4). The writer's relationship with his landlord exists almost entirely in his mind – they have almost no contact – and is a complicated one:

> I was his opposite in every way, social, artistic, sexual. And considering that his family's fortune had grown, but enormously, with the spread of the empire in the nineteenth century, it might be said that an empire lay between us. This empire at the same time linked us. This empire explained my birth in the New World, the language I used, the vocation and ambition I had; this empire in the end explained my presence there in the valley, in that cottage, in the grounds of the manor. But we were – or had started – at opposite ends of wealth, privilege, and in the hearts of different cultures. (174)

The men are opposites, but 'an empire lay between' them. The words suggest distance, separation, but the writer adds: 'This empire at the same time linked us.' It has had a shaping influence on both their lives, 'at opposite ends of wealth, privilege, and in the hearts of different cultures'. They are also both casualties of empire – the writer with what he calls his initial 'disappointment and wounding', the landlord with his 'accidia', his 'curious death of the soul' (193). Like Richard Jefferies, and like those other travellers in their own country, George Orwell and Evelyn Waugh, Naipaul has an anthropological, even an ethnological, eye; he observes people in detail, and recounts their stories; he analyses their social experience, and has a keen perception of their personal and situational limitations.

His landlord has sent the writer poems about Krishna and Shiva in the first year of his tenancy. The ironies of the novel gather about this incident in particular:

> Krishna and Shiva! There, beside that river (Constable and Shepard), in those grounds! There was nothing of contemporary cult or fashion in my landlord's use of these divinities. His Indian romance was in fact older, even antiquated, something he had inherited, like his house, something from the days of imperial

glory, when – out of material satiety and the expectation of the
world continuing to be ordered as it had been ordered for a whole
century and more – power and glory had begun to undo themselves from within.   (192)

Gods from the Hindu pantheon, worshipped by the writer's ancestors in India, figure in poems by his landlord, a son of the empire
which broke up his ancestral cultural pattern and religious rites,
and brought him to Wiltshire, as a tenant on the decaying estate, in
the landscape painted by Constable (notably in his paintings of the
Avon at Salisbury), and in which a gypsy caravan reminds the
writer of E. H. Shepard's illustrations to *The Wind in the Willows*, a
book 'about a river like the one I now saw' (170). The landlord's
'Indian romance' was 'rooted in England, wealth, empire, the idea
of glory, material satiety, a very great security' (192–3). And it par-
took of 'cultivated sensibilities, sensibilities almost drugged by
money' – of the idea of the writer that the Indian from Trinidad was
educated to adopt, and which he has rejected.

Naipaul is not bitter or condemnatory in *The Enigma of Arrival*,
but takes large views. These arise in part from the primeval and
once sacred landscape in which it is set, and in part from the
ancient Hindu tradition with which Naipaul is imaginatively in
touch. Its perspective is that of human life on earth, the perspective of the ancient land and its uses by human beings: land that
'partakes of what we breathe into it, is touched by our moods
and memories'. The writer sees a sheep-shearing, and describes
'the ceremony' as 'like something out of an old novel, perhaps by
Hardy, or out of a Victorian country diary' (18). But the note of
condescension is deceptive: Naipaul's Wiltshire, with its juxtaposition of ancient and modern features, army firing ranges on Salisbury Plain and Stonehenge, has quite a lot in common with
Hardy's Wessex, in which new machines work in the wheat-
fields, and soldiers come to capture Tess as she lies on the Altar
Stone. And there are other features of the past that survive in
Naipaul's characters: in Bray, for example, who has 'the prejudices and strong-headedness and radicalism' of Cobbett, the
social passions of 'a purely agricultural county, the passions connected with manors and big farms and dependent workers'
(222). But *The Enigma of Arrival* is a quite different kind of novel
from Hardy's. It contains stories but has no compelling narrative;
it is mainly analytical, rather than evocative or descriptive.

It is a novel written in keen awareness of the post-colonial present and the predicament facing all peoples to some degree – loss of a sense of the sacred, diminution of 'glory' (a keyword in the novel), and the need to find meaning and adequate rituals in the presence of death. It seems to me that it is Naipaul's awareness of a trans-cultural, world-wide predicament, together with his refusal of a determinant political or religious ideology, that shapes his sympathetic treatment of character in the novel. *The Enigma of Arrival* is also a highly self-conscious book. Novels about writers usually are. It is impossible not to identify the writer in the novel with Naipaul himself. But there is necessarily some imaginative distance between any writer and his self-portrait, whether in fiction or autobiography, and Naipaul is a character in the novel. In any case, his concern is not with his sensibility, but with 'the worlds I contained within myself, the worlds I lived in'. The self-consciousness is not narcissistic or egotistic, I think, but necessary to the theme of voluntary displacement from his native Trinidad, alienation from both his original home and his new environment, in London, and his second life in Wiltshire; and the self-consciousness is a product of alienation, of the self separated from community. What alleviates it in the novel is the sense of place, the manor and the Wiltshire valley, and the life of the seasons, which the writer learns to see. In both respects the novel relates interestingly to the native English tradition of local observation and celebration of the seasons, in painting as well as in various literary forms. It is however the fact of the writer's seeing, rather than the detail of what he sees, that is given prominence. His prose is not heightened, like Golding's, but reflective, diagnostic. His natural descriptions are not lyrical or painterly, like Jefferies', although he too perceives local natural processes as microcosmic, as when snow on the down 'created, in small, the geography of great countries'(45). As Jefferies explained, with an example from Coate Water, in a letter to Oswald Crawfurd: 'You can trace the action of the rain and frost and the waves on its banks, just as Lyell delineates the effect of the ocean on our coast line; of course, on a smaller scale, but the illustration is perfect.'[22] As the reference to Charles Lyell indicates, this was one of the ways in which, in the nineteenth century, geology restored to the land, even in its local details, a sense of the awe-inspiring universal powers which loss of religious

faith, partly as a result of the physical sciences, otherwise dimin-
ished. Hardy, in particular, generates a powerful feeling of awe
by revealing his Wessex landscapes as embodiments of geological time. In Jefferies and Edward Thomas, as well as Hardy, the
'oceanic' space of southern downlands is combined with a sense
of great depth in time to give them an almost preternatural aura.

There is a particularly significant moment at the end of *The
Enigma of Arrival*, when, following his sister's death, the writer
drops his first-person narrative and writes as 'we':

> We were immemorially people of the countryside, far from the
> courts of princes, living according to rituals we didn't always
> understand and yet were unwilling to dishonour because that
> would cut us off from the past, the sacred earth, the gods. Those
> earth rites went back far. They would always have been partly
> mysterious. But we couldn't surrender to them now. We had
> become self-aware. Forty years before, we would not have been so
> self-aware. We would have accepted; we would have felt ourselves
> to be more whole, more in tune with the land and the spirit of the
> earth.   (316)

It is perhaps the trauma of grief that releases in the writer a sense
of solidarity, with his family, but also, surely, with his 'people',
the Indians, who 'were immemorially people of the countryside'.
Like the English writers whose southern landscapes lie under
the shadow of the dying Christian God, or indeed gods, since
Wessex itself may be seen as an 'ancient temple to the Christian
divinities', Naipaul is haunted by 'the past, the sacred earth, the
gods'. But he recognizes that there is no going back to them. The
novel ends affirmatively, nevertheless: 'our sacred world had
vanished. Every generation now was to take us further away
from those sanctities. But we remade the world for ourselves;
every generation does that, as we found when we came together
for the death of this sister and felt the need to honour and
remember' (318).

But does Naipaul slide into sentimentality at the end, and
when the writer says: 'But history, like sanctity, can reside in the
heart; it is enough that there is something there' (318)? This does
indeed seem vague, especially in a world in which, as Naipaul
has good reason to know, humiliated and dispossessed peoples
are turning in large numbers to fundamentalist religion and politics, rather than to humanist sympathy, doubt, and vaguely mys-

tical piety. It may be that the novel is, ultimately, something of a self-justification; the conclusion, certainly, is weaker than the felt loss of the sacred. But the novel is still remarkable for the connections it makes between the relatively small area of its setting and changes affecting the whole world.

It is remarkable, too, for its observation of life in part of Wiltshire in recent decades. Rob Nixon describes Naipaul's 'angle' in the novel as 'ingenious yet perverse'; it 'screens out the violent decrepitude of London and Birmingham's inner cities as well as the monumental industrial collapse of the rusting north'. As Nixon says, these are 'all regions where he could not have nurtured the sensation of his "oddity" or mused with delicate melancholy on the England of Roman conquerors and Camelot'.[23] Nixon's criticism of the novel has to be taken seriously, but he damages his case by his unconscious condescension towards what he takes Naipaul's setting to be: 'a garden county suffused by an ambience of Constable, Ruskin, Goldsmith, Gray's *Elegy*, and Hardy; of chalk downs, brookside strolls, footbridges, bridle paths, Stonehenge, and delicate beds of peonies.'[24] It is evident that for Rob Nixon Wiltshire remains as 'unknown' as it was to the writer at the beginning of his time there, since he wants to see it in pastoral terms, as 'a garden county', instead of as a place where people actually live, and experience the pressures of the changing modern world. But that in fact is what Naipaul shows, whatever he may be 'screening out' in order to concentrate his vision on the writer and on the few neighbours whose stories he tells. The least one can say of this aspect of the novel is that it looks closely at society in southern England, as few writers since Hardy have done. And in doing so, it reveals human needs – for ultimate meaning, for sustaining rituals – that are as integral to lived experience as the great historical movements. This depth of seriousness is one thing that the writers discussed in this book have in common, and they owe it, in part, to a landscape shadowed by 'the past, the sacred earth, the gods'.

Writing about 'driving home across the downs', from Winchester to Salisbury, William Golding describes the magnetic attraction of the cathedral:

> Fifteen miles away you can feel the cathedral begin to pull. It seems ageless as the landscape. You sense that the rivers run towards it, the valleys opening out, each to frame the spike of the

spire. As for the roads, where else should they lead? Even today, though motor traffic is imposing a new pattern on the old one, you can see how the tracks make deeply for the spire and draw together at the ancient bridge just outside the close. It has been a long, steady work, this influencing of the landscape, this engraving and rubbing out, this adjusting and twitching of a whole country into place. And *mana*, however subtle, however indefinable, has at least one quality that aligns it with other forces: it varies inversely as the square of the distance. Fifteen miles away it begins to pull; but stand close to the walls and you feel you might click against them like a nail to a magnet.[25]

This is the landscape of which V. S. Naipaul, too, writes in *The Enigma of Arrival*. He shares with Golding, and with Hardy, the knowledge that the landscape which 'seems ageless' is in fact an historical landscape, shaped by human effort. Golding, though, is not detached like Naipaul; his Salisbury Cathedral is a thing with *mana*; it embodies the power of the elemental forces of nature. If it is sacred, however, that is also because it is part of Golding's life, a place in which he has grown up, and which he sees with a mind 'stocked with memories enough to fill the huge building itself'.[26] It is not a landmark, but part of the writer, 'home'. Such intimacy is a ground of writing, as we see also in Thomas Hardy, Richard Jefferies and John Cowper Powys. But what I have also attempted to show are the complications of the relations between the writers and their places, and of the ways in which they see them. The complications do not dissolve *mana*; the writers share a sense of the sacred quality invested in certain places whose very existence makes them a magnetic force. But it is also all that separates the writer from the original ground – social change, the processes of growth itself, loss of sustaining rituals – that concentrates sacred power in the land, in landscapes, and in particular places. If one could almost forget the purpose for which Salisbury Cathedral was built in reading Golding's description of the 'pull' of the building, that is because he has substituted a complex of powerful feelings, with their roots in personal and historical experience, for its primary meaning for the culture that created it. Would the place remain alive without such transferences? At the end of *A Glastonbury Romance* Powys invokes Cybele, 'that beautiful and terrible Force by which the Lies of great creative Nature give birth to Truth that is to be'.[27] She is the source of the human imagination, the origin of the magical view of life. It is by her, by the imagination, that Stonehenge lives, although with our reason we can only 'number the Stones'. And so it is with all sacred places: while there is someone to breathe their spirit into them, they will live.

Yet it is necessary in conclusion to add a cautionary note. For if the sacred place lives for the individual imagination, it does not live as it did for the culture that produced it. Stonehenge and Salisbury Cathedral were originally products of particular cultures, different from each other in world view, and different from that of the present age. They were built for specific religious purposes, purposes which bound the individual to a common sacred rite (even if, in the case of Stonehenge, we can only speculate about the nature of the rite). The reshaping of such places by the individual imagination – whether Hardy's or Powys's or Golding's, or Constable's or Turner's – may become part of their meaning for us, but what we are responding to is a vision influenced by historical processes that have separated the individual mind from the tribal or religious foundation. This observation may need qualifying in some cases – in that of Constable, for example, who saw equally in the Cathedral and the river and trees the works of God. In the main, however, as I have attempted to show, imaginative perceptions of place in the modern world owe a great deal to displacement and cultural disintegration. If in looking at either religious building, therefore, we see accretions of meaning that suggest continuity throughout the ages, we also see different historical meanings (Stonehenge as 'Druid' temple, or as astronomical observatory, for example), and different personal visions (Stonehenge as the altar of Nature's cruel law, or as a centre of the magical view of life). It is such differences and the questions they raise, more than any clearly definable continuous tradition, that are revealed by explorations of writers in a landscape and their imaginative shaping of place.

Notes

Notes to the Preface

1 C. R. Leslie, *Memoirs of the Life of John Constable* (London: The Phaidon Press, 1951), 203.

2 Samuel J. Looker, ed., *Jefferies' England* (London: Constable, 1937), 176.

3 Ibid., 179.

4 See *The Idea of the Holy* (London: Oxford University Press, 1923), *passim*.

5 'Walks in the Wheat-Fields', *Field and Hedgerow* (London: Longmans & Co., 1890), 125.

6 *Modern Painting and the Northern Romantic Tradition* (London: Thames and Hudson, 1978), 17.

7 *Memoirs of the Life of John Constable*, 282.

8 Ibid., 273.

9 *Tess of the d'Urbervilles* (Harmondsworth: Penguin Books, 1985), 180.

10 *A Glastonbury Romance* (London: John Lane, The Bodley Head, 1933), 909.

11 R. George Thomas, ed., *The Collected Poems of Edward Thomas* (Oxford: Oxford University Press, 1981), 98, 103.

12 Quoted in Thomas Frick, ed., *The Sacred Theory of the Earth* (Berkeley, California: North Atlantic Books, 1986), 37.

13 Quoted in George Steiner, *Heidegger* (Glasgow: Fontana/Collins, 1978), 149.

14 Florence Emily Hardy, *The Life of Thomas Hardy 1840–1928* (London: Macmillan, 1972), 185.

15 Jeremy Hooker, *Solent Shore* (Manchester: Carcanet, 1978), 46–7.

16 'Poem and Place', in *Poetry of Place* (Manchester: Carcanet, 1982).

17 'Thought and Landscape', in D. W. Meinig, ed., *The Interpretation of Ordinary Landscapes* (New York: Oxford University Press, 1979), 92.

18 *The Country and the City* (London: Chatto & Windus, 1973), 258.

19 *Autobiography* (London: Macdonald, 1967), 626.

20 *A Glastonbury Romance*, 328–9.

21 *Autobiography*, 626.

22 Wallace Stegner, 'The Sense of Place', *Where the Bluebird Sings to the Lemonade Springs* (New York: Penguin Books, 1993), 205.

23 *The Anathemata* (London: Faber, 1952), 10.

24 'The Landscape of Home', *The Interpretation of Ordinary Landscapes*, 133.

Notes to Chapter 1

1 Helen Thomas, *Time and Again* (Manchester: Carcanet, 1978), 111–12.

2 I have discussed this subject in 'Honouring Ivor Gurney', *Poetry of Place* (Manchester: Carcanet, 1982), 120–29.

3 See my 'Poem and Place', *Poetry of Place*, 180–90.

4 *Collected Poems of Ivor Gurney*, ed. P. J. Kavanagh (Oxford: Oxford University Press, 1982), 132.

5 Ibid., 117.

6 Ibid., 163.

7 V. S. Naipaul, *The Enigma of Arrival* (Harmondsworth: Penguin Books, 1987), 97.

8 George Eliot, *The Mill on the Floss* (London: The New English Library Limited, 1965), 48.

9 Mircea Eliade, *Myths, Dreams and Mysteries* (London: Collins, The Fontana Library, 1968), 165.

10 Mircea Eliade, *Images and Symbols* (Princeton, New Jersey: Princeton University Press, 1991), 33.

11 *Clare: Selected Poems and Prose*, ed. Eric Robinson and Geoffrey Summerfield (Oxford: Oxford University Press, 1966), 66.

12 The poem is printed at the beginning of what is effectively Hardy's own memoirs, Florence Emily Hardy's *The Life of Thomas Hardy 1840–1928* (one volume edition, Macmillan, 1962), where it is referred to as 'Wordsworthian lines – the earliest discoverable of young Hardy's attempts at verse', and 'written between 1857 and 1860'.

13 Hardy's description of 'Castle Boterel' (Boscastle) and the surrounding area of north Cornwall in his Author's Preface to *A Pair of Blue Eyes* (1873)

14 Donald Davie, *The Poet in the Imaginary Museum* (Manchester: Carcanet, 1977), 226.

15 The original rock of this name lies just off the Dorset Coast, between Bats Head and the Durdle Door, to the east of Weymouth.

16 T. F. Powys, *Mockery Gap* (London: Chatto & Windus, 1925), 35.

17 Llewelyn Powys, *Earth Memories* (London: The Bodley Head, 1934), 169–74.

18 *Mockery Gap*, 182.

19 Richard Jefferies, *Wild Life in a Southern County* (London: Lutter-

worth Press, 1949), 222.

20 Edward Thomas, *The South Country* (London: J. M. Dent, 1932), 158.

21 John Cowper Powys, *Mortal Strife* (London: Village Press, 1974), 156.

22 Richard Jefferies, 'Hours of Spring', 1886, in *Jefferies' England*, ed. Samuel J. Looker (London: Constable, 1937), 5.

23 Quoted in Christopher Neve, *Unquiet Landscape* (London: Faber, 1990), 40.

Notes to Chapter 2

1. *The Letters of Vincent Van Gogh*, ed. Mark Roskill (London: Collins, The Fontana Library, 1963), 295.

2. Richard Jefferies' Preface to *The Natural History of Selborne* (London: The Scott Library, 1887), x.

3. *Amaryllis at the Fair* (London: Duckworth, 1908), 155–56.

4. *Jefferies' England*, ed. Samuel J. Looker (London: Constable, 1937), 99.

5. Included in Richard Jefferies, *Field and Farm*, ed. Samuel J. Looker (London: Phoenix House, 1957), 40–42.

6. Edward Thomas, *Richard Jefferies* (London: Hutchinson, 1909), 1.

7. Ibid., 22.

8. Quoted in Samuel J. Looker and Crichton Porteous, *Richard Jefferies: Man of the Fields* (London: John Baker, 1965), 4.

9. Quoted in *Richard Jefferies: Man of the Fields*, 9.

10. Raymond Williams, *The Country and the City* (London: Chatto & Windus, 1973), 193.

11. Q. D. Leavis, 'Lives and Works of Richard Jefferies', *Scrutiny*, V1 (March 1938), 437.

12. See for example F. C. Happold, *Mysticism* (Harmondsworth: Penguin Books, 1963), and R. C. Zaehner, *Mysticism: Sacred and Profane* (Oxford: Oxford University Press, 1961).

13. W. J. Keith, *Richard Jefferies: A Critical Study* (University of Toronto Press and Oxford University Press, 1965), 21.

14. Richard Jefferies, *Field and Hedgerow* (London: Longmans & Co., 1890), 143.

15. 'John Richard Jefferies, his Worst and his Best', the Centenary Lecture 1987, printed by the Richard Jefferies Society.

16. Richard Jefferies, *The Life of the Fields* (London: Chatto & Windus, 1906), 52.

17. *The Amateur Poacher* (London: Smith, Elder & Co., 1914), 12.

18. 'Sport and Science', *The Life of the Fields*, 160.

19. *Wild Life in a Southern County* (London: Lutterworth Press, 1949), 21.

20. Ibid., 33–4.

21. John Pearson, 'The Rise of Maximin', a talk given to the Richard Jefferies Society in 1980.

22. 'Wild Flowers', 1885, *Jefferies' England*, 121.
23. Ibid., 149.
24. *Amaryllis at the Fair*, 33.
25. *Jefferies' England*, 102.
26. *Amaryllis at the Fair*, 258.
27. Included in Richard Jefferies, *The Toilers of the Fields* (London: Longmans, Green, and Co., 1892).
28. Quoted in Bernard Crick, *George Orwell: A Life* (Harmondsworth: Penguin Books, 1982), 533.
29. David Gervais, *Literary Englands* (Cambridge: Cambridge University Press, 1993), 158.
30. *Field and Hedgerow*, 312–13.
31. *The Open Air* (London: Chatto & Windus, 1926), 97–8.
32. 'Nature in the Louvre', *Field and Hedgerow*, 264.
33. Published by Quartet Books in 1979.
34. *The Amateur Poacher*, 190.
35. *Jefferies' England*, 118.
36. *Bevis: The Story of a Boy* (London: Jonathan Cape, 1932), 355.
37. *Jefferies' England*, 110.
38. *Bevis*, 355.
39. *Round About a Great Estate* (London: Eyre and Spottiswoode, 1948), 82.
40. *The Story of My Heart* (London: Quartet Books, 1979), 65.
41. *Field and Hedgerow*, 35.
42. Ibid., 17–18.
43. *The Old House at Coate* (London: Lutterworth Press, 1948), 66.
44. *The Story of My Heart*, 85.
45. *The Notebooks of Richard Jefferies*, ed. Samuel J. Looker (London: Grey Walls Press, 1948), 128.
46. *Field and Hedgerow*, 32.
47. See John A. T. Robinson, *The Roots of a Radical* (London: SCM Press, 1980), 149–55.
48. *Field and Hedgerow*, 36.
49. *Bevis*, 323–4.
50. Kenneth Clark, *Landscape into Art* (Harmondsworth: Penguin Books, 1956), 120.
51. *The Letters of Vincent Van Gogh*, 286.
52. *The Notebooks of Richard Jefferies*, 251.
53. Ibid., 259.
54. Ibid., 285.

Notes to Chapter 3

1. All page references to *After London* in the text are to the World's Clas-

sics edition (Oxford: Oxford University Press, 1980).

2. J. R. Seeley, *The Expansion of England* (London: Macmillan, second edition, 1895), 2.

3. Ibid., 342.

4. Richard Jefferies, *The Amateur Poacher* (London: Smith, Elder, 1914), 240.

5. John Cowper Powys, *Autobiography* (London: Macdonald, 1967) 1–2.

6. Samuel J. Looker, ed., *Jefferies' England* (London: Constable, 1937), 121.

7. *Bevis*, 88.

8. Ibid., 356.

9. Richard Jefferies, *The Story of My Heart* (London: Quartet Books, 1979), 90.

10. *The Gamekeeper at Home* (London: Smith, Elder, 1910), 12.

11. *The Story of My Heart*, 77.

12. Ibid., 91–2.

13. Richard Shannon, *The Crisis of Imperialism 1865–1915* (St Albans: Paladin, 1976), 270.

14. 'I am a pagan,. and think the heart and soul above crowns.' *Amaryllis at the Fair* (London: Duckworth, 1908), 30.

15. *The Story of My Heart*, 93–4.

16. *The Dewy Morn* (London: Wildwood House, 1982), 92.

17. *Amaryllis at the Fair*, 223.

18. *The Dewy Morn*, 137.

19. *Jefferies' England*, 126–7.

Notes to Chapter 4

1. *The Woodland Life* (Edinburgh and London: William Blackwood & Sons), 9.

2. Samuel J. Looker, ed., *Jefferies' England* (London: Constable, 1937), 24.

3. *The South Country* (London: J. M. Dent, 1932), 36.

4. *The Childhood of Edward Thomas* (London: Faber, 1938), 134.

5. *The Amateur Poacher* (London: Smith, Elder & Co., 1914), 240.

6. *In Pursuit of Spring* (London: Nelson, 1914), 150.

7. *The Country* (London: Batsford, 1913), 39.

8. *Richard Jefferies* (London: Hutchinson, 1909), 305.

9. *Walter Pater* (London: Martin Secker, 1913), 208.

10. *The South Country*, 89.

11. In a notebook, 31 August 1899. Quoted in R. George Thomas, *Edward Thomas: A Portrait* (Oxford: Oxford University Press, 1985), 80.

12. *The South Country*, 7.

13. *The Country*, 31.

14. *The Story of My Heart*, 85.
15. *The Renaissance*, 1873 (London: Collins, The Fontana Library, 1961), 221.
16. *The Heart of England* (London: J. M. Dent, 1932), 133.
17. In a letter of 10 January 1915. Quoted in Eleanor Farjeon, *Edward Thomas: The Last Four Years* (London: Oxford University Press, 1958), 110.
18. *Richard Jefferies*, 49.
19. *Walter Pater*, 73.
20. Ibid., 109.
21. Ibid., 213.
22. Ibid., 108.
23. Ibid., 183.
24. *Richard Jefferies*, 1.
25. From a 1904 review by Edward Thomas of a book by A. B. Paterson. Quoted by Edna Longley in her Introduction to *A Language Not To Be Betrayed* (Manchester: Carcanet, 1981), iv.
26. *Richard Jefferies*, 180.
27. Ibid., 194.
28. From a letter from Edward Thomas to Eleanor Farjeon, in 1913. Quoted in *Edward Thomas: The Last Four Years*, 13.
29. *Richard Jefferies*, 179.
30. Ibid., 313.
31. Review of *North of Boston*, 22 July 1914; in *A Language Not To Be Betrayed*, 125.
32. *Oxford*, (London: A. & C. Black: 1903), 251.
33. *Beautiful Wales* (London: A. & C. Black, 1905), 152–3.
34. *Light and Twilight* (London: Duckworth, 1911), 121–2.
35. *The Childhood of Edward Thomas*, 47.
36. *Rest and Unrest* (London: Duckworth, 1910), 113–14.
37. *The South Country*, 155.
38. *The Country and the City*, 257,
39. *In Pursuit of Spring*, 158–9.
40. *Letters from Edward Thomas to Gordon Bottomley*, ed. R. George Thomas (London: Oxford University Press, 1968), 93.
41. *The Heart of England*, 5.
42. Ibid., 48.
43. *Letters from Edward Thomas to Gordon Bottomley*, 180.
44. *The South Country*, 131.
45. *Rest and Unrest*, 26.
46. *Light and Twilight*, 24–45.
47. *The Happy-Go-Lucky Morgans* (Woodbridge: The Boydell Press, 1983).
48. Ibid., 123.

49. *The South Country*, 75.
50. *The Last Sheaf* (London: Jonathan Cape, 1928), 108.
51. Ibid., 220–1.

Notes to Chapter 5

1. *The Amateur Poacher* (London: Smith, Elder, 1914), 240.
2. Mark Rutherford, *Autobiography and Deliverance* (Leicester: Leicester University Press, 1969), 19.
3. R. George Thomas, ed., *The Collected Poems of Edward Thomas* (Oxford: Oxford University Press, 1981), 3. Except where stated otherwise, all subsequent page references to Edward Thomas's poems, given in the text, will be to this edition.
4. Stan Smith, *Edward Thomas* (London: Faber Student Guides, 1986), 19.
5. *Modern Painters*, edited and abridged by David Barrie (London: André Deutsch, 1989), 399.
6. *The Heart of England* (London: J. M. Dent, 1932), 66.
7. Bill McKibben, *The End of Nature* (Harmondsworth: Penguin Books, 1990), 77.
8. Quoted in Eleanor Farjeon, *Edward Thomas: The Last Four Years* (London: Oxford University Press, 1958), 13.
9. Quoted in Edna Longley, *A Language Not To Be Betrayed* (Manchester: Carcanet Press, 1981), 37–8.
10. Edward Thomas, *The Country* (London: Batsford, 1913), 6.
11. See Peter V. Marinelli, *Pastoral* (London: Methuen, 1971), especially Chapter 5, 'The Retreat into Childhood'.
12. Bruno Snell, *The Discovery of the Mind* (New York: Harper & Row, Harper Torchbook edition, 1960), 292.
13. See for example Mircea Eliade, *Patterns in Comparative Religion* (London: Sheed and Ward, 1958), 382–5.
14. Quoted in R. George Thomas, *Edward Thomas: A Portrait* (Oxford: Oxford University Press, 1985), 80.
15. Edward Thomas, *Richard Jefferies* (London: Hutchinson, 1908), 49.
16. Edward Thomas, *The South Country* (London: J. M. Dent, 1932), 7.
17. Edward Thomas, *The South Country*, 67.
18. These words and the quotation above are from John Cowper Powys, *Obstinate Cymric* (Carmarthen: The Druid Press, 1947), 86.
19. Alwyn Rees and Brinley Rees, *Celtic Heritage* (London: Thames and Hudson, 1961), 344.
20. *Richard Jefferies*, 179.
21. Samuel J. Looker, ed., *Jefferies' England* (London: Constable, 1937), 1.
22. I quote the more familiar version of these lines, from Edna Longley, ed., *Edward Thomas: Poems and Last Poems* (London and Glasgow:

Collins, 1973), 21. 'Stained with all that hour's songs' is, I think, stronger than 'Rich with all that riot of songs' in the version printed by R. George Thomas.

23. *The South Country*, 36.
24. See *The Decline of the West*, abridged edition (London: Allen & Unwin, 1961), 112, 137, 155.
25. In Herbert Read, ed., *Unit One* (London: Cassell, 1934), 81.
26. Anthony Bertram, *Paul Nash: The Portrait of an Artist* (London: Faber, 1955), 99.
27. Roger Cardinal, *The Landscape Vision of Paul Nash* (London: Reaktion Books, 1989), 96.
28. Included in Paul Nash, *Outline: An Autobiography and Other Writings* (London: Faber, 1949), 258–65.
29. Included in Michael Pitt Rivers, *Dorset: A Shell Guide* (London: Faber, 1968), 10–12.
30. Edward Thomas, *Celtic Stories* (Oxford: The Clarendon Press, 1918), 90.
31. For a discussion of 'The Owl' and the significance of its allusion to Shakespeare's 'Winter' from *Love's Labour's Lost*, see my 'The Sad Passion', *Poetry of Place*, 23–4.
32. Again, I quote the more familiar version of the poem, from Longley, 90.
33. In 'The Jungle', Jeremy Hooker and Gweno Lewis, eds., *Selected Poems of Alun Lewis* (London: Unwin Paperbacks, 1981), 100.

Notes to Chapter 6

1. The page numbers in the text refer to the Penguin Classics editions of Thomas Hardy's works.
2. *The Older Hardy* (London: Heinemann, 1978), 8.
3. *Autobiography* (London: Macdonald, 1967), 1–2.
4. Florence Emily Hardy, *The Life of Thomas Hardy 1840–1928*, 15.
5. *Visions and Revisions* (London: Macdonald, 1955), 165.
6. *The Collected Poems of Thomas Hardy* (London: Macmillan, 1965), 331.
7. *The Complex Vision*, 1920 (London: Village Press, 1975), x.
8. *Mortal Strife*, 1942 (London: Village Press, 1974), 157.
9. *The Complex Vision*, 167.
10. *Tess of the d'Urbervilles*, 180.
11. *The Return of the Native*, 56.
12. *Letters of John Cowper Powys to Louis Wilkinson* (London: Macdonald, 1958), 338.
13. *Wood and Stone* (London: Village Press, 1974), xi.
14. *The Meaning of Culture* (London: Cape, 1930), 34.
15. *Autobiography*, 228–9.
16. Ibid., 88.

17. Ibid., 626.
18. Ibid., 224–5.
19. Ibid., 309.
20. Ibid., 15.
21. *Weymouth Sands* (London: Macdonald, 1963), 282.
22. *Wolf Solent* (Harmondsworth: Penguin, 1964), 11.
23. Richard Perceval Graves inclines to the view that the novel was completed in the summer of 1920. See *The Brothers Powys* (London: Routledge & Kegan Paul, 1983), 339, note 23.
24. *After My Fashion* (London: Picador, 1980), 16.
25. Ibid., 16.
26. Ibid., 166.
27. *Visions and Revisions*, 162.
28. *Maiden Castle*, the first full authoritative edition, ed. Ian Hughes (Cardiff: University of Wales Press, 1990), 185.
29. *Mortal Strife*, 148.
30. *Wolf Solent*, 291.
31. *The Meaning of Culture*, 222.
32. *Weymouth Sands*, 65.
33. Ibid., 473.
34. *The Well-Beloved* (London: Macmillan, 1914), 109–10.
35. *Autobiography*, 151.
36. Ibid., 285.
37. *The Meaning of Culture*, 122.
38. *Wood and Stone*, ix–x.
39. *Wolf Solent*, 632.
40. *A Glastonbury Romance* (London: John Lane, The Bodley Head, 1933), 815.

Notes to Chapter 7

1. *Maiden Castle* was first published in 1937, but the first full authoritative edition was not published until 1990. Page numbers in the text refer to the latter edition.
2. *In Defence of Sensuality* (London: Gollancz, 1930), 270.
3. Jeremy Hooker, *John Cowper Powys* (Cardiff: University of Wales Press, 1973), 31.
4. Hardy's Preface to *Jude the Obscure* (Penguin Classics edition), 39.
5. *Porius*, the unabridged edition, ed. Wilbur T. Albrecht (New York: Colgate University Press, 1994), 548.
6. *The Collected Poems of Thomas Hardy*, 531.
7. *Suspended Judgements* (London: Village Press, 1975), 172.
8. John Cowper Powys, *In Spite of* (London: Macdonald, 1953), 168.
9. *A Glastonbury Romance*, 694.

Notes to Chapter 8

1. V. S. Naipaul, *The Enigma of Arrival* (Harmondsworth: Penguin Books, 1987), 301. All subsequent page references given in the text will be to this edition.
2. 'Walks in the Wheat-Fields', *Field and Hedgerow* (London: Longmans & Co., 1890), 155.
3. 'My Old Village', *Field and Hedgerow*, 312.
4. *The Country and the City* (London: Chatto & Windus, 1973), 120.
5. *Wolf Solent* (Harmondsworth: Penguin, 1964), 17.
6. Martin J. Wiener, *English Culture and the Decline of the Industrial Spirit 1850-1980* (Cambridge: Cambridge University Press, 1982), 42.
7. William Golding, *The Moving Target* (London: Faber and Faber, 1982), 17.
8. All page references to the novel in the text are to the Faber paper-covered edition, first published in 1965.
9. 'Belief and Creativity', a talk given in 1980, *The Moving Target*, 199.
10. Mark Kinkead-Weekes and Ian Gregor, *William Golding: A Critical Study* (London: Faber and Faber, revised edition, 1984), 203.
11. *The Moving Target*, 192.
12. Ibid., 167.
13. John Cowper Powys, *Wolf Solent* (Harmondsworth: Penguin Books, 1964), 11.
14. Thomas Hardy, *Far from the Madding Crowd* (Harmondsworth: Penguin Classics Edition, 1985), 48.
15. Thomas Hardy, *The Return of the Native* (Harmondsworth: Penguin Classics edition, 1978), 56.
16. Joseph Conrad, *Heart of Darkness* (Harmondsworth: Penguin Books, 1989), 29.
17. See for example Rob Nixon, *London Calling: V. S. Naipaul, Postcolonial Mandarin* (Oxford: Oxford University Press, 1992).
18. *Richard Jefferies* (London: Hutchinson, 1909), 92.
19. 'Lob', *The Collected Poems of Edward Thomas*, ed. R. George Thomas (Oxford: Oxford University Press, 1981), 57.
20. John Cowper Powys, *Maiden Castle*, 5.
21. *Jude the Obscure* (Harmondsworth: Penguin Classics edition, 1985), 50.
22. Quoted in Looker and Porteus, *Richard Jefferies: Man of the Fields* (London: John Baker, 1965), 29.
23. *London Calling: V. S. Naipaul, Postcolonial Mandarin*, 163.
24. Ibid., 161.
25. 'An Affection for Cathedrals', *The Moving Target*, 14.
26. Ibid., 14.
27. *A Glastonbury Romance* (London: John Lane, The Bodley Head, 1933), 1174.

INDEX